A Speck of Atlantis

BIMINI

THE TOP OF GOD'S MOUNTAIN

Visionary Artwork and Writings of Norbert H. Kox

A Speck of Atlantis

BIMINI

THE TOP OF GOD'S MOUNTAIN

Visionary Artwork and Writings of Norbert H. Kox

Apocalyptic Visual Parables

by

Norbert H. Kox

"LOVE"

אהב

AHB

Apocalypse House Books

New Franken, WI

A SPECK OF ATLANTIS – BIMINI: THE TOP OF GOD'S MOUNTAIN

Apocalypse House, P.O. Box 109, New Franken, WI 54229.

ISBN: 978-0-578-06104-7

Library of Congress Control Number: 2010911090

Please visit our website: **www.apocalypsehouse.com**

For information regarding author interviews, please contact: **nhkox@yahoo.com**

Note: Our apologies, due to variations in the printing process colors may not always be an exact representation of the original paintings.

Spontaneous Symmetrical Surrealism
conceived in Bimini Bahamas
(See pp.71-85)

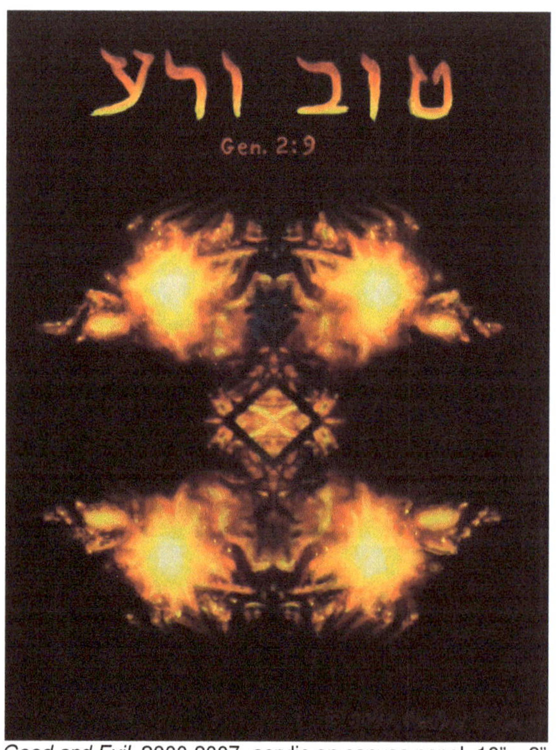

Good and Evil, 2000-2007, acrylic on canvas panel, 10" x 8"

DEDICATION AND ACKNOWLEDGMENTS

This book is dedicated to all Islanders, especially to all the people of the Island of Bimini, for the glory and honor of Yesu Christ, and the setting of his *Yod* (hand and initial) a second time to recover his remnant from the Islands of the seas, in accordance with Isaiah 11:11.

Very special thanks to Mr. Ashley B. Saunders, for his loyal friendship and for accommodating me in the inspirational setting of the Dolphin House, and to Mr. James Pinder for arranging the art exhibits, and to Mrs. Pinder and all the others who help with the setup and details of the receptions. Also a big thank you to the Bahamas Ministry of Education for providing us with exhibition space. Special thanks to Pastor Edmond Ellis and the entire United Church Of God congregation for their continued attendance and support of the exhibitions.

OTHER TITLES TO WATCH FOR
by Norbert H. Kox

The End is Come

The Holy Cipher: Who Changed God's Name?

The Yod of God: Returning His Name, Recovering His Remnant

Masquerade: Antichrist is Here

The White Lie

The Woman's Tail: The Real Star Wars

Sapphire Sphere: Portal to Eternity

Onyx Stones: Key of the Portal

Sound the Shofar

Check for availability at Apocalypse House

http://nkox.homestead.com/BooksByNHK.html

http://apocalypsehouse.com

"LOVE"

אהב

AHB

Apocalypse House Books

* CONTENTS *

A SPECK OF ATLANTIS
BIMINI: THE TOP OF GOD'S MOUNTAIN

MORE BIMINI ART, SELECTED EXHIBITS, SELECTED WORKS

Besides the Bimini Bahamas exhibitions, many of the Bimini series paintings have been exhibited abroad, in Paris, Luxembourg, Brussels, London, Radlett England, Richmond Greater London, and also in Vancouver BC. They have been shown in U.S. exhibitions in New York, Washington DC, Washington (State), California, Oregon, South Carolina, Maryland, Georgia, Texas, New Mexico, Arizona, Georgia, Tennessee, Pennsylvania, Illinois, Wisconsin, and Minnesota.

FOREWORD

Contemporary religious painter Norbert Kox is one of America's most important Visionary artists. His self-described 'apocalyptic visual parables' utilize powerful symbolic metaphors aiming to shake modern man from his spiritual malaise and clear away centuries worth of mistranslations of the Bible. (Richard Metzger, *Disinformation: The Interviews*, p. 116).

Norbert Kox lives today as a semi-hermit... But he is not alone since God (and God's stark message) is ever present in his meditative prayer, in the "bible codes" he finds in a computerized grid of Hebrew letters, and in his lushly visionary paintings and Gothic constructions. Increasingly famous and infamous now for his prophetic images that challenge mainstream religious pieties, Kox is a benign, humble, and intelligent man. Clearly at peace with himself, he does not, however, shy away from confronting us with God's apocalyptic warnings and encrypted revelations. But there are always flashes of light and spirit within the darkness – signs of hope and renewal ...powerfully communicating God's most secret messages through his intensely glowing paintings (he has developed his own techniques of translucent acrylic glazing) and biblically haunted found-object assemblages. Despite the fear that his work sometimes engenders, he has had increasing national success as an artist with a provocatively disturbing vision of the end-time. Most recently, he has been retreating from the bitter Wisconsin winters to the tropical sun of Bimini, and it seems that he has tempered some of the harsh cartoon evil portrayed in many of the early paintings. But no matter how much his recent work shows an ameliorating principle, Kox quietly and passionately persists in his attempt to unveil the mysteries of God's strange missives to humankind.
(Professor Norman J. Girardot, *The End Is A New Beginning: Four Outsider Artists*, p. 20).

Norbert H. Kox has researched the Bible in its original languages for more than 30 years, and presents his startling findings in the form of artworks and writings. As a Visionary Artist and steward of Yesu Christ he paints Apocalyptic Visual Parables that expose religious counterfeits in the light of Biblical truth.

Mine is a ministry of salvation through warnings and admonitions which expose deceptions and reveal truths. Some people comment that my artwork is very disturbing, and filled with negative imagery. This is generally a good observation. My works are Apocalyptic Visual Parables and are mostly warnings. As such they are meant to shock and disturb. You can't tell someone there is a fire without shouting "Fire!" The initial impact can be horrifying, but the negative elements become positive when properly interpreted.

You would not see a flower or a butterfly on a poison bottle. The skull and crossbones appear with the word poison. This imagery and text seems negative, but when interpreted to mean, "do not drink this," the message and image become positive: it will save your life.

In the spiritual sense, my iconography operates in the same way.

My message focuses on exposing mistranslations, misconceptions, and lies, which have been fostered in great part by the religious, and specifically by Modern Christianity.

My art works act much the same as Scripture in presenting hidden messages for the viewer to dig out and decipher.

Whether in writing or artwork the message is often unsettling, simply because it forces us to examine things and to see and recognize the truth. Truth can be intense even frightening. And once that gate has been opened there is no turning away.

Many of the Bimini paintings are more glorious and less confrontational than the usual Apocalyptic Visual Parables but nonetheless leave much to be contemplated by the viewer.

A SPECK OF ATLANTIS

BIMINI

The Top Of God's Mountain

X ON THE WATER

Many of Norbert Kox's visionary works painted in Bimini, Bahamas, are esoteric paintings based on the transference of energy between the physical and spiritual realms. They take into consideration the possibility of portal travel between these realms as postulated by Quantum Physicists, also signified both directly and indirectly within Biblical passages and alluded to in records of Bermuda Triangle encounters.

My first visit to Bimini was on a Blackbeard dive trip, in 1997, when we made an overnight stop. I was a little nervous and stayed close to the ship. The following year I returned again. This time I wandered about the island talking with the natives and looking at apartments. I really didn't know why, because I had no intentions of returning. Yet before I could get back on the ship I felt it burning in my heart, and I knew that I would be coming back to spend some time. The island was calling me and God confirmed it in the Scriptures when he led me to Isaiah 11:11, ending in the phrase, "the islands of the sea." In the Spirit, I knew without a doubt that he wanted me to go to Bimini as his witness to paint Apocalyptic Visual Parables. This was confirmed to me 100% through complex Bible codes. [*What are Bible codes? See definition on p.34*]

Within two weeks I found myself making arrangements to return to the Island.

On my first extended stay I began to notice strange wave patterns along the beach adjacent to the Spook Hill Cemetery. Often the waves would cross forming an X on the water. The waves seemed to come from every direction even defying the wind. High tide, low tide, wind or no wind, there is no way to predict when the wave patterns will be there or when they will not. One day there is action, the next day, nothing.

Upon asking around, I found no one else who had ever witnessed this phenomenon. The local historian Ashley B. Saunders [author of *History of Bimini*, vols. 1 & 2; for purchase contact, *saundersa62@yahoo.com*] when asked what might be causing it, simply stated, "We are on a high-energy grid."

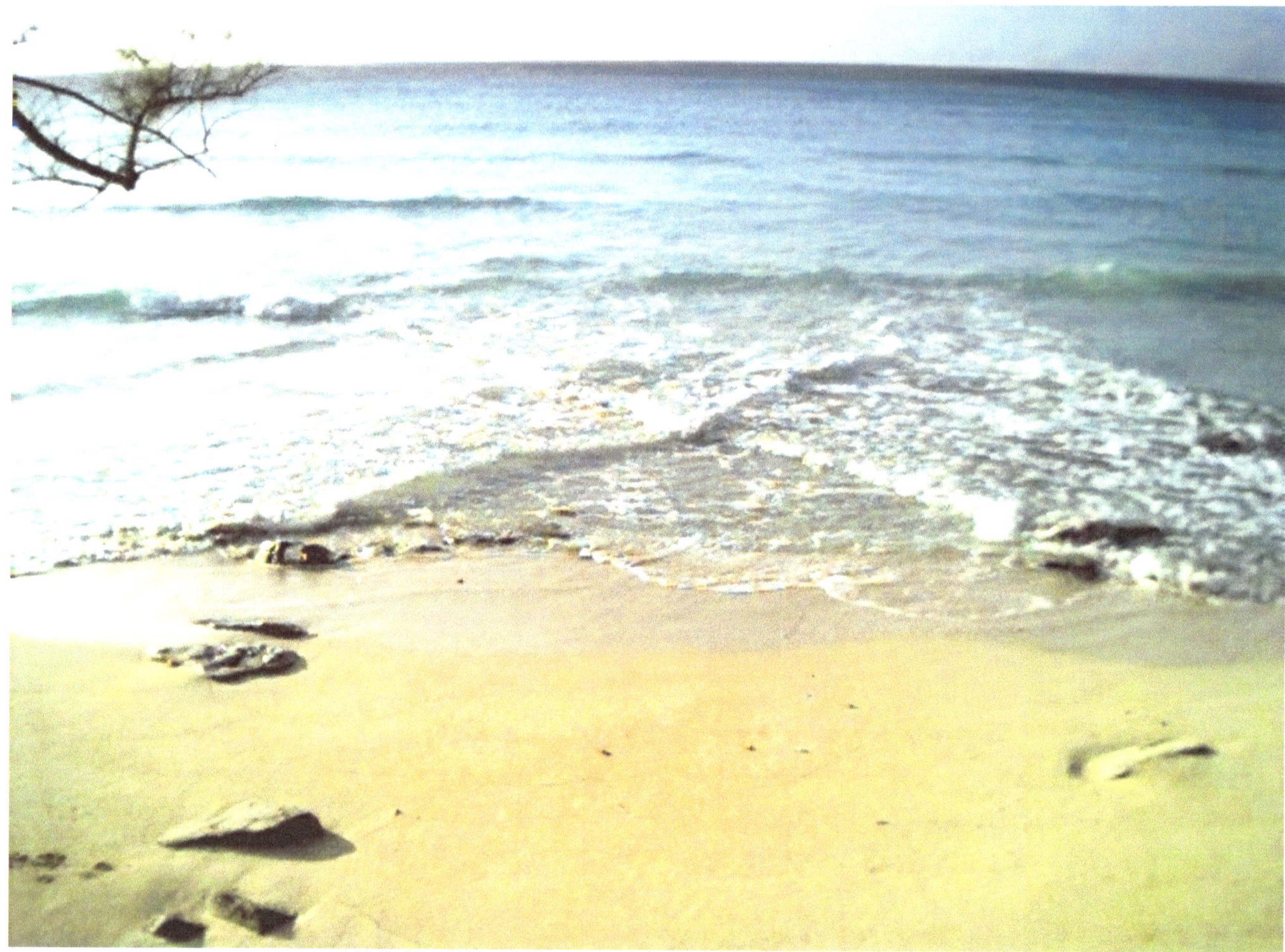

X On The Water, 2000, unaltered photograph, by Norbert H. Kox

The X is the ancient form of the Hebrew letter Tau. It means, "sign," "cross," "mark," or, "musical note." In it's plural form (תוים) it can be interpreted "**Sign of the Sea**." It is also the character of the Greek letter Chi (key), the first initial in Christ. The X on the water is a sign that appears often, in the ocean, at the Island of Bimini, in the Bahamas, just below Spook Hill. This is a point on a high energy grid, in the Bermuda Triangle.

Following notes recorded on 2nd extended visit December 1999-February 2000:

The sea is alive! Waves are coming in. Waves are going out. Waves are running sideways, and on diagonals; each time one wave crosses the other it creates an upward surge. When a wave coming in and a wave going out hit and cross each other, a wall of water shoots upward! When a wave going out hits at a slight angle to the one coming in, it splashes upward and races along the incoming wave like a rooster-tail behind a speed boat, shooting at fantastic speed as it sprays upward into the sky. The waves of the sea are as complex as the crossing of text in the [*octa-directional*] Bible codes. (2/10/2000)

Watching the ocean waves again in the twilight, the action is not as aggressive as last night, but it is all there. The waves coming in and going out, crossing each other, waves traveling perpendicular to the shoreline and the incoming surf. Those waves are traveling in both directions. The diagonal waves are traveling out on both diagonals, crossing each other while the two incoming diagonals cross them. So there are eight directional patterns to the waves [*the Bible codes also run in eight directions*], each crossing the other, changing its appearance to some extent but not destroying it, each variation creates a new variation. (2/11/2000)

Symbolically the "Word" is compared to water. ..."washing of water by means of the word" and "out of his belly shall flow rivers of living water." ...coming in, going out, diagonal, and perpendicular. All the patterns are there. ...The sea is alive. Ever the same, yet ever-changing. Each new ripple is in harmony with the next. Two opposing sets of waves can cross each other without upsetting the harmony of the other. (2/12/2000)

...all the action is here. The same as the past three nights. Must be something about this spot. The water actually seems to have a life of its own. It moves and reacts like a living entity. I can see where the expression "the living waters" comes from. (2/13/2000)

The code is here. All of the crisscross wave patterns are present; I still have not determined what causes them, or why they are there one day and gone the next. But knowing that they are not always there, makes me appreciate them all the more when they are there. When these gently moving waves from various directions collide, there is an explosive action, which sometimes sends a course spray of water straight up into the air. It is a magnificent site to behold. It is an amazing enigma that so many waves can be traveling in all directions at the same time. What causes it? What allows it? In the flat places, the water surface is just shimmering with lively ripples that seem to have no direction, just dancing among themselves. These are crossed by the incoming waves which are 20 to 30 feet apart, and then by the diagonal waves, and the outgoing waves. Yet the ripples are never destroyed. The sea is like a living organism. (2/25/2000)

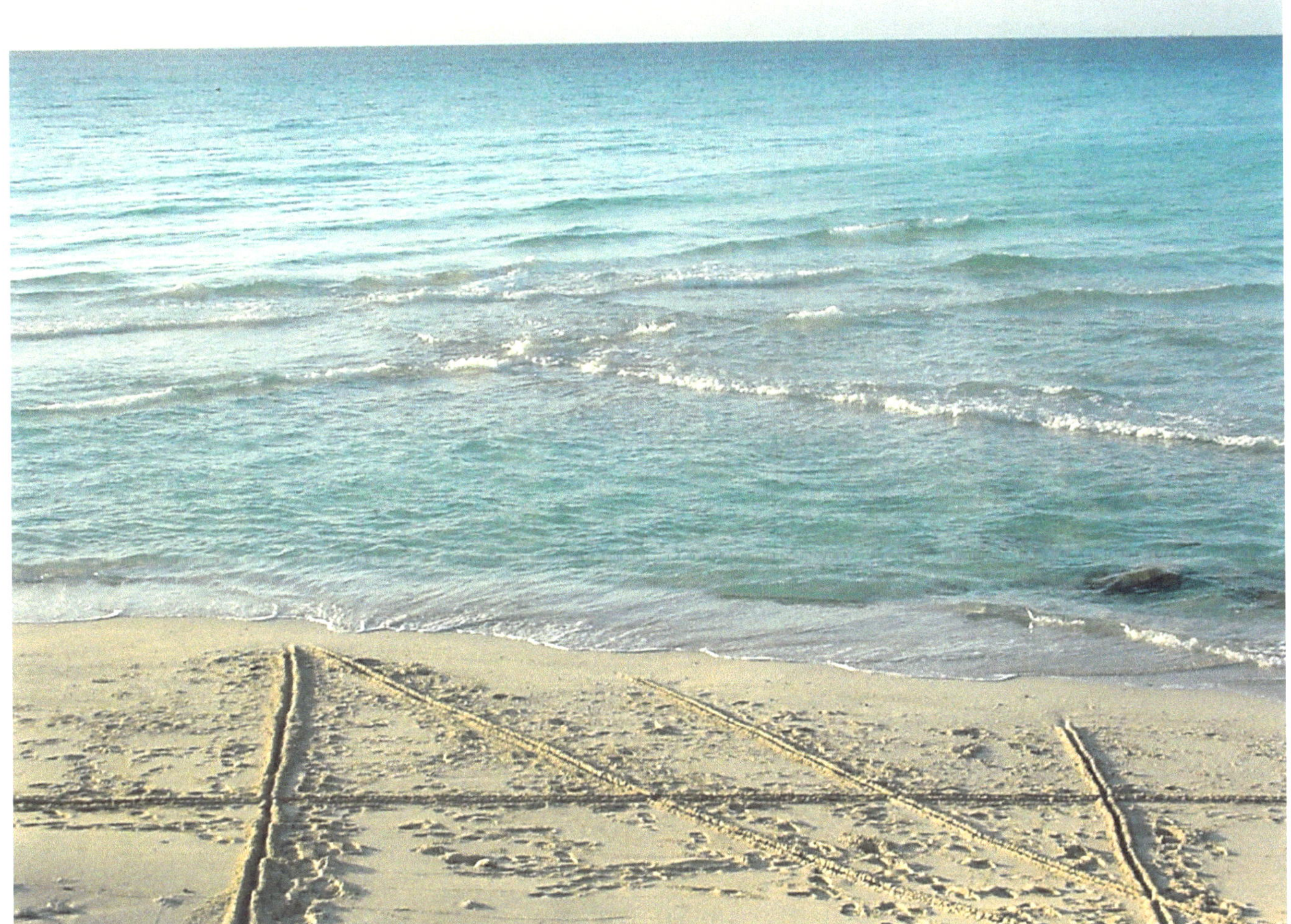

X On The Water & Mapped Telluric Energy Lines/Earth-Currents (Spook Hill Beach) 2005

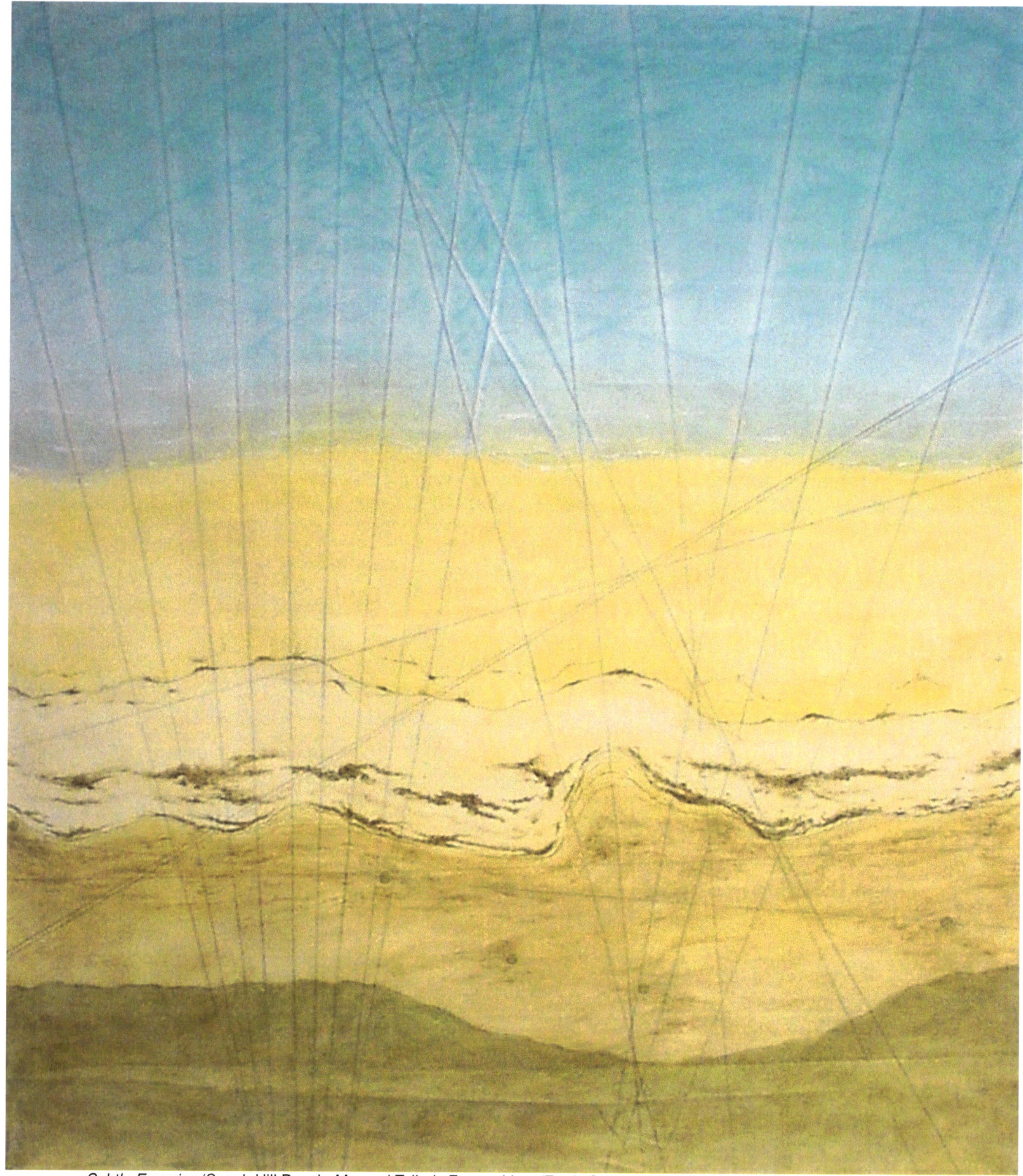

Subtle Energies (Spook Hill Beach, Mapped Telluric Energy Lines/Earth-Currents) 2005-2006, Acrylic on canvas, 61" x 54"

STONES OF ATLANTIS

Bimini is a tiny island within the Bermuda Triangle and is known for a high concentration of spiritual energy and healing vortices, attributed to it's location in the electromagnetic grid. Some believe Bimini is the tiny speck of land that remains of Atlantis. Edgar Cayce (1877-1945) called "the sleeping prophet" (note: his techniques involving trance are not to be advocated) had predicted that evidence of Atlantis would be found in 1968 or 1969 in the waters of Bimini. An amazing discovery was made in 1968 when a plane flying over Bimini spotted an underwater structure that has become known as the Bimini Road or the Stones of Atlantis. The subject of these mysterious stones quickly became controversial but the matter seems to have been put to rest in 2005, when underwater archaeologists disclosed irrefutable evidence of perhaps the world's oldest seaport, in about 15 feet of water just off Bimini's north-west shoreline (*The Ancient Bimini Harbor: Uncovering The Great Bimini Hoax*, Dr. Gregory L. Little, 2005 DVD) . The Bimini Road was in fact an ancient harbor of a long forgotten civilization, and perhaps as some have speculated, a seaport of the lost continent of Atlantis.

EUREKA! TOP OF THE MOUNTAIN

Eureka! was the excited cry of the prospectors who struck it rich during the California gold rush. In 1927, Edgar Cayce predicted gold in Bimini. He also stated that Bimini is the mountain top of an ancient continent that sunk beneath the floodwaters of the great deluge. To date, the gold vein has not been found, and though we have not been able to shout Eureka over the discovery of a hidden gold vein, we can shout Hallelujah as we stand with our feet upon the holy mountaintop.

Cayce had referred to the Bimini Islands as "these mountain tops," possibly the remnants of an ancient twin-peaked volcano related to Atlantis.

Geologist William Hutton states:

> Geoscientists think that the Bahama Banks were built by coral reefs on a spreading ocean crust with volcanic extrusions. ...An extrusion could have produced a twin-peaked volcanic mountain that became surrounded and then covered by coral reefs ...If a twin-peaked volcano underlies North and South Bimini, it is probably buried deeply. But the morphology of that volcano could be preserved somewhat in the overlying carbonate rocks. ...if, there is a buried carbonatite volcano at some depth beneath Bimini, one might further speculate that the "vein of gold, spar, and ijolite" could be part of the ijolite and related magma materials of a volcano center core.... Pure ("native") gold has been found in many of the volcanic terranes of the ocean floor ...reactivation to have occurred in the recent geological past in order for gold-bearing fluids to penetrate the late-Pleistocene rocks that underlie Bimini. Such reactivation could be related to the postulated sinking of Atlantis...
>
> (*TREASURE ISLAND: Edgar Cayce Predicted Gold in Bimini*, http://www.huttoncommentaries.com/Other/Bimini/VolcanoLinkG&S.htm)
>
> The oldest mention of Atlantis is found in two of Greek philosopher Plato's dialogues "Timaeus" and "Critias" which date back to 300 B.C. Plato introduces Atlantis ...as a huge island, existing in about 10,000 B.C. ...the island was violently destroyed by volcanoes.
>
> (*History Of Bimini*, volume 1, p.45, by Ashley B. Saunders)

Image on following page, *Bimini (Mountain Top of Atlantis) In My Right Hand*, 2006-2007, acrylic on canvas, 36" x 24"

In this painting the spiritual mountaintop is represented symbolically by the pyramidal capstone that the builders rejected (Psalms 118:22; 1Peter 2:4,7) i.e. Yesu Christ. Inside the capstone you see the Hebrew letter *Yod*, the initial of Yesu and of Yahweh, above the crystal blue pearl of great price, sending out electrical beams of energy (symbolizing the Holy Spirit) to all who will receive. You are living stones in the temple of God (1Peter 2:5) and Yesu is the "top corner stone" that ties everything together completing the mountain of the House of Yahweh. It may have been in Atlantis where the angels first entered the physical realm against the will of God. The capstone represents the portal of heaven through which those who are obedient to God may now find their way of entrance into the spiritual realm of the heavenly kingdom (Psalms 118:19-20). In the Hebrew Language Bimini means "In my right hand."

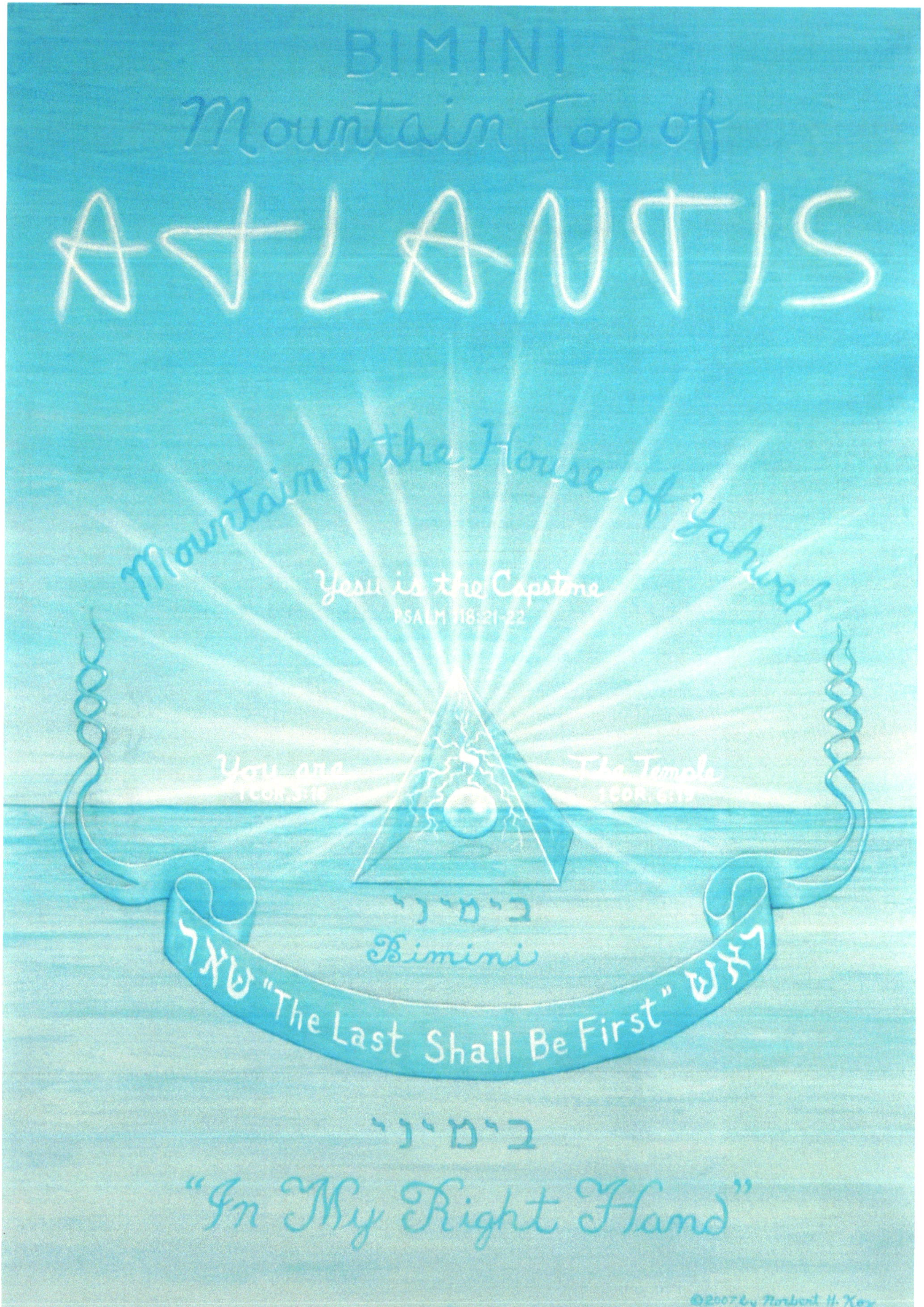
BIMINI
Mountain Top of
ATLANTIS
Mountain of the House of Yahweh
Yesu is the Capstone
PSALM 118:21-22
You are
1 COR. 3:16
The Temple
1 COR. 6:19
בימיני
Bimini
שאר "The Last Shall Be First" ראש
בימיני
"In My Right Hand"
©2007 by Norbert H. Kox

MOUNTAIN TOP IN THE SEA

Great excitement arose in 1968 when Edgar Cayce's prophecy that evidence of the lost Atlantis would appear in the shallow water along the west side of North Bimini seemed to be fulfilled. The main stone structure that was discovered has been dubbed the Bimini Wall or Bimini Road, also called the Atlantis Road. From the airplane, "The 'Road' appears to be the largest ruin, and it is shaped like an inverted 'J,' extending for some 1,900 feet, about half a mile off Bimini's northwest shore. Nearby 'fallen walls' start and stop without any reason, giving a perplexity to the entire meaning of the site." (http://www.bermuda-triangle.org/html/prophecy_fulfillment.html).

Cayce referred to North and South Bimini as two mountain tops of Atlantis. "He spoke of Atlantis as being under the water in the area of the Bermuda Triangle. The island of Bimini was supposed to be the highest peak of the mountain of Atlantis that never sunk." (http://www.merrybattles.com/ articles/article1.html).

> Edgar Cayce referred to Bimini as one of the mountaintops of ancient Atlantis. While few would consider the island a mountain, 12,000-years ago it was one of the highest points on the vast land formation in the region. Bimini and Andros Island, lying about 100 miles to the east of Bimini, were a part of the same island in 10,000 B.C.—called "Poseidia" by Cayce. Cayce related that a Hall of Records containing the records of Atlantis was constructed somewhere in the region. The Hall of Records was in a temple which sunk in 10,000 B.C.
> (http://www.edgarcayce.org/AM/atlantisnews.html)

Could this sunken temple have been the temple-pyramid discovered by Dr. Ray Brown in 1970? The television series, *In Search Of* (1976-1982) hosted by Leonard Nimoy, presented a segment on the discovery of "The Bimini Wall," in which Dr. Ray Brown spoke about his 1970 discovery of a sunken pyramid in the Bahamas near the Berry Islands, [east] of Bimini, in the Tongue of the Ocean. Dr. Brown removed a crystal ball from the temple pyramid. In the film this crystal ball containing powerful forces can be seen repelling a piece of steel, causing it to float up in the air like a feather in the wind. "Kirlian photographs, which record impressions beyond our limited range of vision, showed an eye inside the crystal not visible to the naked eye." (http://www.hiddenmysteries.org/mysteries/atlantis/evidence.html).

"Out of all the 700 plus islands of the Bahamas, only once did [Cayce] mention one by name, and this island was Bimini. The now famous Bimini prophecy does not just concern the island, but concerns the power crystals that directed the electromagnetic energy of Atlantis." (http://www.bermuda-triangle.org/html/prophecy_fulfillment.html).

> As for a description of the manner of construction of the [crystal] stone: we find it was large cylindrical glass (as would be termed today); cut with facets in such manner that the capstone on top of it made for centralizing the power or force that concentrated between the end of the cylinder and the capstone itself. As indicated, the records as to ways of constructing same are in three places in the Earth, as it stands today: in the sunken portion of Atlantis, or Poseidia, where a portion of the temple may yet be discovered under the slime of the ages of sea water—near what is known as Bimini, off the coast of Florida . . . reading from December 20, 1933, *Edgar Cayce on Atlantis* (*ibid.*)

Atlantis was the land where gods and humans cohabited. This aligns it with the Biblical land of Genesis chapter six, as can be seen in the writings of Enoch. The gods (the Elohim, mighty ones) were the angels that left their first estate to mingle with humans on earth. Their first estate was the heavenly realm. They came through an interdimensional portal, the gate of heaven (star-gate, in Egyptian literature) from the spirit world into the physical realm. Many wondrous things were learned as a result of their great knowledge, but according to Enoch they soon corrupted the human race. This wickedness resulted in Yahweh's decision to destroy them. They had created a race of giants, possibly through genetic manipulation, who were subsequently drowned in the flood. Evidently the floodwaters never completely subsided and as a result Atlantis remained mostly submerged beneath the ocean. Perhaps Cayce was right and the Biminis are the mountain tops of Atlantis.

> Before the end of the last Ice Age (12,000-years ago) the ocean levels were at least 300 feet below their current levels. A vast "island" was in the area in those remote times rather than chains of islands. Edgar Cayce referred to Bimini as one of the mountaintops of ancient Atlantis. (http://www.edgarcayce.org/ancient_mysteries/atlantis.asp)

Bimini is possibly one of the lowest islands in the sea, its major portion being hardly a few feet above sea level and its highest point rising only to about 20 feet, yet it may have been one of the highest mountain tops of Atlantis.

THE BIMINI CALL

With the words of Isaiah 11:11, God called me to the Islands of the sea in 1998. He took me to the Island of Bimini, which means "In my right hand" when transcribed into Hebrew, בימיני.

The numbers 11:11 are extremely significant. Symmetrical numbers are often very powerful in symbolic meaning. Some of the Internet references to 11:11, claim that it is an esoteric allusion to a portal gate of ascension… This would correlate it to Psalms 118:20, "the portal of Yahweh into which the righteous shall enter."

When you multiply 1111 by 1111 you get the symmetrical number 1234321, representing a pyramid, which in essence represents a portal.

One of the great "Swallows" crop formations has an 11:11 incorporated into it which is supposedly a symbolic connection to the alleged 11:11 Doorway in the Belt of Orion. New Agers claim there is a wormhole between Orion's Belt and the Earth.

New Agers have many truths about the laws of the universe and quantum physics, but this has nothing to do with salvation. Be cautious of their spiritual teachings. Anyone who believes he is his own saviour is in trouble. Scripture says that Yesu Christ is the portal and anyone who enters by any other way is a thief and a robber (John 10:1, 7-11).

Supposedly the 2012 Mayan end year is timed at 11:11 Universal time. This link at the US naval observatory indicates the possibility that these people could have been connecting in to the 2012 phenomenon. According to this page, the 2012 winter solstice (12/21/12) will occur at 11:11 universal time (*Earth's Seasons*, etc. 1992-2020, U.S. Naval Observatory, http://aa.usno.navy.mil/data/docs/EarthSeasons.php).

Is there anything to this 11:11 phenomenon, or is it all shear coincidence? Could it actually relate to Isaiah 11:11 and Yahweh gathering the remnant of his people?

REVELATIONS IN PAINT

During my first extended stay in Bimini, 1999, while painting an Apocalyptic Visual Parable of the Island (4-ft x 18-ft), God revealed many things to me in the Bible codes which went into the painting, including the destruction of the twin towers of the World Trade Center (2 ½ years prior to the event). Even though he gave me the code that revealed the terrible destruction, I was not allowed to completely decipher it at the time. But none-the-less it was in the painting for anyone with the proper enlightenment to see. He also revealed the depths and many layers of the Hebrew word for island, אי [*aleph-yod*].

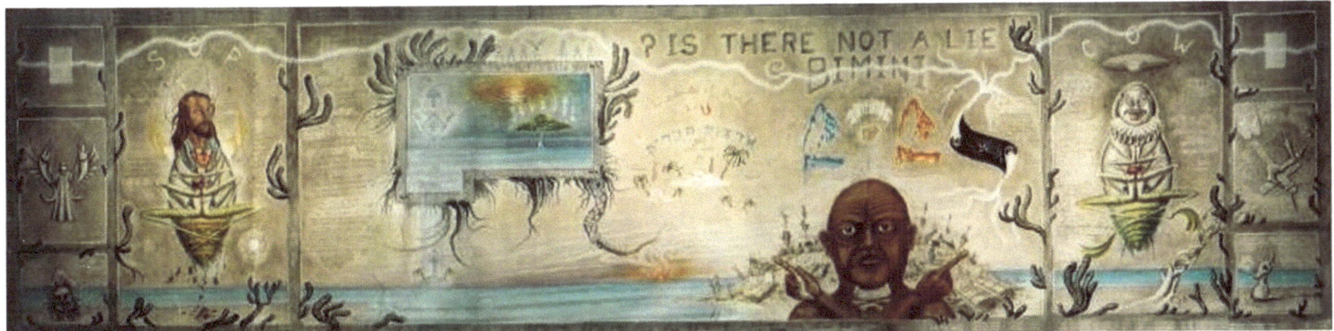

Bimini, 1999, acrylic on canvas, 48" x 216" (4-ft X 18-ft)

This painting was first exhibited in March of 1999, at Precious de Paris in Bimini, Bahamas, where it was well received. Next it was exhibited at Neville Public Museum in Green Bay, Wisconsin, in the solo exhibition *To hell And Back* (July-October 1999) where it stirred a great controversy and remained in the news for more than 3 ½ months. The museum was picketed by a radical Marian group, and was also protested in the media by the Catholic Defense League of New York. Neville Museum attendance reached an all-time record high and during the show donations increased to 40% higher than ever before. The painting was also shown in Wisconsin Classic 2000, at Milwaukee Institute Of Art And Design.

In January 2001, Channel 4 in the United Kingdom broadcasted an episode of Disinfo Nation (by *The Disinformation Co.*) hosted by Richard Metzger, in which the *Bimini* painting was prominently featured and explained by Norbert Kox.

Partial description of *Bimini*:

The painting is riddled with Bible codes, most of which have not been translated into English but remain in pure Hebrew. "I had intended to include the English translations but was impressed in the Spirit to leave the Codes untranslated because they are for the Hebrew speaking people." The man in the foreground is one of the last day judges of Israel; "My Judge" is written on his forehead in Hebrew. Above his head is a partial Bible code matrix from Psalms 118, at skip-26, which reveals the phrase "Man of Yah" or God-Man, superimposed by the words "My blood," and the name of Yesu crisscrossed on each side, so that the name is seen four times in a symmetrical pattern. This is exactly how you would see it within the full gridwork of a Bible Code program. Higher up is a loaf of the famous Bimini bread with the name of Yesu inscribed on it, and on the banner the three vowels (*yods*) of Bimini form the phrase "My God" the remaining letter's say "In Bread." In Scripture Yesu says, "I am the bread of life." In Hebrew the word Bimini means "In my right hand." The judge is pictured with his arms crossed and two right hands, essentially saying, "You decide; What will you hold in your right hand, truth or falsehood?"

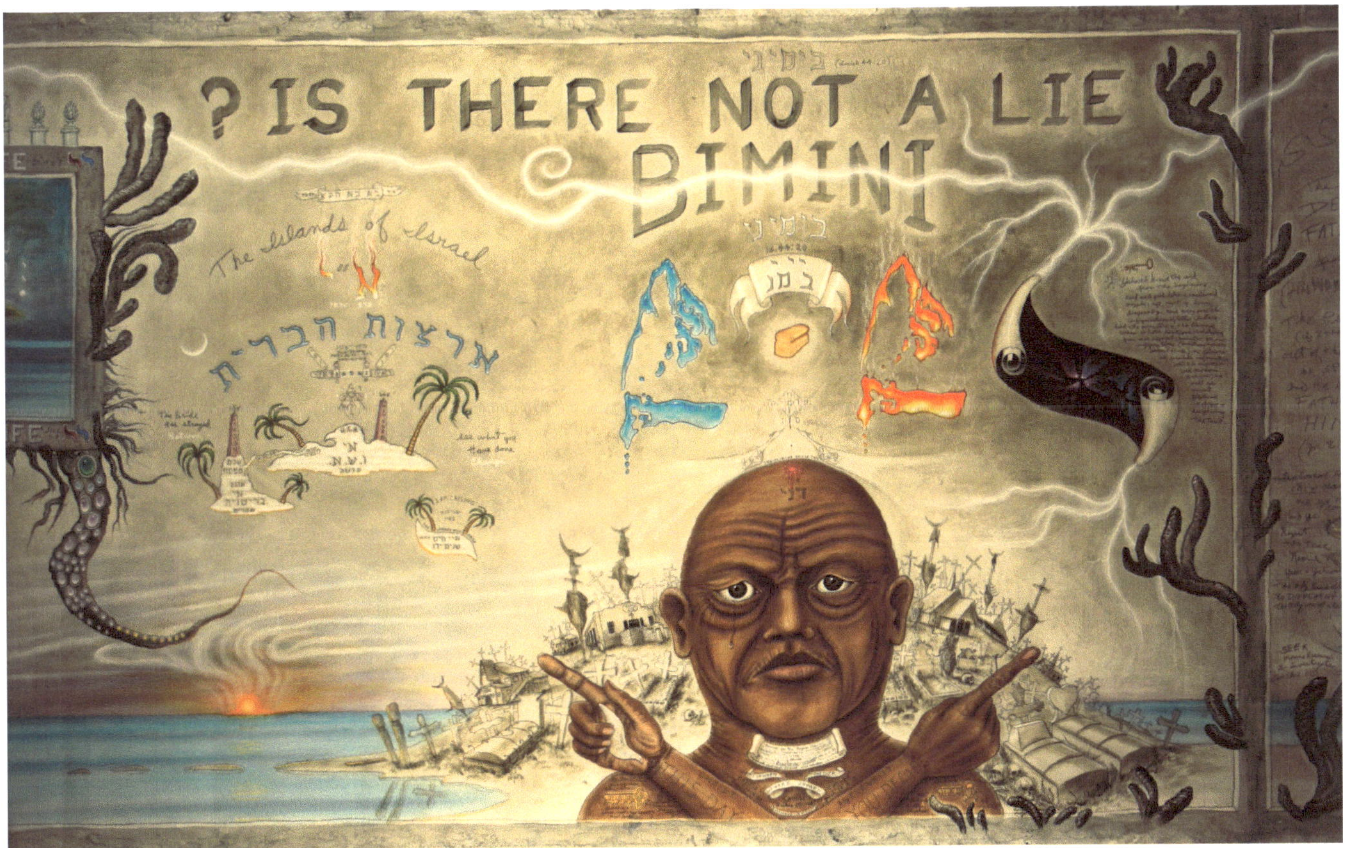

Bimini (detail) 1999, acrylic on canvas

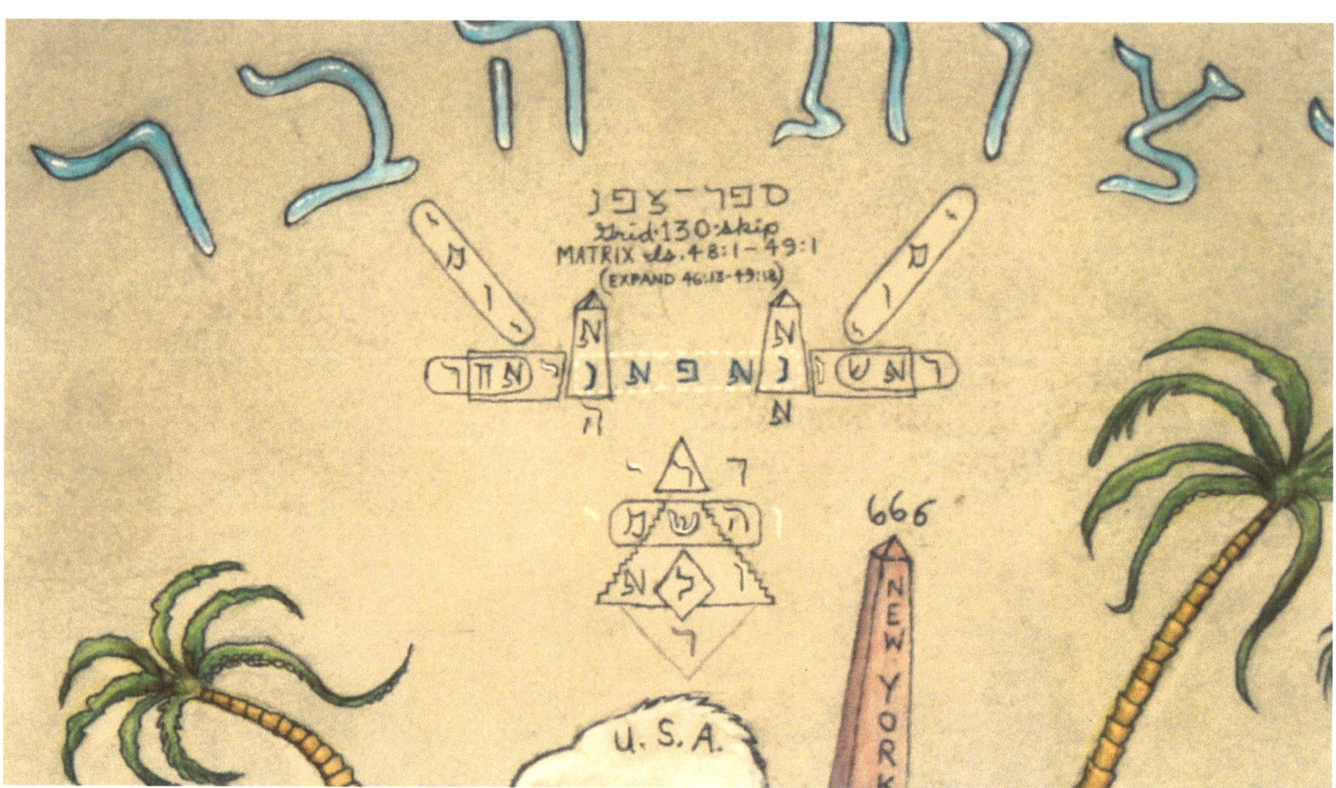

Bimini (detail, symmetrical Bible code of twin tower inferno) 1999, acrylic on canvas

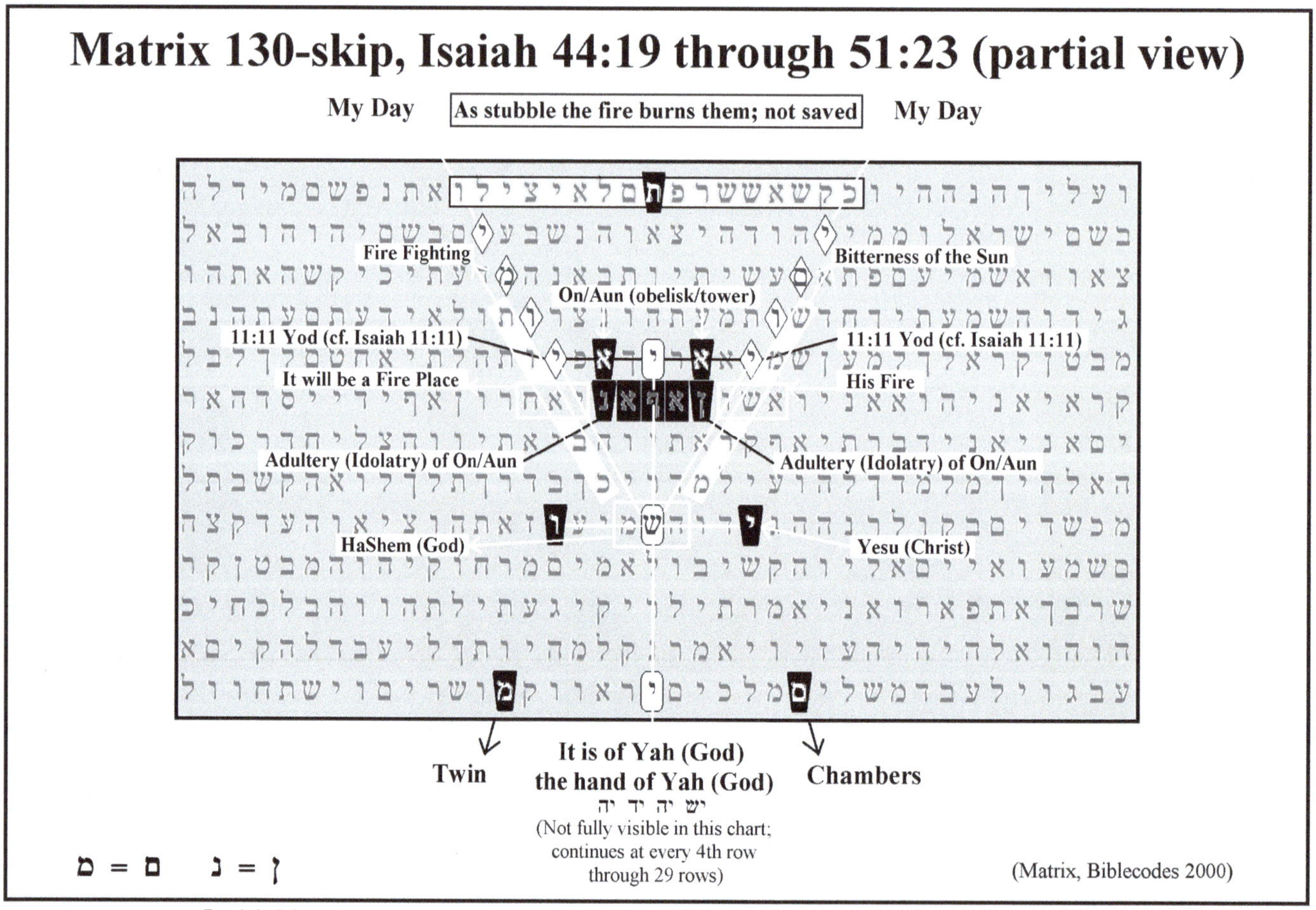

Matrix 130-skip, Isaiah 44:19 through 51:23 (partial view)

My Day | As stubble the fire burns them; not saved | My Day

Fire Fighting
Bitterness of the Sun
On/Aun (obelisk/tower)
11:11 Yod (cf. Isaiah 11:11)
11:11 Yod (cf. Isaiah 11:11)
It will be a Fire Place
His Fire
Adultery (Idolatry) of On/Aun
Adultery (Idolatry) of On/Aun
HaShem (God)
Yesu (Christ)

Twin | It is of Yah (God) the hand of Yah (God) | Chambers

יש יה יד יה

(Not fully visible in this chart; continues at every 4th row through 29 rows)

מ = ם   נ = ן

(Matrix, Biblecodes 2000)

Partial elaboration on the symmetrical grid from the 1999 *Bimini* painting (*The End Is Come*, p.35)

The section of Isaiah under scrutiny holds hidden messages in an elaborate symmetrical matrix (Isaiah 44:19 through 51:23; Equidistant Letter Sequence, 130-skip) encoding in great detail the events of 911 (this was partially shown, 2 1/2 years before 911, in the 1999 epic painting titled "Bimini"). In this Isaiah grid the words "twin" and "chambers," intersected by the double appearance of the word On/Aun [city where Cleopatra's Needles originated] signify the Twin Towers; and "it will be as a fireplace." The term "His firepalce," is "U.S.A." in reverse. The dual term "My day" rises symmetrically from the letter *Shin* in the middle of Yesu and HaShem; *Shin* is the Hebrew *mother letter* symbolizing fire. The same *Shin* is crossed by the phrase, "It is of Yah, the hand of Yah," indicating the fire was God's judgment. "As stubble the fire burns them; not saved," is the portion of the surface text of Isaiah 47:14 that falls here symmetrically at the top of this chart, and the phrase "Declaring the bitterness of my fire" [not shown here] also appears symmetrically, higher up in the expanded matrix (Isaiah 46:10).

The word On (אָן also אֹנ) connects Manasseh to the U.S. (Genesis 41:45-52) seen twice vertically, *viz.* the standing towers, and twice horizontally, the two fallen towers. AUN, spelled with the Hebrew vowel-letter, has the alternate meanings "wealth" and "wickedness."

ISLANDS OF THE SEA

Many of the symmetrically numbered Scripture verses are highly significant keys in God's eternal plan. Isaiah 11:11, is one such passage.

God has chosen to work in symmetry and with synonyms and antonyms. All through Scripture he works in pairs, twins. Starting in Genesis with darkness and light, good and evil, Cain and Abel, things are done symmetrically all through the Bible, of course, culminating with Christ and Antichrist, and finally at judgment day, eternal death versus eternal life and a new heaven and new earth.

On the third day of creation, God caused dry land to come forth. The dry land he called **ארץ**, *eretz*, and the collection of the waters he called **ימים**, *yamim*. The initials of *land* **א** (*a*) and *sea* **י** (*i*) spell island, **אי** [*ai*]. So the initials of the term "land of the sea," spell the Hebrew word for "island," and an island is essentially the *land of the sea*. "The Bahama Islands" are encoded into this third day Scripture (see, p.39).

The "Islands of the sea," is a term with deep hidden meaning. First we look at the surface. The islands of the sea are literal places. Every piece of land in the seas constitutes an island of the sea.

According to Dov Ben-Abba, the letter "I" means *Yod* (י), or **אי**, [*ai*: *aleph-yod*] (*Hebrew-English English-Hebrew Dictionary*, p. 146, "I"). What an astonishing prophetic revelation! Second and third levels of the word for island, **אי**, are designated as the *Yod* and *I*. These are extremely significant, since Yahweh will re-establish his *Yod* to recover the remnant of his people from the Islands of the Sea. These three levels are a type of triple witness, *ai=I*, *ai=Yod*, *ai=island*; *viz.* *"I"* will set my *"Yod"* ...to the *"Islands"* of the sea.

Besides meaning *Yod*, *I* and *island*, in still a fourth level the letters *aleph-yod*, **אי** (*ai*) are also an abbreviation for the *Land of Israel* [*Eretz Yisrael*: **ארץ ישראל**]. So the mission to the Islands is also a mission to the Land of Israel, to return his *Yod*.

There is yet a fifth significant level of this word connected symbolically to the "United States."

How is the U.S. Related to Israel? The name of Israel was conferred upon Ephraim and Manasseh, by their paternal grandfather Jacob (Israel) in Genesis 48. Cleopatra's Needles, in London and New York, are the twin obelisks that stood in front of the Sun Temple where the maternal grandfather of Ephraim and Manasseh was the great high priest of the sun-god (Genesis 41:45-52). The Needles identify our hidden heritage. Great Britain and the United States are Israel (Egypto-Israel) the descendants of Ephraim and Manasseh. Thus the title Israel, conferred upon Ephraim and Manasseh, is rightfully applied to Great Britain and the United States (Bimini is also Ephraim/Israel, having been part of Great Britain).

This identity is affirmed in Hebrew dictionaries. United States is, **ארצות הברית**, "Lands of the Covenant." Everyone knows that Israel is the Land of the Covenant. Why would the Jews attach that name to the United States? Because they see it as the land of the promise, the new Israel. Therefore the United States is a fifth level of the word Island, **אי**, "the Land of Israel." The U.S.A. is *Island Israel*. It is one of the Islands of the Sea, the Lands of Israel of the Sea, the scattered and dispersed Israel that Yahweh wants to recover.

Great Britain is another set of Islands. British is a Hebrew compound word. *Brit* means "covenant," and *ish* means "man." The British Isles are the "Islands of the Covenant-Man."

America and Britain are Islands of Israel. The Bahamas are also Islands of the Covenant-Man."

Island, *aleph yod* (*ai*) has a numerical value of eleven. In Hebrew, the number 11, is written *yod aleph* (*ia*). "Island of the Land of Israel," is abbreviated *ai-ai*. In reverse it is *ia-ia*, which is the symmetrical number, 11:11, the same chapter and verse where Isaiah prophesied the return of the *Yod* of Yahweh.

Since the Scriptures say Yahweh is to recover his remnant from the nations and the Islands, by setting his *Yod* a second time, his name must be very important. We need to know and use his name, not the counterfeit versions.

APOCALYPTIC MISSION

God has shown me some astounding things and he has inspired me to present them to the world. This is a time of judgment; the Day of Yahweh is at hand. The kingdom is in you and is determining your destiny at this moment.

> Neither shall they say, Lo here! or, lo there! for, behold, the kingdom of God is *within* [Greek, *entos,* "inside"] you. (Luke 17:21)

Yesu said not one *Yod* [KJV, "Jot"] would pass from the Torah till all things be fulfilled (Matthew 5:18). The *Yod* is the tenth letter of the Hebrew alphabet and the initial of the names Yesu and Yahweh. It has not passed from the Hebrew Torah. But it has been lost in English. Even though it still exists in the Hebrew Scriptures, the Jews do not pronounce the name of Yahweh, and most of them reject Yesu as Messiah. God is displeased with both these practices by the Jews and the English nations, and has determined to correct the matter, for those who will receive his word.

If you are Jewish, please do not take offense at the use of the Name Yahweh in this book. To understand the importance of pronouncing his name please read, *The Holy Cipher: Who Changed God's Name?* (Norbert H. Kox, 2007, Apocalypse House).

The Hebrew letter *Yod* means "hand" (*yad*), and in ancient times was represented by the pictograph of a hand. Scripture has encoded within the surface text, "O Yahweh our God ...thine holy name is from thy *hand* [*yad/Yod*]." (1Chronicles29:16). Yahweh's initial *Yod* represents his "hand" and his power. He wants to give back power to his name by returning his *Yod* as he has promised,

> And in that day there shall be a root of Jesse, which shall stand for an ensign of the people; to it shall the Gentiles [*Goyim*] seek: and his rest shall be glorious.
>
> And it shall come to pass in that day, that Yahweh shall set his hand [*yad/yod*] again the second time to recover the remnant of his people, which shall be left, from Assyria, and from Egypt, and from Pathros, and from Cush, and from Elam, and from Shinar, and from Hamath, and *from the islands of the sea.* [11:11]
>
> And he shall set up an ensign for the nations, and shall assemble the outcasts of Israel, and gather together the dispersed of Judah from the four corners of the earth.
>
> The envy also of Ephraim shall depart, and the adversaries of Judah shall be cut off: Ephraim shall not envy Judah, and Judah shall not vex Ephraim.
>
> (Isaiah 11: 10-13).

Israel and Judah had split into two separate nations after the end of Solomon's reign but according to the prophets they will reunite in the last days.

Joseph's sons, Ephraim and Manasseh were given the name and birthright of Israel. Often the name Ephraim is used in reference to Nation Israel. Ephraim and Manasseh are Nation Israel, otherwise called Gentiles (Hebrew, *Goyim*) and have been traced, respectively, to Great Britain (Bahamas were British until 1973) and the United States.

The root of Jesse to whom the *Goyim* seek is Yesu. The English-speaking nations are remnants of Israel, descended through Ephraim and Manasseh. It is the English Bibles that have taken away the *Yod* (the Hebrew Y and I) and replaced it with a J that never existed until a few hundred years ago. "Yahweh shall set his *Yod* again the second time to recover the remnant of his people." He wants to give the *Yod* to us the second time, so that through the names of Yahweh Yesu he can recover us.

He is reaching out to recover his remnant from Assyria, Egypt, Pathros, Cush, Elam, Shinar, Hamath, and *from the islands of the sea.*

The words of the Torah are compared to the waters of the sea. As the waters of the sea contain great depths with many marvelous secrets hidden in the darkness far beneath the surface, so does God's word hold wonderful secrets for those who are willing and able to retrieve them.

RECOVERING AND REUNITING

Yahweh seeks to recover his remnant from the Islands of the Sea, while simultaneously reuniting Judah and Israel. This probably seems like an odd statement to most people, not realizing they were even separated. The modern State of Israel is actually not Israel at all. It is Judah. In ancient Biblical times the sons of Israel were split into two nations, Judah and Israel. They never reunited. Those referred to as the lost tribes of Israel, or the *Nations/Goyim*, are essentially the descendants of Jacob that migrated through Europe to the British Isles and eventually to the United States. Many of the Black African slaves who were brought as captives to Babylon (U.S.A.) are also related to Israel.

> *Biblical Truth* tells us what the Book of Genesis says concerning the present day identity, and future destiny, of the Israelite tribes including those whose descendants are unaware of their Hebrew ancestry. ...The USA with Britain and her daughters descend from Joseph who was to receive the major blessings. Judah represents the Jews. Judah and Joseph each have their own tasks. They are two parts of one whole.
>
> The Israelites were to possess the "gate of his enemies" and "the gate of those that hate them" (Genesis 24:60). This means major strategic points giving an edge over all potential adversaries. The USA and Britain have had this advantage and still do. Descendants of Joseph were to become the most powerful nations in the world, and to bring a blessing to all the peoples of the earth. Genesis identifies the Lost Ten Tribes of Israel with the USA, Britain and related nations. This is *Biblical Truth*.
>
> (http://www.christianreality.com/Books/bs-bok133.htm, *Biblical Truth*, by Yair Davidiy, Orthodox Jew living in Jerusalem). Note: Davidy has done some very thorough research but is biased in certain areas, therefore prudence is advised the reader.

IN THE BEGINNING

On my first extended stay in Bimini (Winter of 1998-1999) while working on the epic painting "Bimini is there not a lie," God began to open to me the great mystery of the "Key of David" (Psalm 22:22; Revelation 3:7). It is the key that opens and closes heavenly portals. He showed me through the Bible code that the key on the shoulder of the high priest refers to the onyx stones (Exodus 39:6) which held up the breastplate of righteousness/judgment. The shoulder stones had the names of the twelve sons of Israel

(Jacob), six of them engraved on each stone indexed by their birth order, and the same Hebrew word for key also means "index."

> The shoulder attachments were flesh colored onyx stones inscribed with the names of the 12 tribes in birth order. Attached to the ephod in front was the breastplate that had 12 precious stones representing the tribes in marching order. This breastplate weighed 40 pounds! The priest "carried" the tribes (the people of Israel) on his shoulders and over his heart. (http://www.abundantword.org/pages/freestuff.htm)

The two stones were thinly cut flesh colored translucent onyx with red veins running through them, to represent flesh and blood. This may have been a prophetic symbolism of the coming messiah, prior to John's writing of its fulfillment, "The Word was made flesh and dwelt among us."

LIVING ORACLES AND DIAMOND CODES

In Psalms 88:9, there is an Equidistant Letter Sequences code (ELS-3) within the phrase, "Yahweh in every day." In the Hebrew text, יהוה בכל יום, every third letter spells יהלם, (*yahalom*) "diamond." *Yahweh in every day* is our diamond!

Notes from my first extended visit to the Island of Bimini:

> February 24, 1999
>
> Living oracles, concerning Bible Code:
>
> There are things happening here that cannot happen by chance, far out of the realm of coincidence. Yet, far too sophisticated to have been contrived by any human brain. There are so many variations, so many encoded, detailed and intricate, messages emanating from any given section of Scripture, that it is doubtful that such a thing could be accomplished by any human even with the use of supercomputers. It is in the realm of impossibility.
>
> The true guide and creator, Yahweh-Yesu is the author of Scripture, knowing the end from the beginning, and having the capability to encode it all in one small book, to be deciphered by us in these latter days of time.

> March 2, 1999, 7:20 AM
>
> Diamond code:
>
> There are keywords around which the diamonds form. When the proper key is hit upon there are countless variations within a short section of Scripture, e.g. Psalm 11:1-7. I think it would probably take years to decipher completely; I'm not sure it would be completely. God keeps showing me ways to get deeper into the code and it seems infinite.
>
> If we could teach every scholar in the world these techniques of breaking the code, and everyone took a section of Scripture to decipher, we would still only be scratching the surface. [Once when I said "We are only scratching the surface," one very wise Jewish lady in London replied, "We do not even know where the surface is".]
>
> ...All that God has revealed in the codes to me over a period of about a year [with over 600 hours in six months] marvelous as it has been it was just a drop in the bucket compared to what has been revealed in the past week here in Bimini.
>
> ...11:25 PM, I just shut the computer off. Worked over 36 hours straight and most of it was extremely rewarding. For 24 hours it seemed like I could not miss. Everything was an amazing discovery and it all fell together.

> March 3, 1999, 4 PM
>
> I've been into the divine living oracles for the past twelve days, and over 150 hours in that short time. Yahweh has shown me more wonders in this little time in Bimini ("In my right hand") than in

my whole life. He has taken me so deep into his word to show me the importance of his unchanged name and the letter yod, which is his hand [and his initial].

Bud Kraus had told me of the vision he had of Yahweh's throne and the many faceted diamond that turns and gives new light through all eternity. I've seen the blueprint. It is marvelous. I know I've only seen a speck of it, but of that little piece there is no end.

March 6, 1999, 1 PM

Diamond Code key:

The importance of Yahweh-Yesu's initial yod is very evident in the diamond code. If one "jot" (*Iota, Iot* = *Yot* = *Yod* = *Yad* = י) had failed (before heaven and earth pass - Matthew 5:18) it would delete important, essential information from "the book of life."

The *yod* is Yahweh's hand and pointer. Often there are yods at the points of the diamonds, and/or in the center facet. Sometimes the *yods* will form an outline, either dotted, or uninterrupted, to dictate the confines of that diamond code.

A number of these diamond codes found their way into the epic *Bimini* painting.

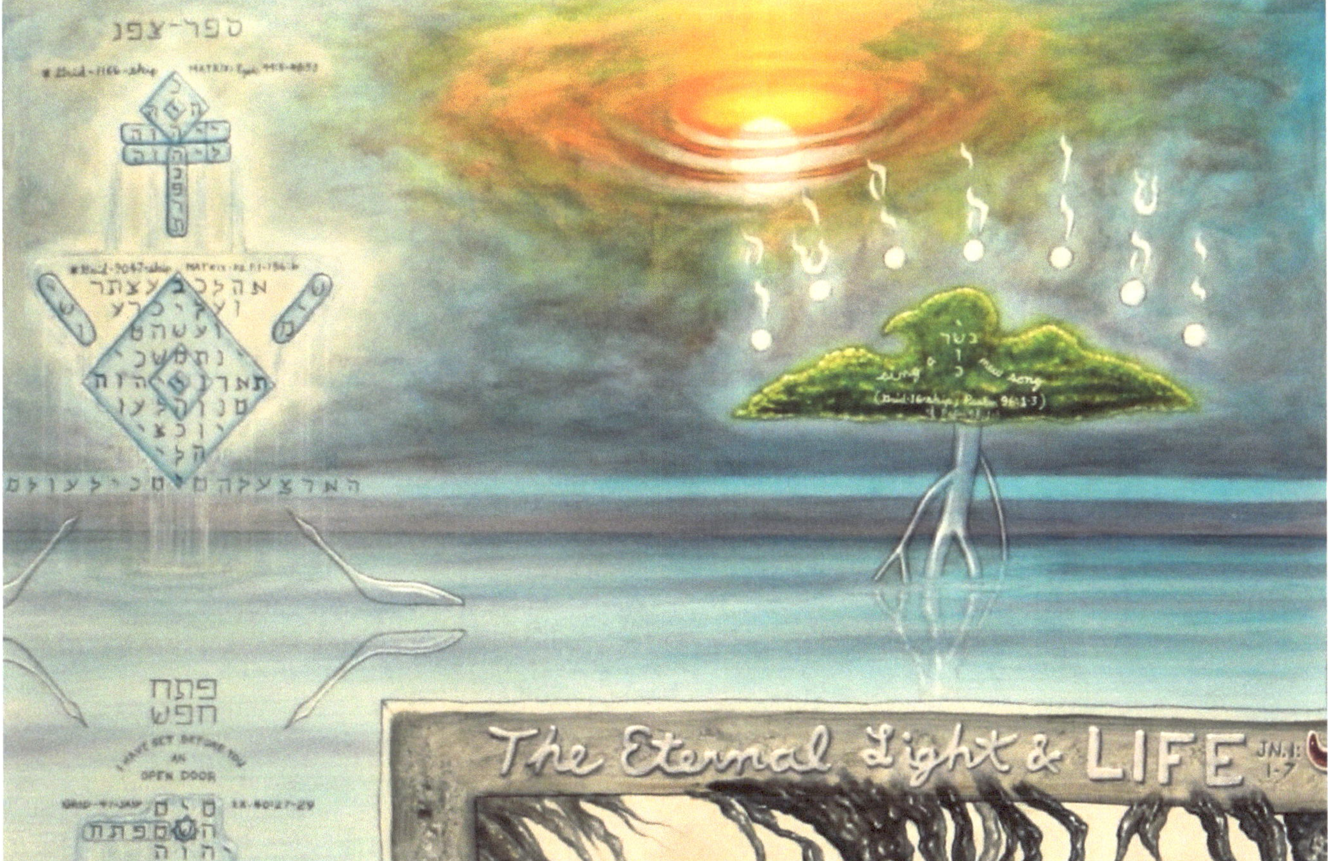

Bimini (detail, symmetrical diamond Bible codes) 1999, acrylic on canvas

DIAMOND-SHAPED ONYX STONES

With all that had been shown to me in the diamond codes for some reason I did not catch on to the shape of the onyx stones. It should have been something to immediately explore, but it took several years of hard research before it was revealed. At first I had thought the stones would appear as we normally think a square should look, the way they have been pictured in drawings and paintings before, but now through much research, it seems that they would have basically been turned on edge to form diamonds rather than squares. This affects the placement of the letters.

These stones were engraved as an index of the names of Jacob's 12 sons, with the letters arranged as crossword puzzles, thus enabling the code within them. The Hebrew word for crossword puzzle, תשבץ, even appears in the surface text that speaks about the holy garments of the high priest in Exodus 28:4.

Upon intense prolonged examination of the word puzzles and the messages within, it seems quite apparent that the onyx stones on the high priest's shoulders would have been in the diamond shape with the letters of the names arranged accordingly.

When the proper letter arrangements of the names that were on the onyx stones are written into two grids representing the two diamond-shaped stones, each one reveals an identical cluster-pattern of four Hebrew characters, Shin, Waw, Lamed, Yod (s, w, l, y).

Shin, *Waw*, *Lamed*, *Yod* spells the Hebrew word *shuli* (שולי) meaning "my train" or "my hem." It is a direct reference to the throne room of God, as seen in Isaiah 6:1, where Yahweh was raised up on a high throne and "his train filled the temple." It also references the hem of Yesu's garment by which all who touched it immediately experienced the power of God and were healed (see Matthew 9:20-22; & 14:35-36). As an anagram the four letters also spell, לישו, "For Yesu," or "to Yesu." Paul said, "Whatsoever ye do in word or in deed, do all in the name of the Lord Yesu" (Colossians 3:17).

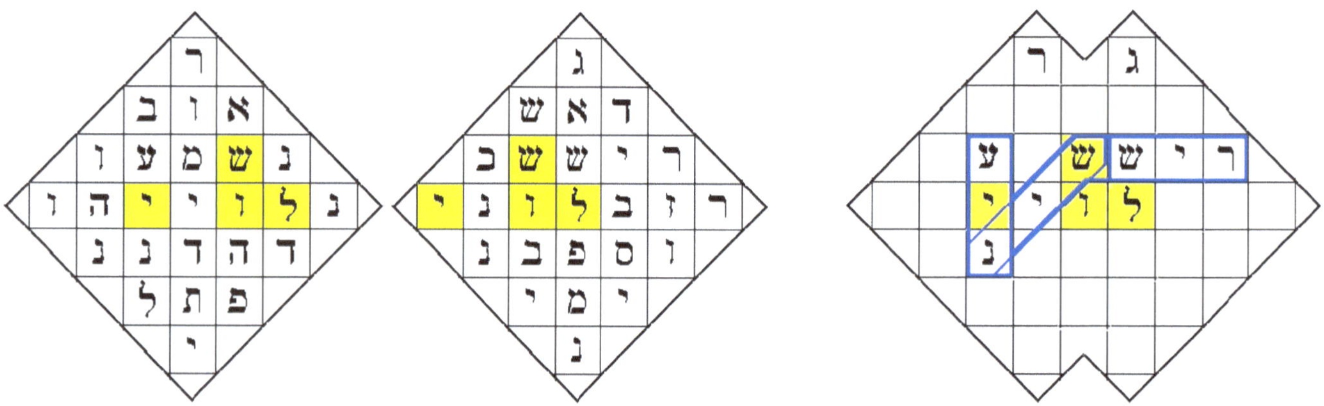

These diamond-shaped grids are facsimiles of the onyx stones on the high priest's shoulders. The one on the far left has the names of the first six sons of Jacob/Israel, and was worn on the right shoulder. The next one has the second set of six names and was on the left shoulder. Notice the two sets of identical key-letters. The image to the far right shows how overlapping the stones on these key-letters causes the words *shin-ayin* from stone-1 to connect to the word *resh* on stone-2; the Hebrew letters *shin-ayin-resh* spell *shaar*, or "portal." The pattern curiously resembles a square root symbol.

When the thinly cut translucent stones are placed one on top of the other and the identical four-letter patterns of *Shin*, *Waw*, *Lamed*, *Yod* (ש, ו, ל, י) are overlaid and lined up as a key, we see that three Hebrew letters which are spelled out in the stones, *Resh*, *Ayin*, *Shin*, all interconnect to resemble a square root symbol (what this symbol applies to here is not yet certain). *Resh*, *Ayin*, *Shin*, רעש, means earthquake or vibration, but reversed, שער, it means PORTAL. When the Hebrew numerical values of these three letters (300-70-200) are transmuted onto a 360 degree circle, and then connected by three straight lines, they format a perfect isosceles triangle with an apex of 50 degrees and two base angles of 65 degrees each. This is the exact same format as the capstone eye over the pyramid on the Great Seal of the United States, found on the backside of the one dollar bill. In the *Shin-Ayin-Resh* portal triangle, the *Ayin* is at the apex, and the Hebrew word *Ayin* means EYE. It all lines up with the eye over the pyramid representing the portal of heaven. In ancient Egypt the capstone pyramidion was believed to be a portal that transported the gods between this world and the heavens.

The *Ayin* is also a symbol for portal. Another interesting note is that the Hebrew word for key (מפתח) also means opening or aperture, which is exactly what a portal is. This means we have at least three references of portal within the onyx stones that are the key on Yesu's shoulder.

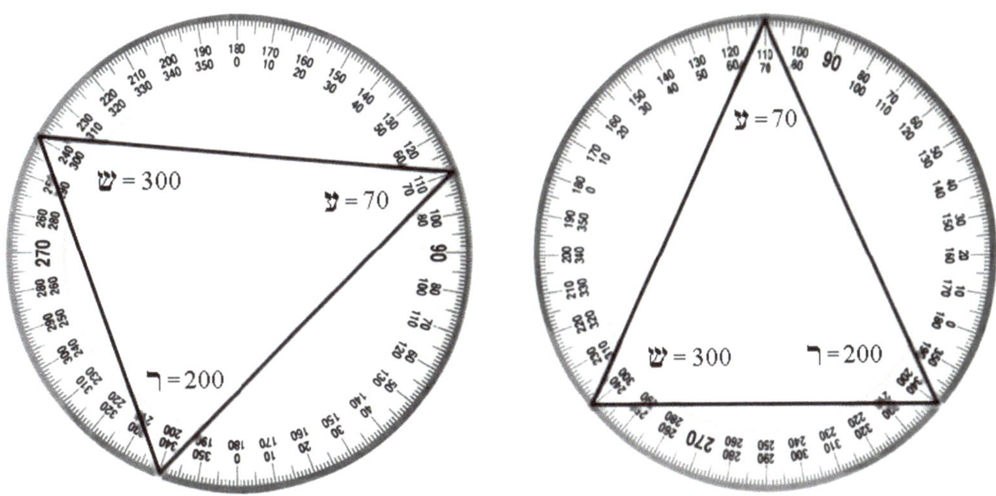

The numerical equivalents of the letters *Shin-ayin-resh* plotted on a circle reveal a perfect isosceles triangle with an apex of 50 degrees and two base angles of 65 degrees each. The letter *ayin*, or "eye" is at the apex of the pyramid.

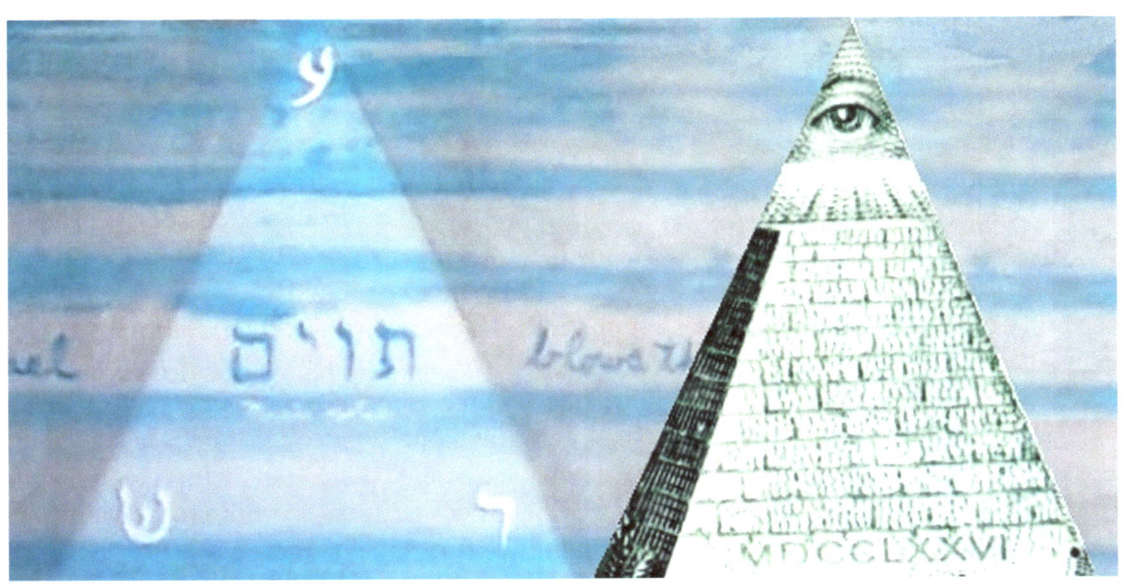

Detail of *Opening The Portal* (2004-2005) with superimposed eye and pyramid from the Great Seal of the United States, as pictured on the one dollar bill. The *Shin-ayin-resh* as demonstrated has produced a perfect isosceles triangle which correlates exactly to the format of the eye over the pyramid on the seal.

Many people see the eye/pyramid symbol as Satanic, but it is actually one of Yahweh's symbols that has been appropriated by the occult in their endeavor to stand as God in the place of God, and as a fulfillment of Satan's boast, "I shall be like the most high."

The pyramid is actually outlined symmetrically within the onyx stones, as a symbol of the portal. The first stone has the Hebrew word *amin*, "authentic," running through it diagonally. The second stone, symmetrically to the first, contains the phrase "that precious stone," or "that agate." The Hebrew word for agate is שבו. That is the spelling of the stone of Asher, the Firestone agate on the breastplate of the high priest, the stone that opened the portal for Jacob. The anagram of agate is "a gate," in essence a portal.

When the two stones are overlapped on the key, as previously described, the diagonal words "authentic" and "that precious stone (agate)" are joined at the top creating a pyramid-shape. At the apex of the pyramid the letters *aleph* and *shin* are joined giving us the Hebrew word for "fire." There it is, the capstone of Fire, that precious stone, "a gate." Scripture tells us that Yesu Christ is a gate, a portal (John 10:7) and that he is that "precious" stone, the capstone (1 Peter 2:6-7).

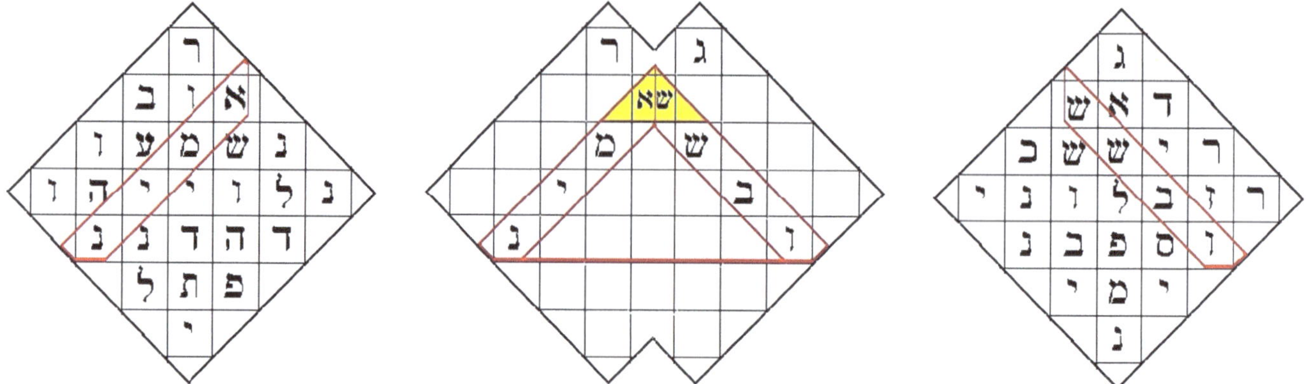

Stone 1, אמינ = authentic. Stone 2, ששבו = that precious stone; that agate. When overlapped, as indicated by the key, a perfect similitude of a pyramid is formed with the letters א and ש joined in the place of the capstone. The Hebrew word אש means fire. This code states, "That precious stone (fire agate) is authentic." In confirmation the code forms a pyramid with the word "fire" in the capstone position. The word pyramid actually means "fire in the middle." According to a code in the surface text of Genesis 28:10-22, the portal stone that Jacob laid at his head was probably a pyramid-shaped fire agate and is the same type of stone (שבו) in Asher's position on the Breastplate of Righteousness and Judgment. The Hebrew word for agate (שבו, *shebuw*) means "to flame," *i.e.* sparkle as *tongues of fire*. The anagram of agate is "a gate," *viz.* a portal. The Egyptians actually did believe the capstone was the portal of the gods.

THINKING LIKE EINSTEIN

While visiting an acquaintance in Baltimore who had been a very dear friend of Albert Einstein, I was in the midst of relating some things that had been revealed to me by the Holy Spirit when she became very interested. She said it sounded much like what Einstein had talked to her about. She began to explain some of the theories he had confided in her, and then she sketched a diagram that he had shown her illustrating the nature of time and how past present and future exist simultaneously in a vortex allowing for the possibility of time travel. Another visitor changed the subject of the conversation several times and I was never able to hear all of the details in order to have any chance at understanding. When I had explained some of my discoveries in the Bible code to this friend she said this sounds like kabbalah (cabala). I was aware that various writers have drawn the same connection between kabbalah and the Bible codes. I really did not like to hear this, having associated kabbalah with occult magic and the modern Hollywood version of the movie stars, but she assured me it had nothing to do with that and was actually a spiritual deciphering of the Hebrew scriptures by the ancient Jewish mystics. Kabbalah means "receiving," and has to do with the receiving of spiritual revelation and knowledge of God combined with intense study and deciphering of the Hebrew Scriptures. This is very much what is done in the true Bible code by serious researchers. Not to advocate kabbalah, it is used by some for evil and by others for good.

It was through the kabbalah that Einstein discovered the string theory, and that everything is made of light (energy). He once remarked, "We have been all wrong. What we have called matter is energy, whose vibration has been so lowered as to be perceptible to the senses. There is no matter." (*Conscious Healing: Book One on the Regenetics Method*, p.105). According to kabbalah God is light. He created a dark void within himself and then sent a thread of light into the void, and all that exists is made from that string as it is influenced by the various frequencies of the letters of the Hebrew alphabet relating to the word. Quantum physicists working with Einstein's string theory say that everything that exists is made of clusters of tiny strings of energy vibrating at various rates causing the illusion of matter. The Apostle John saw this back in the first century A.D. when he wrote that God is light, and the emanation of the light is his word that created all things and is the light and life of every person who comes into the world (John 1:1-ff).

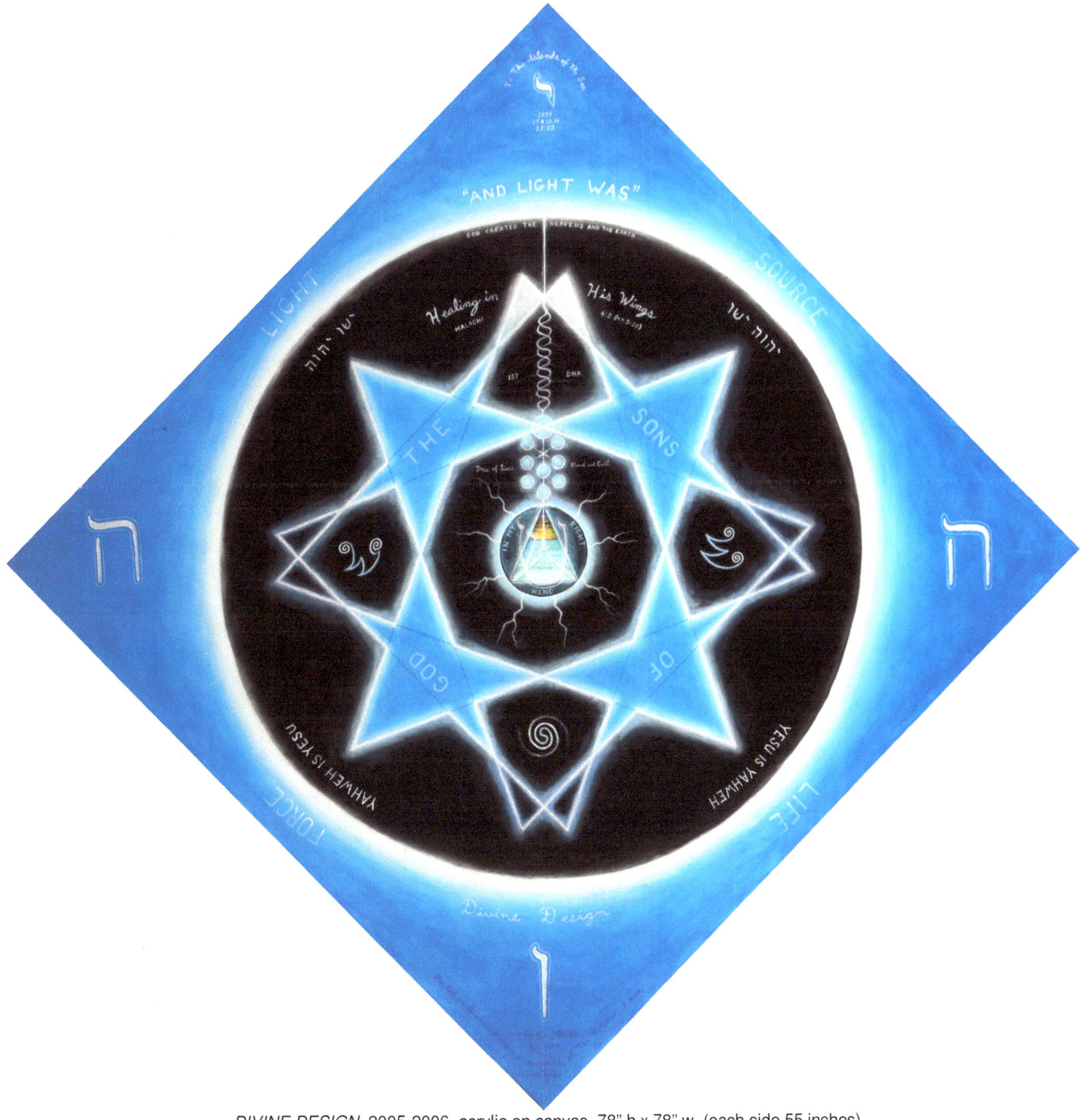

DIVINE DESIGN, 2005-2006, acrylic on canvas, 78" h x 78" w (each side 55 inches)

"He created a dark void within himself and then sent a thread of light into the void, and all that exists is made from that string..."

GOD'S OASIS

Prior to the 1980's, scientists thought that if they could ever see beyond the Quasars (the brightest and most distant objects in the known universe) there would be only total darkness, but with advancements in radio and x-ray telescopes they were able to reach beyond the quasars and discovered that we are surrounded on all sides by a wall of light. We exist within the light. Our universe exists within the blackness of outer space which is just an oasis in the light. The ancient Jewish mystics saw it all in the pattern of the tree of life. The tree was a reflection of God and the spiritual pattern of man. This tree shoots out lines or beams of energy in all directions to vitalize all of creation.

HEAVENLY VIBRATIONS

Until recently, the theme of portal travel had been relegated to science fiction books and movies. Modern Science now acknowledges that it is a conceivable reality. Physicists have reopened Einstein's unfinished work in the realm of "string theory," which allows for inter-dimensional portals, even time travel.

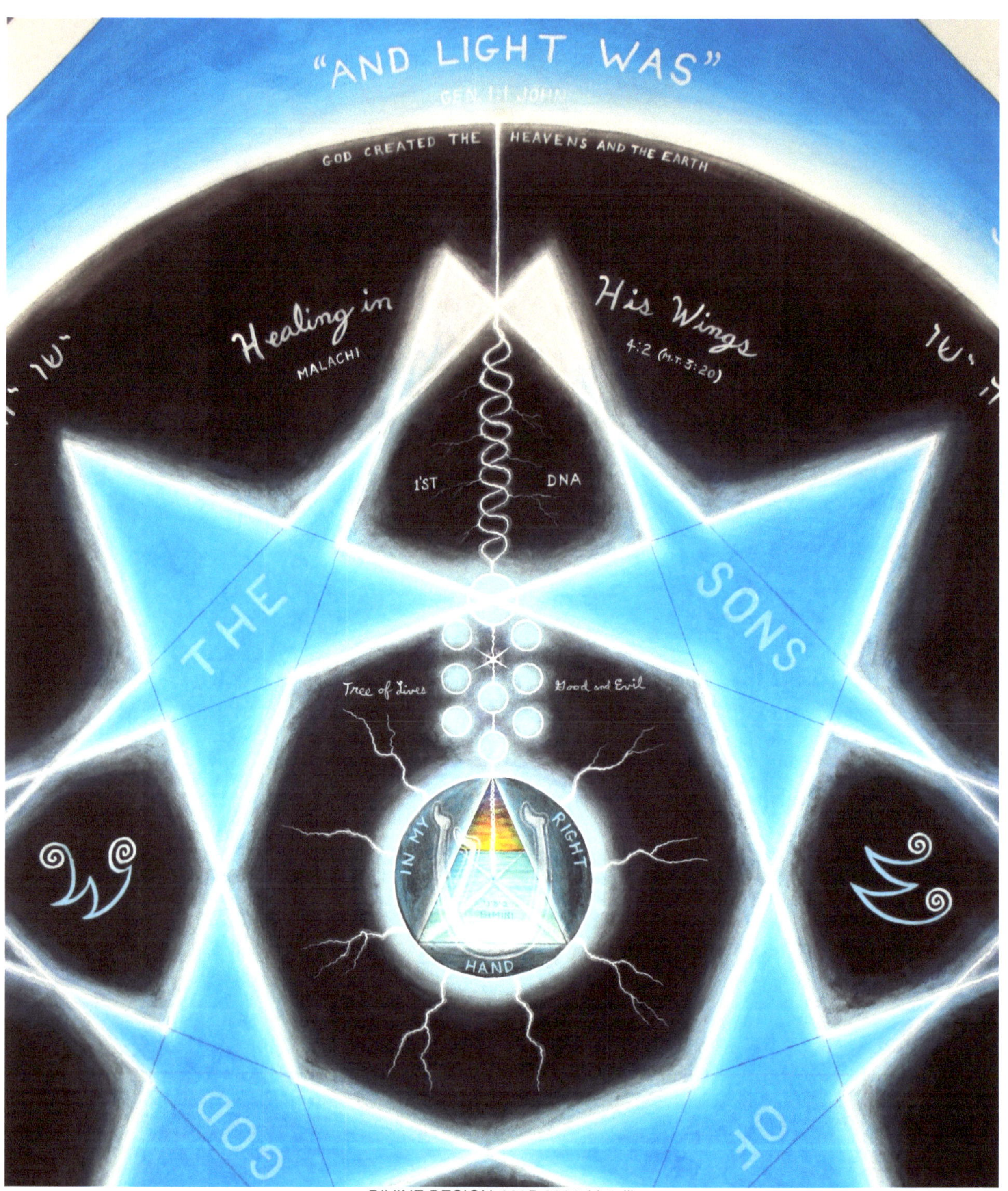

DIVINE DESIGN, 2005-2006 (detail)

Everything that exists is manifested as the result of vibrations of pure energy. According to *The Elegant Universe*, all matter is comprised of submicroscopic vibrating strings of energy. Quantum Physicists have discovered that a photon (particle/wave of light) can be present in more than one place at the same time, without splitting or duplicating itself; it is the same photon appearing simultaneously. In essence there is only one. It is both a wave and a particle. As a wave it vibrates creating strings of energy. Everything in existence consists of these strings of energy. This is called "The Theory Of Everything." Ancient Jewish mystics knew of this omnipresent eternal source energy, *Ein Sof* (without end). It was God, and the light of God.

As these strings of light (electromagnetic energy) vibrate, the different wavelengths determine what substances we see and feel. What is manifest to our senses visually and audibly is minuscule compared to all the invisible waves around us. Physicists are now telling us all those invisible strings make up other dimensions and even parallel universes. There are other realms co-existing with us simultaneously in the same space. According to the model it is theoretically possible to create a wormhole portal in the fabric of time and space through which we could physically travel. They say we could step into a portal in one city and step out in another. We could travel to a distant point on this Earth, or to another world in another dimension, perhaps another time. This is Science speaking. The top quantum physicists in the world are working on this right now. And it was all told in the Bible, recorded thousands of years ago. Some of the Biblical figures who traveled in and out of portals through time and space were Enoch, Elijah, Jacob, Moses, Ezekiel, Daniel, Yesu, Philip, Paul and John The Revelator.

The heavenly kingdom is right here with us. We exist in the same space with heaven. God, the angels and the demons are all right here among us. The spirit world exists at a frequency that is normally undetectable to our physical senses. At certain times and in certain places it becomes possible for people to see angels or demons. Frequencies may shift allowing them to temporarily become visible to us. Some people seem to be more sensitive to the vibrations and are able to see these manifestations when the rest of us cannot. Sometimes special film or electronic cameras are able to bridge the gap and capture images of the otherwise invisible world. Beyond our realm of time, the past, present and future may all exist simultaneously, at various levels within parallel universes.

Portals have been known to open randomly in different locations on the Earth, quite notably in the Bermuda Triangle (which includes Bimini) and in the Devil's Sea. They have been reported in many places, but are unpredictable and uncontrollable. Sometimes people are transported to another place on Earth, and have to make their way back home. Other people go into apparently different dimensions, sometimes returning with stories of angels or demons in another world. Some report various strange ordeals, even abductions. Others have altogether lost their sanity, while some just never return at all.

We have lost the key that is necessary to gain access to enter in and out of portals freely and safely. We have no control over them. The answer is in heavenly vibrations. Yesu Christ said that his followers would be able to come in and out of the portal at will (John 10: 1-9). He scolded the religious leaders for taking away the key of knowledge (*gnosis*: knowing) so they could not enter in, and for preventing others who might have entered (Luke 11: 52).

PORTAL OF HEAVEN

In the period of the Old Testament portals were abundant. Jacob's portal and stairway to heaven opened to him in a dream. The stones that were set by his head, where he laid down, generated a frequency that caused him to experience the spirit realm in his sleep. He entered another dimension where he saw a ladder, a spiral staircase, with its top reaching to heaven, and angels ascending and descending on it. Yahweh stood above it and spoke to him (Genesis 28: 12-13). Jacob awoke frightened, and exclaimed, "How dreadful is this place! This is none other but the house of God, and this is the *portal* (שער) of heaven." (Genesis 28: 17). He set up a pillar of the stones that had activated the portal frequency around his head while he slept. On top of the pillar, he placed the capstone ("stone of Asher," האבן אשר; "the stone of fire," האבן אש, i.e. pyra-mid) that was the main generator of the portal frequency. It was apparently a pyramid-shaped stone, probably a crystal, that emitted constant energy and was a pre-figuration symbolic of Christ Yesu, the "chief cornerstone," literally translated from Hebrew, the "head," or "top" stone. He is the *top-stone* that the builders rejected (Psalm 118: 22; 1 Peter 2: 4-7).

MOUNTAINTOP PORTAL

The mountaintop is a natural representation of the pyramidal capstone. Yahweh visited Moses through a blazing portal, over a bush on top of the mountain. Moses received a set of plans to build a traveling tabernacle with an inner cubicle that would be called the Holy of Holies and the Oracle. This special room housed the Ark of the Covenant which was the most powerful instrument in the world.

When the ark interacted with the circuitry of interconnected gemstones on the breastplate of the high priest, the Holy of Holies was energized. It was a portal of heaven. The first-Century historian, Josephus, recognized this when he referred to it as, "a heaven peculiar to God." He knew that when the high priest interacted with the ark something miraculous happened. The Holy of Holies was transformed, and was no longer just a room in the tabernacle. The physical and spiritual realms united in the same space. The invisible came into view. The cubicle became the throne room of Yahweh. While God came to earth the high priest simultaneously found himself standing in heaven. At that moment heaven and earth were one.

The power of the Ark of the Covenant energized and amplified the frequencies of the breastplate stones, altering the vibrations in the cubicle and opening the portal.

God is the highest form of energy, and the source of all energy. God calls himself a rock. It is he that set up the frequencies in the stones and in everything else that exists. Stones are an important source of stored frequencies. Modern technology has devised many important uses for the frequencies held within crystals. These natural vibrations are energy from God.

The same frequencies that emanated from the stone of Asher, the "stone of fire" on the breastplate, are what had activated and opened a spiritual portal for Jacob. After his vision he built an obelisk pillar (another symbol appropriated by the Occult) and placed the miraculous capstone on it, proclaiming, "This stone …will be God's house." (Genesis 28: 22). Of course we know that God did not live inside of the stone, but that it would somehow create the proper frequencies to activate and open the door/portal to his otherwise invisible realm.

When Moses first saw the light of God the stones on the mountaintop created the portal frequencies.

At the time when the first covenant was given, Yahweh's voice sounded as the voice of the shofar, ram's horn trumpet. There was fire, smoke, lightning and thunder, and the whole mountain quaked greatly. The frequencies on the mountaintop were altered and a portal opened where heaven and earth converged. When Moses went into the cloud he literally walked into heaven and interacted with Yahweh.

God instructed Moses in the proper design of a mobile tabernacle portal, through which he would funnel his power and presence into this physical world. It was an assemblage that could be carried by the Israelites on their journeys through the wilderness. The structure was a pre-figuration and typology of the true temple portal, Yesu Christ, the great high priest.

Yesu was the word made flesh, to tabernacle among us (John 1:14). He is the temple of God, torn down and rebuilt again. He said, "I am the portal: by me if any man enter in, he shall be saved, and shall go in and out, and find pasture." (John 10: 9). The proper entrance is through Yesu. He said no man cometh to the father but through me. Entering by another way is possible but the end may be tragic.

At times we are able to open spiritual portals. Why do we not have control over physical portals also? We need to rediscover Yesu's key.

Christ walked through solid walls in his physical body. He was able to make himself invisible, and to travel instantaneously through time and space, because he was master of the portal.

ENERGIZE THE PORTAL – RIVER OF LIGHT

When we are able to reconstruct the Biblical and scientific data necessary to reactivate the Portal of Heaven, we will witness first-hand the awesome glory of the almighty Yahweh as he once again descends in the whirlwind pillar of cloud and fire. God's people were able to travel the portals 2,000 years ago, and earlier. Enoch was one of the first. We will do it again.

The unchangeable God Almighty is pure energy. The light that emanates eternally from this source, according to ancient mysticism, and the Bible, is what created all that exists. This is exactly what quantum physicists following in Einstein's footsteps are telling us today, with the string theory. Scripture says that this light is Yesu Christ, the foundation stone. The mystics have believed there is a heavenly tabernacle, patterned after the tree of life and tree of knowledge of good and evil. Within the holy of holies is a foundation stone from which roots and branches reach out as paths or rays of "light" (energy) to supply the electrical sustenance necessary for all existence, heavenly and earthly to continue.

I have seen a River of Light. It is the same type of light that flows from before Yahweh's throne, only on a small scale, that God allowed me to see. It flowed from the side of a gigantic Van de Graaff Generator we had made to simulate the power coming from the Ark of the Covenant. There was some leakage around the base of the generator's globe, where a half-million volt stream of light was flowing to the discharge wand. We said, almost simultaneously, "The light is flowing like water." There was a six-inch diameter flow of light that reached downward and then curved back up to the discharge wand (Angel Food cake pans) thirteen inches away. You could actually see the movement of the light resembling the look of swift moving water. It looked like water blasting from the end of a fireman's hose. Within this river of light were scattered sparks, like sparkles on the water. Occasional lightning bolts shot forth within the flow. It was a spectacular display of awesome beauty and power.

When Scripture says a "fiery stream" issued forth from before God's throne, the Hebrew words of Daniel are actually, "river of light." At the time the Bible was translated into English this Hebrew term probably seemed unimaginable. It is easy to picture a stream of fire shooting out, like some kind of a flame-thrower, but who could visualize a river of light? Unless I had seen it with my own eyes, coming from the Van de Graaff machine, I could never have imagined such a thing. The scientists of our time must also have seen this in their experiments. It is an awesome sight for anyone to see. But finding the reference hidden within the wording of Scripture, made it even more awesome, just to realize we were viewing a small model of the actual River of Light that flows from the presence of Yahweh.

Daniel saw the "Ancient of days," upon his fiery throne of light. "His throne was like sparks of light, its whirlwinds of fiery-light. A *river of light* flowed in the presence from before him" (Daniel 7: 9-10).

Yahweh also opened a portal of heaven for the Apostle John to view the things recorded in the book of Revelation. John saw the throne of light and the luminous river of life.

> After this I looked, and, behold, a *portal* was opened in heaven: and the first voice which I heard was as it were of a trumpet [*shofar*: ram's horn] talking with me; which said, Come up hither, and I will show thee things which must be hereafter.
>
> And immediately I was in the spirit: and, behold, a throne was set in heaven, and ONE sat on the throne.
>
> And he that sat was to look upon like a jasper and a sardine stone: and there was a rainbow round about the throne, in sight like unto an emerald.
>
> And round about the throne were four and twenty seats: and upon the seats I saw four and twenty elders sitting, clothed in white raiment; and they had on their heads crowns of gold.
>
> And out of the throne proceeded lightnings and thunderings and voices: and there were seven lamps of fire burning before the throne, which are the seven Spirits of God.
>
> And before the throne there was a sea of glass like unto crystal... (Revelation 4: 1-6).
>
> And I saw a throne of great *brilliant light* (Greek, *leukon*), and him that sat on it, from whose face the earth and the heaven fled away; and there was found no place for them. (Revelation 20: 11).
>
> And he shewed me a *luminous* (Greek, *lampron*) river of water of life, clear as crystal, proceeding out

> of the throne of God and of the Lamb. ...
>
> And they shall see his face; and his name shall be in their foreheads.
>
> And there shall be no night there; and they need no candle, neither light of the sun; for Yahweh God giveth them light: and they shall reign for ever and ever. (Revelation 22: 1, 4-5).

> The river of light is the life-force of men (John 1: 1-14). We run on electrical impulses. If something interrupts or impedes our electrical circuits we are in trouble. Without electricity we die. In Scripture, water, fire and light symbolize the regenerating life of the Holy Spirit.
>
> God is pure unfathomable energy, emanating from an infinite eternal source. He is endlessly creating and recreating within himself. He is all the energy in string theory that keeps the vibration frequencies in motion and keyed to the perfect harmonic symphony of the universes. He is all the light of every star and sun, dwelling in the vast unending darkness of empty space, and all the hidden energy pulsating in every other dimension. He was the flash that brought it all into being and he will be the final unifying flash that completes his plan.
>
> He is the fiery whirlwind portal that went before the Israelites to guide them through the wilderness. Everywhere he appeared he brought fire and light. To some it was destruction. To others it was Life.
>
> Right now, we cannot walk through walls, and we cannot travel the fiery whirlwinds to distant places. We do not yet have access to the physical portals that can carry us away and bring us back. But, we can communicate with God in the spirit, and enter the spiritual portals of heaven. We can feel the real presence of God in his glory. We can feel the healing touch of his Holy Spirit as he communicates directly to our inner being. You are the temple of God. Let the veil be opened. (*Sapphire Sphere: Portal To Eternity*).

The Heavenly Temple is the center point where all the branches of the Tree of Life connect with their roots, sending a flow of sustenance and blessing to the all of creation. There is one body, united through an invisible head, the *rosh* stone, the Tree of Life in heaven. From that heavenly capstone, the Living Rock, all the branches of light reach out to nourish heaven and all the roots of light reach throughout the earth, so that all of existence receives its essence from the one great celestial *Ayin*, the Source.

> The inner meaning and purpose of the Future Temple are explained in full in *Mishkney Elyon*, a priceless jewel from the legacy of towering 18th century mystical genius Rabbi Moshe Chaim Luzzato ("Ramchal", 1707-47). The Temple is the center point where all the branches of the Tree of Life connect with their roots, channeling a flow of sustenance and blessing to the entire world. ...where all these roots come together, there is a single "stone". [This is in the Holy of Holies of the Heavenly Temple.] This stone is most precious. ...It is called the Foundation Stone (*Even Shetiyah*). ...Stretching out in all directions from this stone are channels and pathways leading to all things. ...Branching off from these highways are countless smaller pathways containing the individual roots of every single being in creation ...they all join together in the stone in the middle of this place ...this stone stands at the heart of the universe... This place is hidden and secret. Only the King may come there. No one may enter except for Him. This place contains all the beauty of this light and all its radiance and perfection. ...This hidden and concealed place...the Holy of Holies, where the Ark and the Testimony are situated, and where the Foundation Stone stands in all its power. (*SECRETS OF THE FUTURE TEMPLE: Mishkney Elyon*, by Rabbi Moshe Chaim Luzzatto).

The New Testament writings tell us that Christ Yesu is that one king who alone has entered that perfect light, "...who is the blessed and only Potentate, the King of kings, and Lord of lords; Who only hath immortality, dwelling in the light which no man can approach unto; whom no man hath seen, nor can see..." (1 Timothy 6:15-16).

He is the high priest in the holy of holies, and People of Bimini, you are the temple of God standing on his holy mountain top in the islands of the sea.

THE NAME OF SALVATION

The name Yesu is said to mean *salvation* or *saviour.* It more fully means *Yahweh Saviour.* "Neither is there salvation in any other: for there is none other name under heaven given among men, whereby we must be saved" (Acts 4:12). His name in the Biblical languages, Greek, Hebrew and Latin, is Yesu. This was translated in old English and early modern English as Iesu and pronounced yay-soo, just like in the Biblical languages. Over a period of a few hundred years it gradually morphed into the English name Jesus. This removal and replacement of the name Yesu had been prophesied in the Bible. One such reference is found in Jeremiah 11:19, "I was like a lamb or an ox that is brought to the slaughter, and I knew not that they had devised devices against me, saying, Let us destroy the tree with the fruit thereof, and let us cut him off from the land of the living, that his name may be no more remembered." (For detailed information on the etymology and importance of the saviour's name please refer to *The Holy Cipher: Who Changed God's Name?* or, *The End Is Come*, both by Norbert H. Kox).

There is a Jewish curse that states, "His name and his memory shall be obliterated." This is undoubtedly related to Jeremiah 11:19, "...that his name may be no more remembered." The curse is represented by the letters YMS or, according to some, YShW, which they associate with the name Yeshu, or Yesu.

THE NAME THAT CANNOT BE DESTROYED

Many Christian scholars believe that the name of Christ in Hebrew was *Yeshua*. But the name which is pronounced Yeshua (yay-shoo-ah, or, y'shua) by Modern Christian scholars is not pronounced that way by the Jews (with few exceptions) in reference to Christ. The final letter, *ayin* (eye-in) represented by ` is not heard in the pronunciation (*Dictionary of the Bible*, p. 71, McKenzie). The *ayin* is usually neglected, although it appears in writing (cf. *Beginners' Hebrew Grammar*, Rev. Harold L. Creager, B.D., p. 6). An *ayin* at the end of a word does not necessarily change its pronunciation, neither would an *alef* or *he*. Modern Hebrew dictionaries do not even print the *ayin* in the name Yesu, but simply print the three-letter spelling, *yod*, *shin*, *waw.*

In his Bible Code book, Scholar and researcher, Jeffrey Satinover, states, "The silent letters in Hebrew are '*aleph*' and '*ayin*', which can take on any vowel sound. Many words are spelled with them or without them." (*Cracking The Bible Code,* p. 312). The "a" vowel of the final syllable in Yeshua is not derived from the *ayin,* but from the deceptive Masoretic points which did not appear before the 8th century AD. "One has to be careful not to grant the same canonical authority to the Masoretes as to Moses and the prophets. Nor should one be too critical of the modern Old Testament scholar who thinks he has just cause to alter one or two of the signs the Masoretes had introduced." (*Do It Yourself Hebrew and Greek: Everybody's Guide to the Language Tools, p.* 14:3).

If the *ayin* had been pronounced it could have represented either of two sounds, *g* or *h*, according to various Hebrew Grammars and *Septuagint* study. But in the name which we are scrutinizing, we can be relatively certain that it was ignored or practically silent, because it was not transliterated in the *Septuagint.* A *g*-sound would have called for a Greek rendering of *Iesoug*, which never appears. An *h*-sound, preceded by a vowel, would scarcely be heard and need not appear in transliteration. "*Ayin* is an aspiration midway in strength between *alef* and *he*. We transliterate it by a rough breathing [`], and practically neglect it in pronunciation." (*Beginners' Hebrew Grammar*, p. 6). Yesu and Yesuh would be identical in pronunciation. A word can be closed with an unsounded consonant. The "moveable" *ayin* (even when not pronounced, *ayin* is categorized as a *moveable* letter) could be used in closing, the same as a "silent" *alef* or *he.*

In the Talmudic spelling of the same name, the *ayin* has actually disappeared. Rather than YSW` (*yod, shin, waw, ayin*) the name is simply YSW (ישו, *yod, shin, waw*). This leaves no reason to doubt the "Yesu" pronunciation. The Talmud refers to him as YSW HNOTSRY (*Yesu ha Notsriy*: Yesu the Nazarene; *Notsriy* also means Christian).

Like the *Jews for Jesus*, Grant Jeffrey and Yacov Rambsel, in their Bible Code books, use the name Yeshua synonymously with Jesus. Grant Jeffrey says Yeshua is "Jesus," and promotes the name Yeshua over the name Yeshu (Yesu) which he insinuates is incorrect. What he does not realize is that the Hebrew/Aramaic three-letter and four-letter spellings of the Saviour's name are pronounced the same, Yesu or Yeshu, not Yeshua. The Bible Code programs all have the three-letter spelling, not the four, in their data bases. All the Hebrew dictionaries have the three-letter spelling also, and not the four-letter spelling. Mr. Jeffrey suggests the name of Yeshu (Yesu) comes from a derogatory acronym, *Yimach Shemo Uzikhro* [or, *yemach shemo vezichro*] "May his name and memory be blotted out" (*The Mysterious Bible Codes*, pp. 99-100). The initial letters of these three words, the *Yod Shin Waw* (YSW) do spell the name of Yesu. The curse is actually pronounced with the words *Yemach shemo,* "his name shall be erased." According to *Ben Yehuda's English-Hebrew/Hebrew-English Pocket Dictionary* (p. xxiii) the abbreviation for the *yemach shemo vezichro* curse is YMS, *Yod Mem Shin*, for *Yemach shemo.* If a person's name were to be blotted out and remembered no more, it would have to never be written again, otherwise the purpose would be defeated. It would perpetuate that name rather than destroy it. If the YSW acronym were used as an abbreviation for the curse, every time it was written down it would proclaim the name of Yesu. Rather than blot out his name it would actually preserve it. And, if this is the case, his name cannot be obliterated.

(*Who Changed God's Name?* pp. 40-42; *Masquerade: Antichrist is Here*, pp. 54-56)

His name cannot be obliterated. In fact, every time the curse would be pronounced upon someone, their name would be obliterated while simultaneously being overwritten by the name of Yesu (YSW). In a sense, this happens to us. We are cursed because of sin. When we repent and are baptized, Yesu's name is called out over us. We are superimposed by his name and he has become the "curse" for us (Galatians 3:13). "Cursed is everyone that hangeth on a tree" (Deuteronomy 21: 22-23). It is only appropriate that the letters of his name, ישו (YSW) would stand as an acronym for the curse.

These letters (ישו) also spell, "his existence." Reversed, they spell, "and gift." The primary meaning of the name Yesu is, "Yahweh the Saviour." The symmetrical analysis of the name, when it is read forward and then backward, says, "His existence and Gift."

(*The End Is Come*, p.153; *The Holy Cipher: Who Changed God's Name?*, pp.69-70)

HIS EXISTENCE AND GIFT

Yahweh's *existence and gift* was and is Yesu Christ, the chief cornerstone, the capstone portal of the resurrected living temple of God. In essence Yesu is Yahweh and the "name which is above every name" (Philippians 2:9).

Yesu is the WORD of God. He said, "I am the way, the truth, and the life: no man cometh unto the father but *through* me." His name, which was made a curse by those who cursed him, is the name that is exalted above all other names, and his name is anagrammed into the key of the onyx stones (see, p.24).

BIBLE CODE: DELIGHT OF THE SCRIBE

Genesis 2:9, speaks of the tree of life and the tree of good and evil knowledge; the nine letters centered within that phrase give us, "Delight of the scribe," when read in reverse. This was the seed of inspiration and the impetus for the painting *Delight of the Scribe: The Tree of Life and The Tree of Knowledge of Good and Evil* (2002-2003).

Delight of the Scribe incorporates a Bible Code grid as the central theme. The Biblecode is a scientific analysis of the Hebrew text of the Bible. When each letter is placed in a grid, the matrix becomes a cross-word puzzle, a word-search with words and phrases interlocking in all directions, right, left, up, down, and diagonally. The use of computer programs help to discover the number skip-sequences (Equidistant Letter Sequences, or ELS) at which God has encoded and "sealed the cipher" of his messages for his people to unravel and decode in the last days, "the time of the end...when knowledge will be multiplied" (Daniel 12:4).

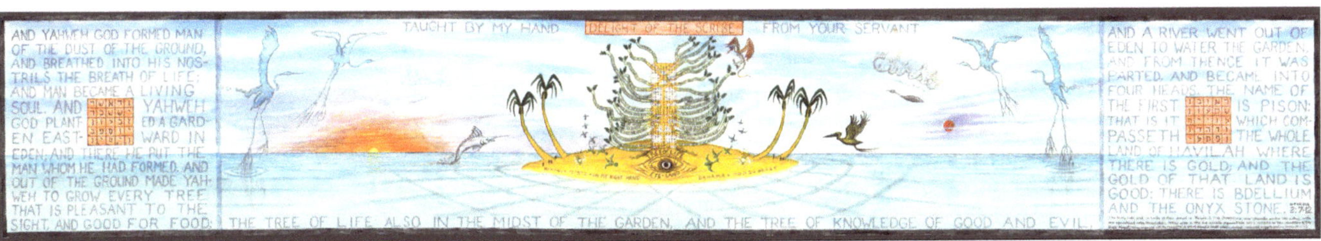

Delight of the Scribe: The Tree of Life and The Tree of Knowledge of Good and Evil, 2002-2003, Acrylic on canvas, 24" x 144" (2-ft x 12-ft)

Here is a description of the painting:

The nine Hebrew letters located between the tree of life and the tree of knowledge of good and evil, "in the midst (middle) of the garden", when read in reverse translate into English as "Delight of the scribe." The tree of life and the tree of knowledge of good and evil may be the same tree in the middle of the garden, and may represent the Word of God, the Living Word, the delight (enjoyment) of the scribe.

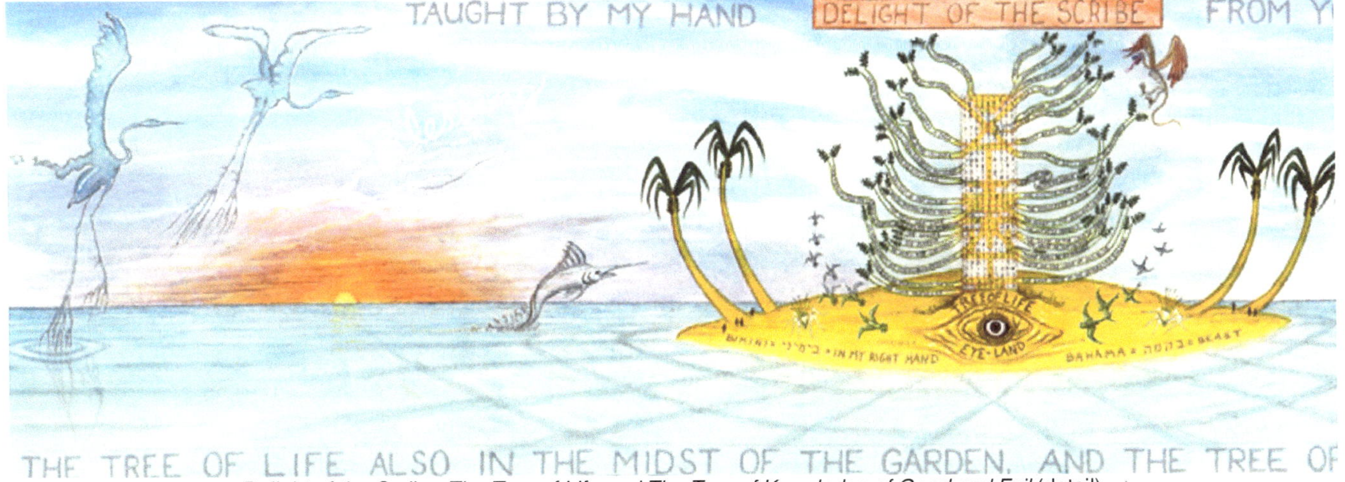

Delight of the Scribe: The Tree of Life and The Tree of Knowledge of Good and Evil (detail)

Following is one writer's concept of the great tree:

> "The majestic tree was the first temple of God and the original tabernacle man. Beneath its spreading branches and swinging boughs man first held conscious communion with the Divine Spirit of the universe. In its checkered shade the first offspring of God's creation gamboled and frolicked." (A Dictionary of Trees, p. 5, "The Tree", by Fred Walden; 1963, Great Outdoors Publishing Co., St. Petersburg 14, Florida).

It is interesting that this author chose the word "checkered" in reference to the shade of the great tree.

The Hebrew word for "crossword puzzle" also means "checkered work", and contains the root meaning "checkered".

In the painting, "Delight of the Scribe", I have rendered the Living Tree and Tree of Knowledge of Good and Evil as a Biblecode matrix, which is in essence a checkered work crossword puzzle.

The Bible Code is a scientific analysis of the Hebrew text of the bible. When each letter is placed in a grid, the matrix becomes a cross-word puzzle, a word search with words and phrases interlocking in all directions, right, left, up, down, and diagonally.

The scientific principle which is incorporated into the Bible Code is what cryptographers refer to as equidistant letter sequence (ELS). It simply means that each letter in a code is an equal distance from its preceding letter. So if a code is on a five letter skip, every fifth letter is part of the code which spells out a word, or phrase, or sentence.

The grid in this painting is based on a nine-letter-line code matrix, simply because the key phrase "Delight of the scribe" is comprised of nine letters. Because it is a nine letter grid, all the nine-skip ELS codes fall in the vertical columns.

God's system depends heavily upon symmetries, which can be seen throughout the Bible.

This matrix, which contains the Hebrew text of Genesis 2: 7-12, has been scrutinized specifically for its symmetrical codes. The first code at the top of the grid is "Created of Yahweh." Beneath that is the phrase "My agreement." Located centrally (symmetrically) within this phrase is the word "Symmetry".

(http://inmyrighthand.homestead.com/delighttext1.html).

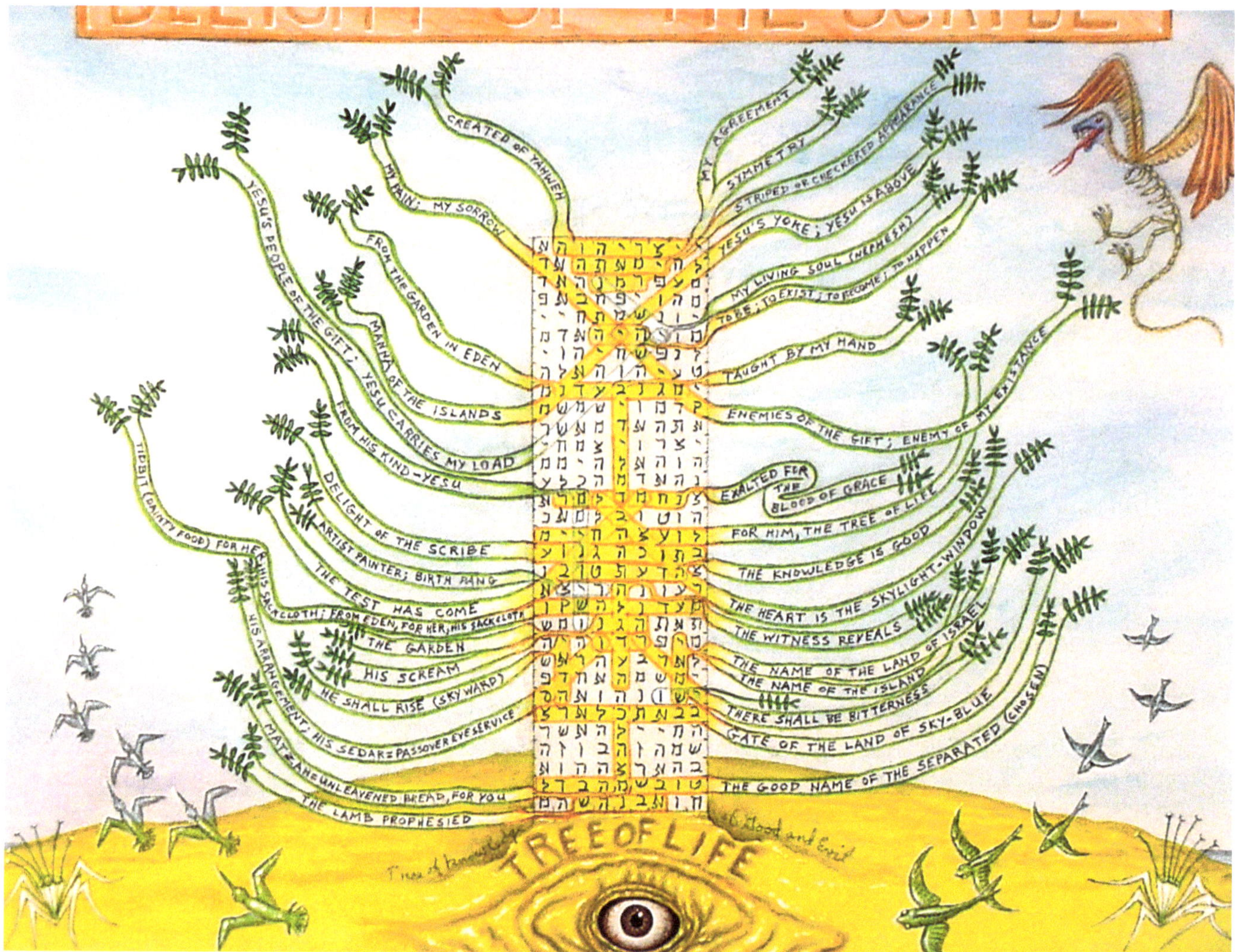

Delight of the Scribe: The Tree of Life and The Tree of Knowledge of Good and Evil (detail).
The branches translate the codes and are sprouting with leaves of the *lignum vitae*, the national tree of the Bahamas. *Lignum vitae* means "Tree of Life." The subtle serpent appears as a flying fossil of the archaeopteryx, a prehistoric winged reptile, truly a tiny dragon. This creature closely resembles the fabulous flying serpent described as Satan in Revelation 12:9. It had feathers like a bird but teeth like a snake, rather than a bird beak. The archaeopteryx has been found in many locations around the world by modern archaeologists.

Noted below is a list of the highlighted symmetrical Biblecodes within this matrix:

1. Created of Yahweh
2. My Agreement; Symmetry
3. Striped, or checkered appearance
4. My pain; My sorrow
5. Yesu's yoke; Yesu is above
6. From the Garden in Eden
7. Taught by my hand
8. Manna of the Islands
9. Enemies of the gift; Enemy of my existence
10. Exalted for the blood of grace
11. Delight of the scribe
12. For him the Tree of Life (Living Tree)
13. The knowledge is good
14. The test has come
15. The heart is the skylight-window
16. Tidbit (dainty food) for her, his sackcloth; From Eden, for her, his sackcloth

17. The witness reveals
18. The garden
19. His scream
20. He shall rise (skyward)
21. The name of the Land of Israel; The name of the Island
22. His arrangement; His Seder = Passover Eve service
23. Matzah = unleavened bread for you
24. There shall be bitterness
25. Gate of the land of sky-blue
26. The Lamb prophesied
27. The good name of the separated (chosen)

Symmetrical codes not highlighted:

1. Pages of Yah (Yahweh); God's pages
2. From still waters

Other codes in this matrix:

1. The empowered word (not highlighted)
2. My living soul (nephesh)
3. Yesu's people of the gift; Yesu carries my load
4. From his kind-Yesu
5. Artist, painter; Birth pang
6. Yesu

Following is the English translation of the plain text in the code matrix of Genesis 2: 7-12:

> And YAHWEH God formed man of the dust of the ground, and breathed into his nostrils the breath of life; and man became a living soul.
>
> And YAHWEH God planted a garden eastward in Eden; and there he put the man whom he had formed.
>
> And out of the ground made YAHWEH God to grow every tree that is pleasant to the sight, and good for food; the tree of life also in the midst of the garden, and the tree of knowledge of good and evil.
>
> And a river went out of Eden to water the garden; and from thence it was parted, and became into four heads.
>
> The name of the first is Pison: that is it which compasseth the whole land of Havilah, where there is gold;
>
> And the gold of that land is good: there is bdellium (gum Arabic) and the onyx stone.

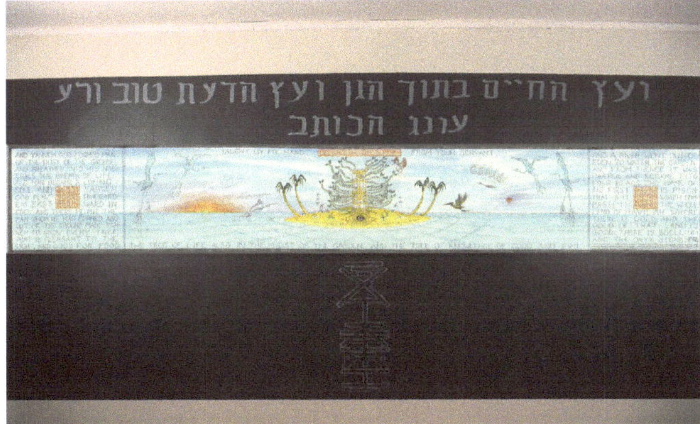

Delight of the Scribe, exhibited on black painted background with Hebrew text and symmetrical pattern from the code duplicated below.

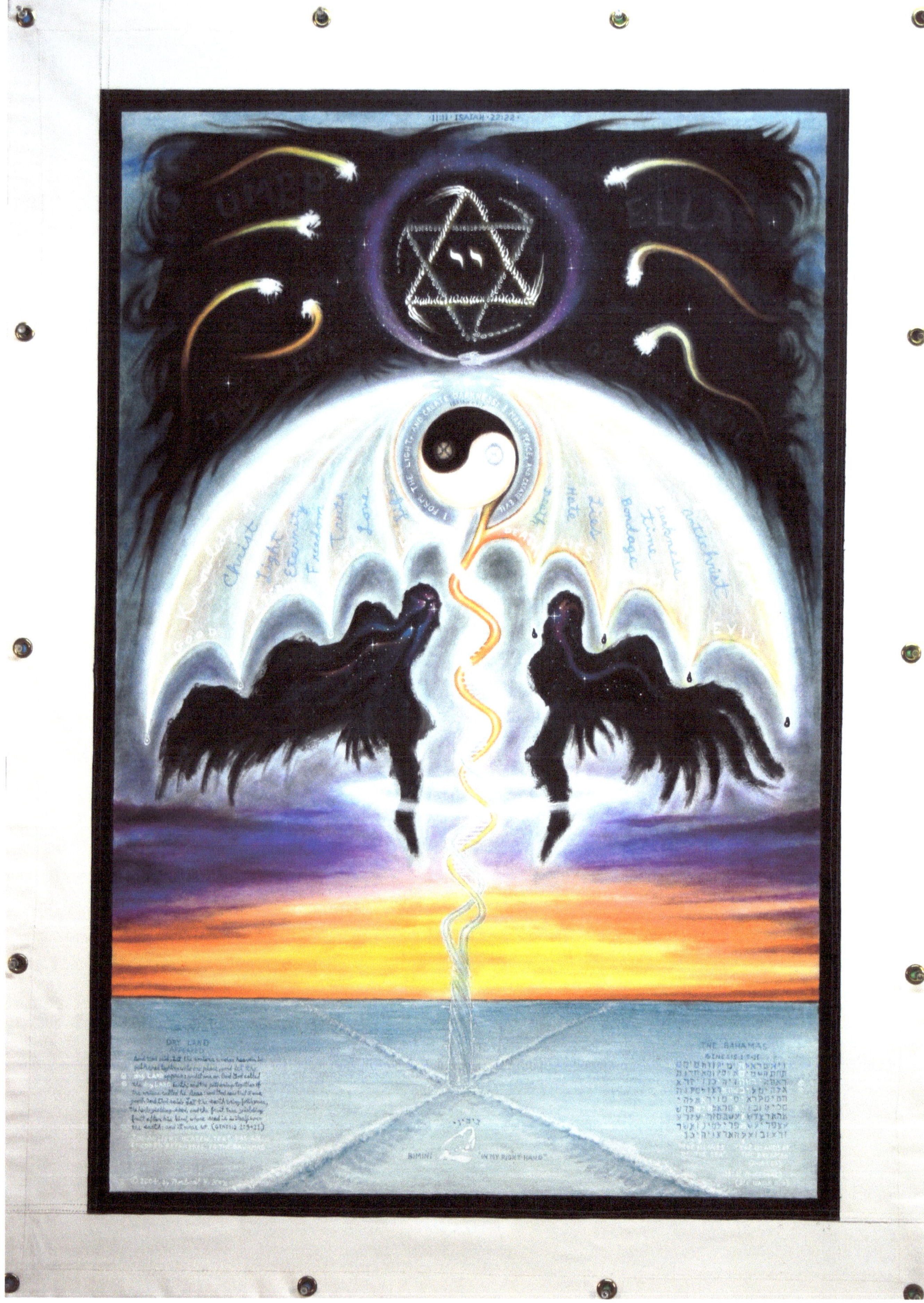
1:11 ISAIAH 22:22
I FORM THE LIGHT, AND CREATE DARKNESS: I MAKE PEACE, AND CREATE EVIL
Christ
Light
Eternity
Freedom
Truth
Love
Life
Death
Hate
Lies
Bondage
Time
Antichrist
GOOD
EVIL
DRY LAND
APPEARED
THE BAHAMAS
BIMINI
"IN MY RIGHT HAND"

Image on previous page, *Umbrella: Tree of Life, Good and Evil*, 2003-2004, acrylic on canvas (banner) 53" x 38"

UMBRELLA

On my way to Bimini in December of 2003, while waiting in Chalk's terminal at Fort Lauderdale, I began to have a vision for the painting I call *Umbrella*. I started to sketch it immediately; then while flying over the ocean in the seaplane more details came. By the time I reached Bimini I could hardly wait to start painting. During the time that I worked on the painting God led me into some very amazing Bible codes that were destined to go into the work.

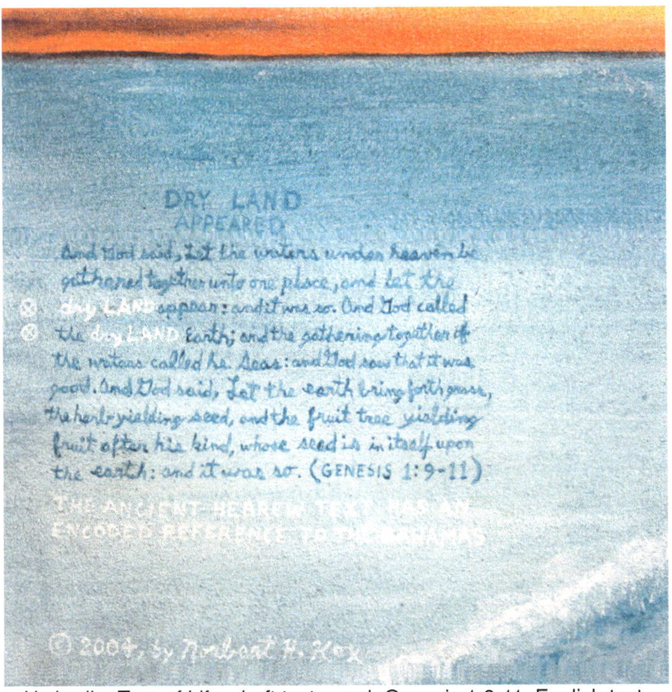

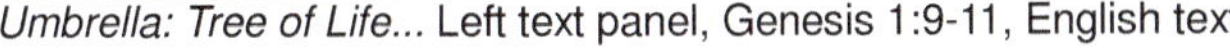
Umbrella: Tree of Life... Left text panel, Genesis 1:9-11, English text

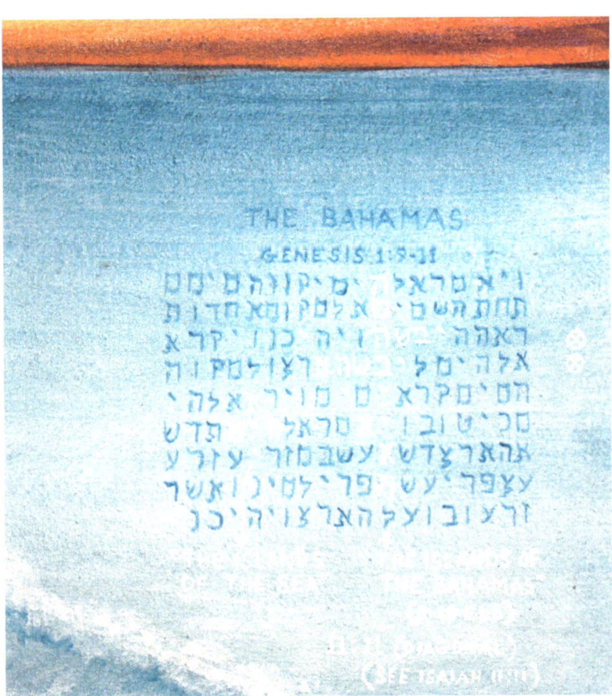

Right text panel Genesis 1:9-11, Hebrew text with Bible code

Genesis 1:9-11, declares how Yahweh gathered the waters and brought forth dry land from the seas. When those same verses are placed into a matrix with nineteen Hebrew letters per line, they produce the Bible code phrases, "The Islands of the sea," "The Islands of the Bahamas" or "The Bahama Islands," and "11:11." The Hebrew words for "dry land" (יבשה) appear twice, running through Bahamas and 11:11. *Dry land*, which is here referenced to the Islands, when read in reverse, השבי, says "My restoring" or "My returning." The two occurrences run through Bahamas. The second one actually connects Bahamas and 11:11, and it is Isaiah 11:11 in which Yahweh says he is returning his hand (*yad/yod*) a second time to the Islands of the seas to recover his remnant.

THE TREE IN THE MIDDLE OF THE GARDEN

In this painting the tree of life and of knowledge of good and evil is interpreted as one tree and symbolized as the DNA ladder seen rising from the sea. It splits into the light and darkness covering mankind. The heads of the two seraphim entwine to form the Tao (dow) symbol of balance. The X-ed eyes are a representation of the first microscopic photograph of DNA. Around the Tao are written Yahweh's words, "I form the light and create darkness, I make peace and create evil" (Isaiah 45:7).

The two angel-like figures (representing the Human Race before the fall) under the umbrella are made up of darkness and light, illustrating the potential of man for good or evil.

The seraphim wrapped around the ankles of humanity is a symbol of the bondage that resulted from the

Edenic fall. The Hebrew Bible Code (Equidistant Letter Sequence) painted in the sea reveals that when God ordered the dry land to come forth he simultaneously gave a reference to the Bahama Islands. Also noted, the word Bimini spelled in the Hebrew Language means "In my right hand."

At the top of the painting, above the Tao, is the Earth's solar system. The Ouroboros-seraphim, with its head over the sun, represents the Earth's ages. The six-pointed star with its powerful symbols of fire and water enshrines two Hebrew *yods*. The double *yod* is a symbol for God. Fire and water represent the Spirit and the Word.

Last but not least, the heavenly seraphim frolic in worship of the Creator (*viz.* Isaiah 6:2-3).

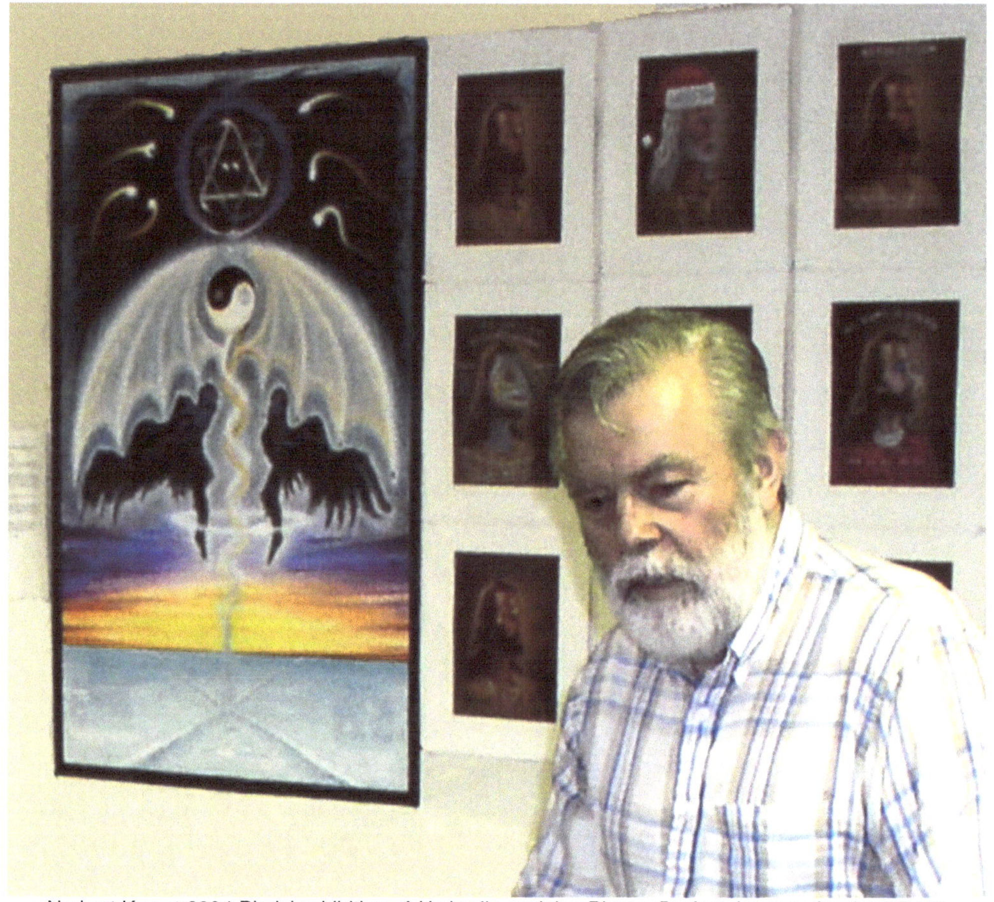

Norbert Kox at 2004 Bimini exhibition of *Umbrella*, and the *Picture Perfect Jesus* series (pp.87-96) exposing the fraudulent Head of Christ by Warner Sallman. (photo by James Pinder)

SEA OF TRUTH

On the Island of Bimini, in December of 1999, I received a vision over the ocean looking southwest, toward southern Florida. A colossal pillar of fire appeared on the surface of the ocean and extended upwards high above the clouds. It remained about five minutes with its flames swirling around in the sky. The words "Sea of Truth" burned themselves into my mind. When I realized this was what I was supposed to paint I got out a pencil and paper, that I carry in my pocket, and began to draw. The fire remained long enough for me to make my rough sketch (later I found a picture of a pillar of fire that became my model).

Back at the apartment I got on the computer and searched the Scriptures for the Bible Code "Sea of Truth." In Genesis at an ELS of 1,032, I found the key words, "God encoded; God is the sea of truth." It was in the very same code that researchers from Israel had found: "God encoded; God is truth." The letters in the key cluster can be accurately translated into either of the two phrases mentioned.

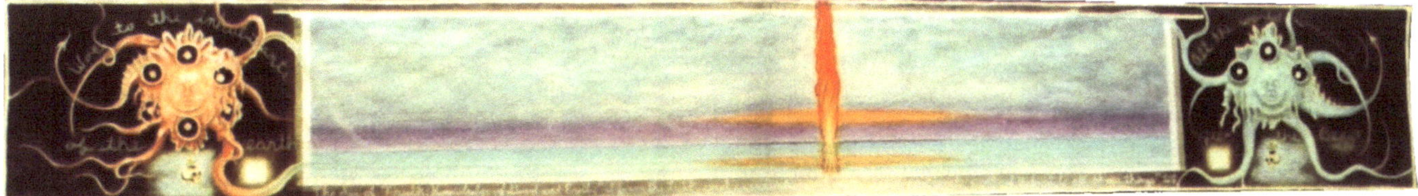

Sea of Truth (Sea of Knowledge of Good and Evil) 1999-2000, Acrylic on canvas (banner) 28" x 215"

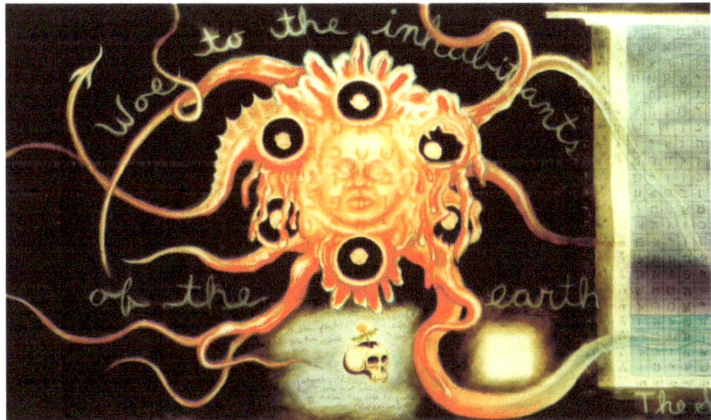

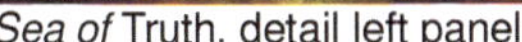

Sea of Truth, detail left panel

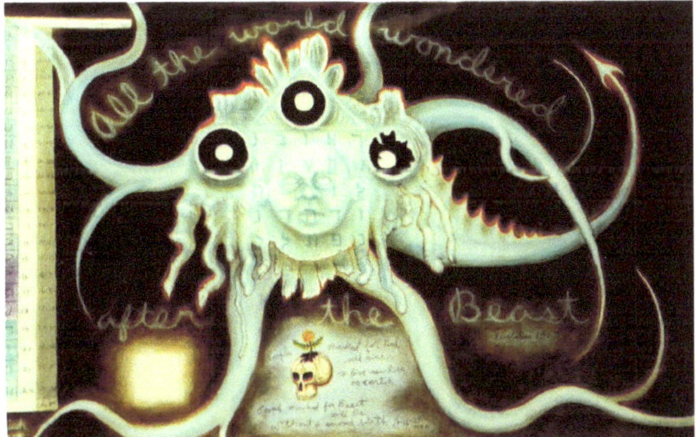

Sea of Truth, detail right panel

This painting is meant to alert the viewer to approach the Bible codes with caution, since they are a record of all things both good and evil. The Dragons on each end are warnings from the book of Revelation. These references are meant to call attention to the fact that the Dragon has his tentacles into the code. The subtle tentacles enter the matrix with the words "Leviathan" and "the Dragon," at various equidistant letter sequences (ELS). Two serpents cross each other directly over the word "two." The serpents are overlain upon two variant Hebrew spellings of "the Dragon." a string of letters connecting their tails spell out the phrase from hydrogen, bringing to mind the detonation process of the atomic bomb called "tickling the dragons tail."

The painting is laid out on a Bible code matrix from the book of Genesis, with a grid work containing 2,882 Hebrew alphabet characters. The key code, "God encoded; God is truth" was first discovered by Hebrew scientists and cryptologists in Jerusalem working with computer programs specially designed to break the code. The phrase that they found contains within itself the additional term "the sea of truth," and can be correctly translated "God encoded; God is the sea of truth."

The phrase "the sea of truth" is also found in other parts of this matrix as well. The pillar of fire that inspired this painting is superimposed directly over the phrase "God encoded; God is the sea of truth."

The *Sea of Truth* painting was chosen as a logo for the 2000-2001 exhibition, "The End Is A New Beginning," at Lehigh University in Bethlehem, Pennsylvania. Represented in this show were major works of four outsider artists, Mr. Imagination, Lonnie B. Holley, Charlie Lucas, and Norbert H. Kox. The pillar of fire appeared on the invitation cards and also on the exhibition posters, and was presented as the theme painting in the exhibit.

The *Sea of Truth* had premiered at Precious de Paris in Bimini, 2000. Later it was shown prominently in the 2005 exhibition Elohim The Apocalyptic Time Machine, at UW-Green Bay, Lawton Art Gallery.

Image on following page, *The Sea Of Truth*, pillar of fire logo; "The End Is A New Beginning," Exhibition poster 19" x 12.5"

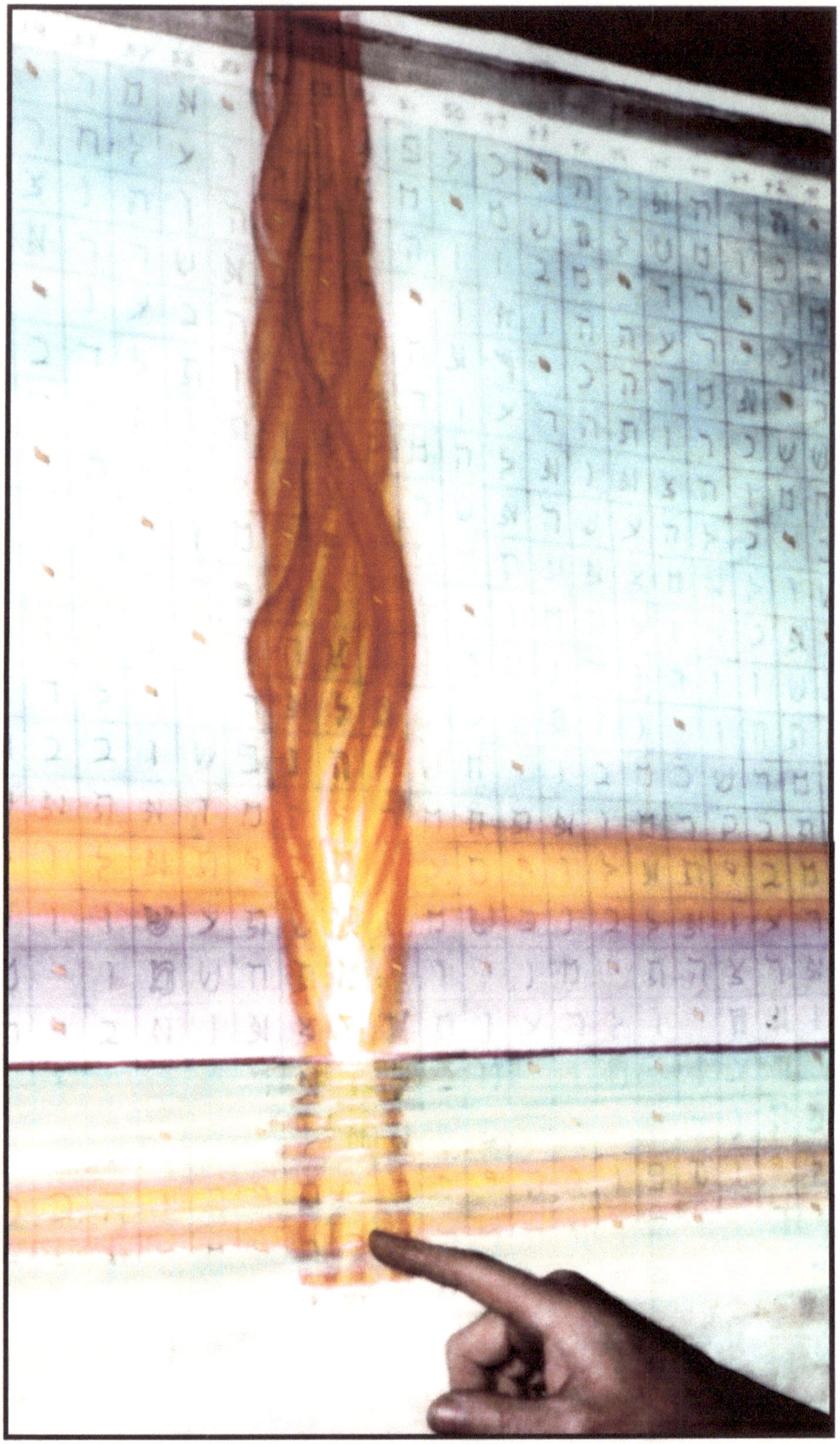

Photography by: Matt Nawada; Design by rvdesignconsulting and Laura Mardon

Exhibit Logo, detail: Norbert Kox, "The Sea of Truth"

FOUR OUTSIDER ARTISTS

the end is a new beginning

November 29, 2000 – February 25, 2001

An Installation at the Turn of the Millennium

Zoellner Arts Center Main Gallery • Lehigh University, Bethlehem, Pennsylvania

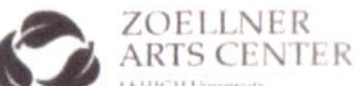

INSIDE THE PILLAR OF FIRE

Sometimes I refer to myself as NHK, those are my primary initials. In Hebrew, NHK is נהק, *nahak*, meaning to *bray*, or to *cry wildly*. That describes me in my mission to proclaim the end times and repentance from idolatry, although it is not always a verbal cry, nonetheless my paintings are screaming and shouting out. For those who would rather ignore it, the cry is quite loud.

In the early morning hours of March 4, 2006, I discovered NHK in the pillar of fire, on the *Sea of Truth* painting. Directly in the middle of the pillar of fire, centered symmetrically on the very first letter of the phrase "the sea of truth," are the Hebrew letters שפנהקשח; reading left to right this says, "Crushed! NHK bent down" (for the Hebrew reader that would simply be reversed, שפ נהק שח).

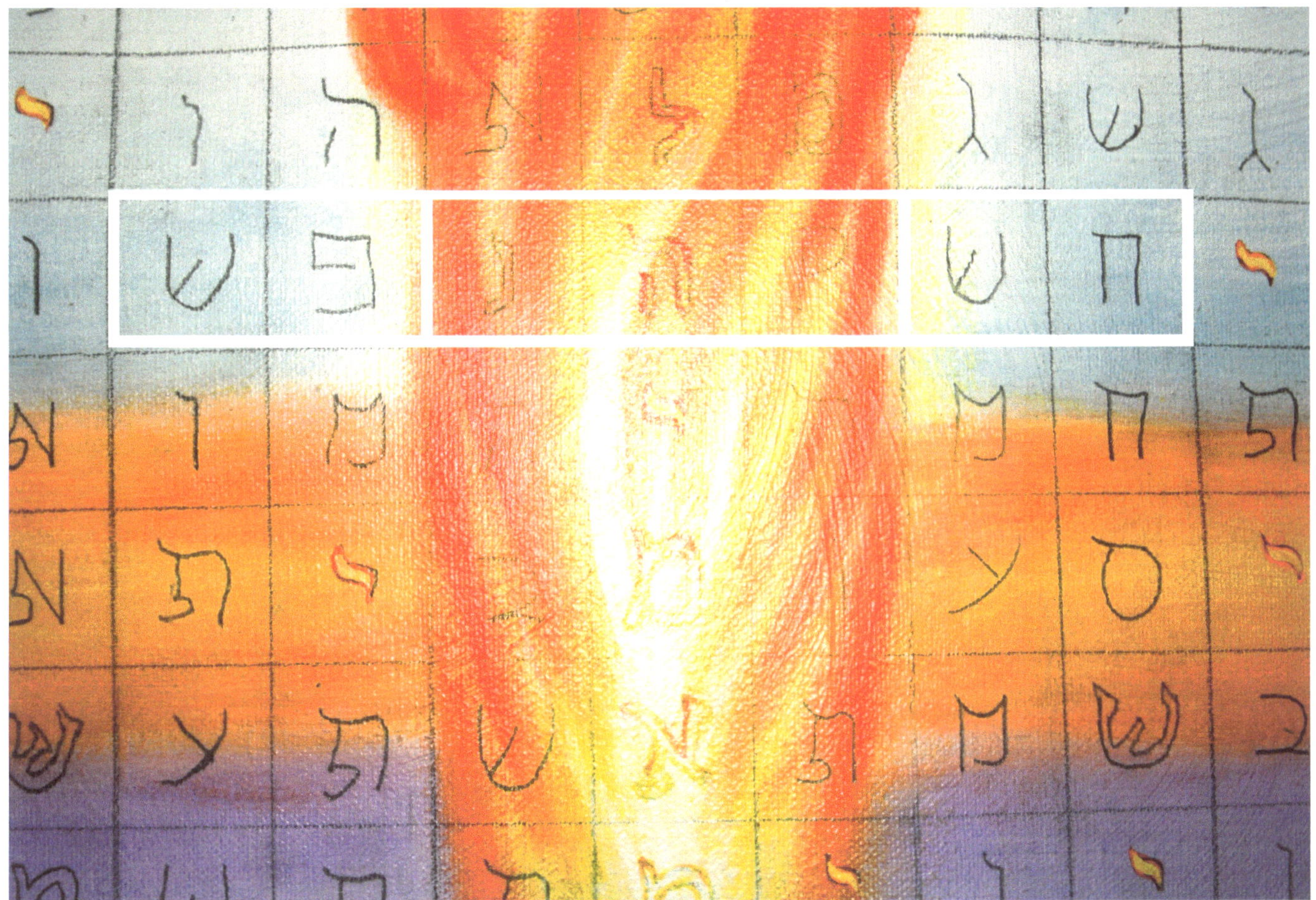

Sea of Truth (detail) with symmetrical reverse code highlighted: שפנהקשח; reading left to right, "Crushed! NHK bent down"

That phrase really troubled me and I could not get it out of my mind. About six hours after I had found it, I was on my way to Michigan with my son and grandson to go skiing. I had not skied in forty-five years, but saw it as an opportunity to spend time with my loved ones.

On the way up I explained what I had found to my son and told him how it was bothering me not to know what it meant. He simply assured me that I would figure it out and that when the time was right I would know the meaning.

Just twelve hours after I had discovered the code, I was laying on the ground in the snow dying of a heart attack. I had fallen hard on my shoulder and shaken something loose. My son had training and quickly ascertained that I was experiencing a heart attack. He immediately called for help. I sat down on a bench, but soon slid to the ground and curled up into a fetal position.

While laying on the ground, I lost track of the world around me and went into a deep communion with

God. I asked him to take me into the portal for a little while, and I felt that I was with him in the pillar of fire. I had no fear and in what is supposed to be one of the most painful things one can experience, I felt no pain. But I was immobile and at perfect peace. I told Yesu that if my work was finished here, I was ready to go, but if he still had work that I could do then please let me stay to finish the job. The next thing I knew I was in the hospital with my son and grandson standing next to the bed. As I questioned, why this would happen to me when my life is completely dedicated to the work of God and serving him in the capacity that he allows me, my son said, "Just remember what you found in the Bible code this morning." That is all it took to turn what had seemed like a curse into a blessing. The tears of joy streamed down my face as I thanked God for his wonderful blessings and for accounting me worthy of serving him. That was a moment of realizing how great our God really is.

The code said, "Crushed! NHK bent down," and that is exactly what happened, and God allowed me to find it before it happened. It was actually in my painting from six years earlier but Yahweh did not allow me to see it until twelve hours before it was fulfilled. He chose not to have me dwelling on it for six years.

Thinking it was all over, I jumped out of bed and was about to tear off the wires and walk out of the hospital, when the nurse gave me such an alarmed look that it startled me. Just then I felt a little woozy and fell backward, slipping into unconsciousness. They had to put the defibrillators on me and hit me with some high voltage to stop my heart so that it could regain proper rhythm again.

Note: Here is a little trivia. In Australia, defibrillators are called "Packer Whackers," named after Kerry Packer who donated them to all the ambulances in New South Wales. Since Packer Whackers rhymes with Packer Backers it seems the Wisconsinites might get a kick out of it. The Green Bay Packer fans in Bimini might also get a laugh.

After a short stay in the hospital my son took me into his home till I recuperated. We picked up my laptop computer and brought it to his house so I could research and run code searches.

I used the code I had found in the pillar of fire as a search term, "Crushed! NHK bent down." It turned up at a -564 ELS, in a matrix that stretched from Lamentations 1:17 through 4:2. Crossing symmetrically through my first initial, N, was a cluster of 23 Hebrew letters (כורותשיחעלינפשיזאתאשיבא) that translate to "His smelting furnace; My soul/life is bowed down within me. This my fire is come." This phrase links back to the *Sea of Truth* painting in which NHK is embedded directly into the pillar of fire, perhaps symbolizing my trial by fire.

בותעירבהשתפכנפשמאלחיקאמתממהאעידכמהאדמהלכה
כמשאותשואומדוחימספקועליככפימכלעברידרכשרקו
שקוינהומצאנוראינועשהיהוהאשרזממבצעאמרתואשר
אלתדמבתעינכקומירניבליללראשאשמרותשפכיכמימל
פחימאמיהרגבמקדשאדניכהנונביאשכבולארצחוצותנ
תיורביתיאיביכלמאניהגברראהעניבשבטעברתואותי
בעדיולאאצאהכבידנחשתיגמכיאזעקואשועשתמתפלתי
אשפתוהייתישחקלכלעמינגינתמכלהיומהשביעניבמר
ראשזכורתזכורותשיחעלינפשיזאתאשיבאללביעלכנא

Detail: Partial matrix of skip-141, displaying text from Lamentations 2:12 – 3:21. The full grid includes texts from Ruth 4:14 through Ecclesiastes 1:2. The full key phrase is not seen in this visible portion of the grid but only the section containing NHK, seen in red letters (running upward) with the related symmetrical codes. The purple/pink says, poor skier, and the blue says, shoulder in the snow. The green says, His smelting furnace; My soul/life is bowed down within me. This my fire is come.

When the Lamentations -564 matrix is reconfigured by a row-splitting of four, it becomes a grid of 141 letters per line (Ruth-Eccl.). The afore mentioned terms are still present, but these additional terms also appear crossing symmetrically over the key phrase, מכגלש = "poor skier," and, בשלגכתפ = "shoulder in the snow." In addition to these pertinent terms relating accurately to the accident that caused the heart attack and crossing symmetrically through the key search term, "Crushed! NHK bent down," which defines the result of the heart attack, there is also the exact date that it happened, March 4, 2006 (4 Adar, at the bottom of the grid, and 5766 at the top). If that is not enough, my surname, Kox, runs diagonally through the key phrase giving it additional legitimacy.

There it is, an accurate description of the accident and heart attack, along with the exact date 4 Adar 5766 (March 4, 2006) with my initials and my surname, all in one matrix with three critical phrases running symmetrically through the search key phrase. Had I not discovered my initials in the pillar of fire I would never have had the key phrase to enter into the search and this significant Lamentations code would not have been found.

אמרנההנשימאלנעמיברוכיהוהאשרלאהשביתלכגאלהי
תהובחיקהותהילולאמנתותקראנהלוהשכנותשמלאמרי
ינדבהולידאתנחשונונחשונהולידאתשלמהושלמונהו
ותהיתהלמסבכותבכהבלילהודמעתהעללחיהאינלהמנח
יציונאבלותמבליבאימועדכלשעריהשוממינכהניהנא
יושריהכאילימלאמצאומרעהוילכובלאכחלפנירודפז
כנלנידההיתהכלמכבדיההזילוהכיראוערותהגמהיאנ
הגוימבאומקדשהאשרצויתהלאיבאובקהללככלעמהנאנ
ביאשרעוללליאשרהוגהיהוהביומחרונאפוממרומשלח
בידילאאוכלקומסלהכלאביריאדניבקרביקראעלימוע
יבפרשהציונבידיהאינמנחמלהצוהיהוהליעקבסביבי
מהרמוניכהניוזקניבעירגועוכיבקשואכללמווישיב
מעורעתיששוכיאתהעשיתהבאתיומקראתויהיוכמונית
ישראלולאזכרהדמרגליוביומאפובלעאדנילאחמלאתכ
בכאשלהבהאכלהסביבדרכקשתוכאויבנצבימינוכצרוי
מסכגנשכושחתמועדושכחיהוהבציונמועדושבתוינאצ
ציוננטהקולאהשיבידומבלעויאבלחלוחומהיחדואמל
רעלראשמחגרושקימהורידולארצראשנבתולתירושלמכ
בותעירבהשתפכנפשמאלחיקאמתממהאעידכמהאדמהלכה
כמשאותשואומדוחימספקועליככפימכלעברידרכשרקו
שקוינהומצאנוראינועשהיהוהאשרזממבצעאמרתואשר
אלתדמבתעינכקומירניבליללראשאשמרותשפכיכמימל
פחימאמיהרגבמקדשאדניכהנונביאשכבולארצחוצותנ
תיורביתיאיביכלמאניהגברראהעניבשבטעברתואותי
בעדיולאאצאהכבידנחשתיגמכיאזעקואשועשתמתפלתי
אשפתוהייתישחקלכלעמינגינתמכלהיומהשביעניבמר
ראשזכורתזכורותשיחעלינפשיזאתאשיבאללביעלכנא
טובויחילודוממלתשועתיהוהטובלגברכיישאעלבנעו
ילאענהמלבוויגהבניאישלדכאתחתרגליוכלאסיריאר
יגברעלחטאונחפשהדרכינוונחקרהונשובהעדיהוהנש
מנובקרבהעמימפצועלינופיהמכלאיבינופחדופחתהי
ותעיריצודצדוניכצפוראיביחנמצמתובבורחייוידו
ירארבתאדניריבינפשיגאלתחייראיתהיהוהעותתישפ
מתשיבלהמגמוליהוהכמעשהידיהמתתנלהממגנתלבתאל
ואיכהנחשבולנבליחרשמעשהידייוצרגמתנינחלצושד
מנימעליתולעחבקואשפתותויגדלעונבתעמימחטאתסד
לעצממיבשהיהכעצטובימהיוחלליחרבמחללירעבשהמי
כליסודתיהלאהאמינומלכיארצוכלישביתבלכייבאצר
וטמאקראולמוסורוסורואלתגעוכינצוגמנעואמרובג
צפינואלגוילאיושעצדוצעדינומלכתברחבתינוקרבק
מרנובצלונחיהבגוימשישיושמחיבתאדומיושבתיבאר
האתחרפתנונחלתנונהפכהלזרימבתינולנכרימיתומי
לחמאבתינוחטאואינמאנחנועונתיהמסבלנועבדימשל
ידמנתלופניזקנימלאנהדרובחורימטחוננשאוונערי
עלאלהחשכועינינועלהרציונששממשועלימהלכובואת
לינועדמאדדבריקהלתבנדודמלכבירושלמהבלהבלימא

Full matrix displaying texts from Ruth 4:14 through Ecclesiastes 1:2. The full key phrase, **"Crushed! NHK bent down,"** is seen in this grid in red letters, running from bottom to top.

ELOHIM THE APOCALYPTIC TIME MACHINE

Elohim is the Hebrew word we translate as "God," and "apocalypse" is the New Testament word for revelation. The concept of "Elohim The Apocalyptic Time Machine," is very simple and at the same time quite complex. Elohim, God, exists in a limitless eternity, outside of our realm of measured time. According to Scripture he knows and sees the end from the beginning. This is what makes prophecy possible. He sees what has happened before we experience it. To him it has already taken place. All past, present and future are recorded in the eternal archives of the omniscient Elohim. At times he chooses to allow certain people to glimpse the future. This is a prophetic revelation, an apocalypse of things to come, an actual view of God's memory. Since he holds all knowledge of past, present and future, Elohim is a virtual time capsule, a time machine: Elohim the Apocalyptic Time Machine.

Norbert H. Kox and William Thomas Thompson held a joint exhibition, from February 24 through March 24, 2005, titled Elohim the Apocalyptic Time Machine, showcasing their specific artworks as well as collaborative works. They feel that their paintings have been inspired and guided by the hand of Elohim, the Master of time and space, to allow others to see beyond the confines of the moment into the Eye of the Eternal.

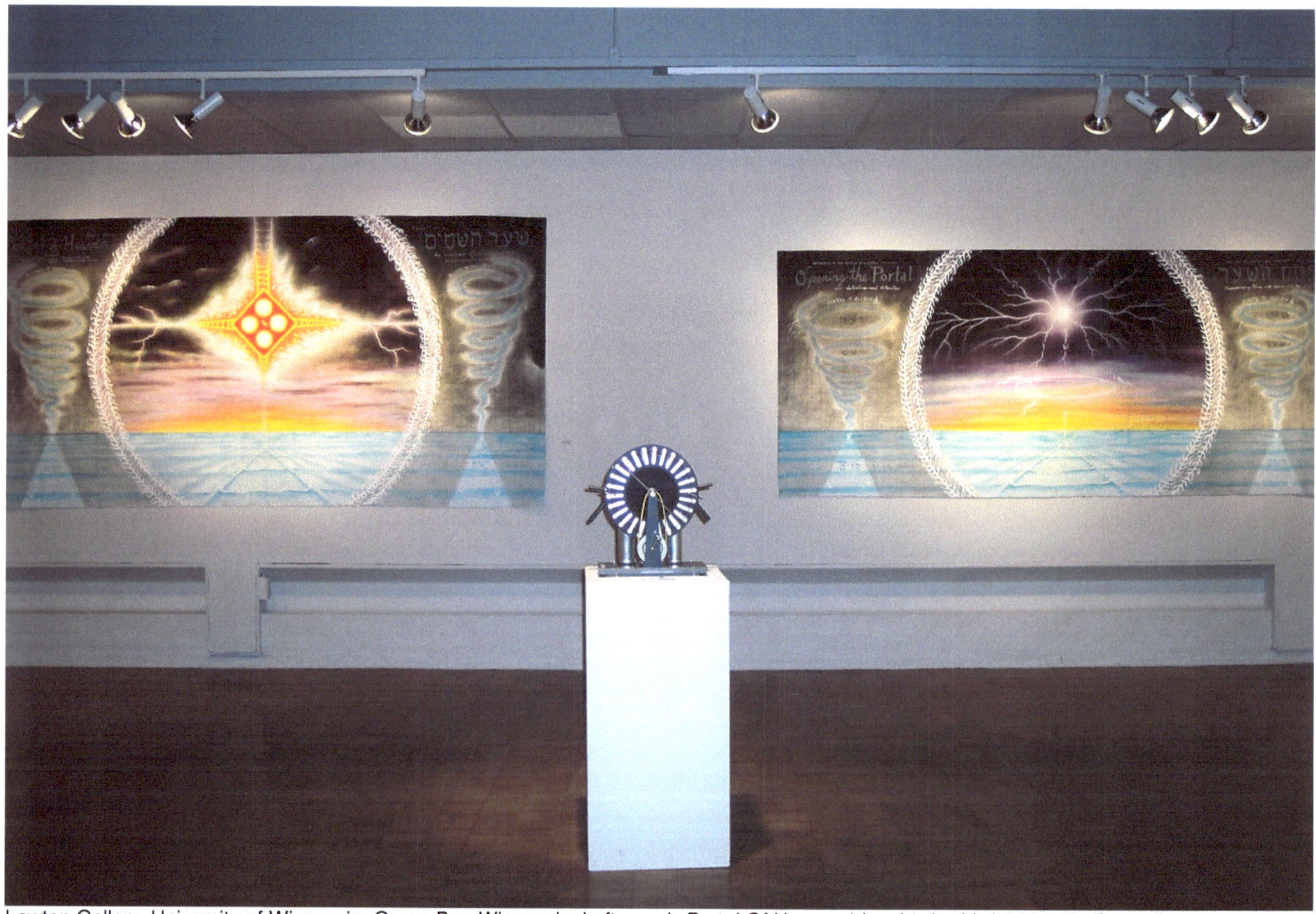

Lawton Gallery, University of Wisconsin, Green Bay, Wisconsin. Left panel, *Portal Of Heaven* (*Jacob's Ladder*) 2004-2005, acrylic on canvas, 60" x 124". Right panel, *Opening The Portal*, 2004-2005, acrylic on canvas, 50" x 124". (Both paintings were painted on the Island of Bimini). Center pedestal, Wimshurst Wheel generator; creates tiny high voltage lightning bolts and a loud crack. Actually blasts holes through light-weight cardboard in experimental demonstration.

MEANING OF THE LIGHTNING

The lightning bolts depicted throughout this exhibit, and brought to reality through the Van de Graaff Generators within the cubicle [built to the dimensions of the Holy of Holies in the ancient tabernacle of Yahweh] symbolize and represent the power of God (Elohim) in the Ark of the Covenant. The ark was a powerful capacitor which collected and stored energy within itself. Whenever this energy was discharged it often brought great destruction and death to those within its range. Moses appointed a specially trained group of priests with knowledge of how to safely handle and transport the extremely dangerous ark.

When Israel was not on the move the ark was placed within a tent, inside a cubicle the size of the one in this exhibit. This cubicle was called "The Holy of Holies," and "The Oracle." It was a portal to the spirit realm, and a virtual time machine, which connected the temporal world to the eternal, when the proper frequencies were attained. Josephus, a first-century Jewish historian, referred to the Holy of Holies as, "a heaven peculiar to God." That is, the private dwelling of Elohim. When the portal was activated it was no longer just a room in the tabernacle, it became an actual doorway between heaven and earth. When the High Priest entered the Oracle Chamber, there was an interaction between the energy of the ark and the crystals in the breastplate he wore. The circuit was completed and the frequency within the chamber had such an effect on the physical and spiritual realms that the invisible became manifest and tangible.

The physical and spiritual worlds exist in the same space at the same time, but at different frequencies. Everything that exists is made up of waves (frequencies). Our limited physical senses can only comprehend and process a small segment of the electromagnetic spectrum. Wavelengths above or below this narrow corridor go undetected by our natural senses. When there is some anomaly present within the veil that normally keeps other worlds invisible, time and space may be temporarily transcended revealing the spirit realm. In a sense heaven is brought to earth, or earth is brought to heaven. Like when the High Priest entered the Holy of Holies and found himself transported to "a heaven peculiar to God." When the priest activated the Ark of the Covenant, Elohim manifested in an energy form above the mercy seat (lid) of the ark. From this manifestation of pure energy Yahweh spoke and instructed the Israelites.

Above the tent was a pillar-cloud of fire and smoke, a flaming whirlwind teaming with uncontainable energy, hurling lightning bolts as it churned the atmosphere. It was the same portal of heaven that was seen by Jacob when he had laid his head at the Chief Cornerstone (the pyramidal capstone representing Yesu Christ). It was the same whirlwind-portal that carried Elijah into the heavens. Ezekiel saw it. He called it a wheel in the middle of a wheel, and was transported by it through time and space. God spoke to Job out of the same portal. Yesu Christ traveled through portals many times in Scripture. So did his apostles and disciples.

In the Biblical writings, Elohim enters this world through a portal, in a whirlwind swirling with fire and lightning, accompanied by roaring thunder and quaking earth.

God's presence and awesome energy was always with the ark, and people died by simply touching it. But to those who had reverence and the knowledge to use it properly, the Ark of the Covenant was a key to the portal of heaven.

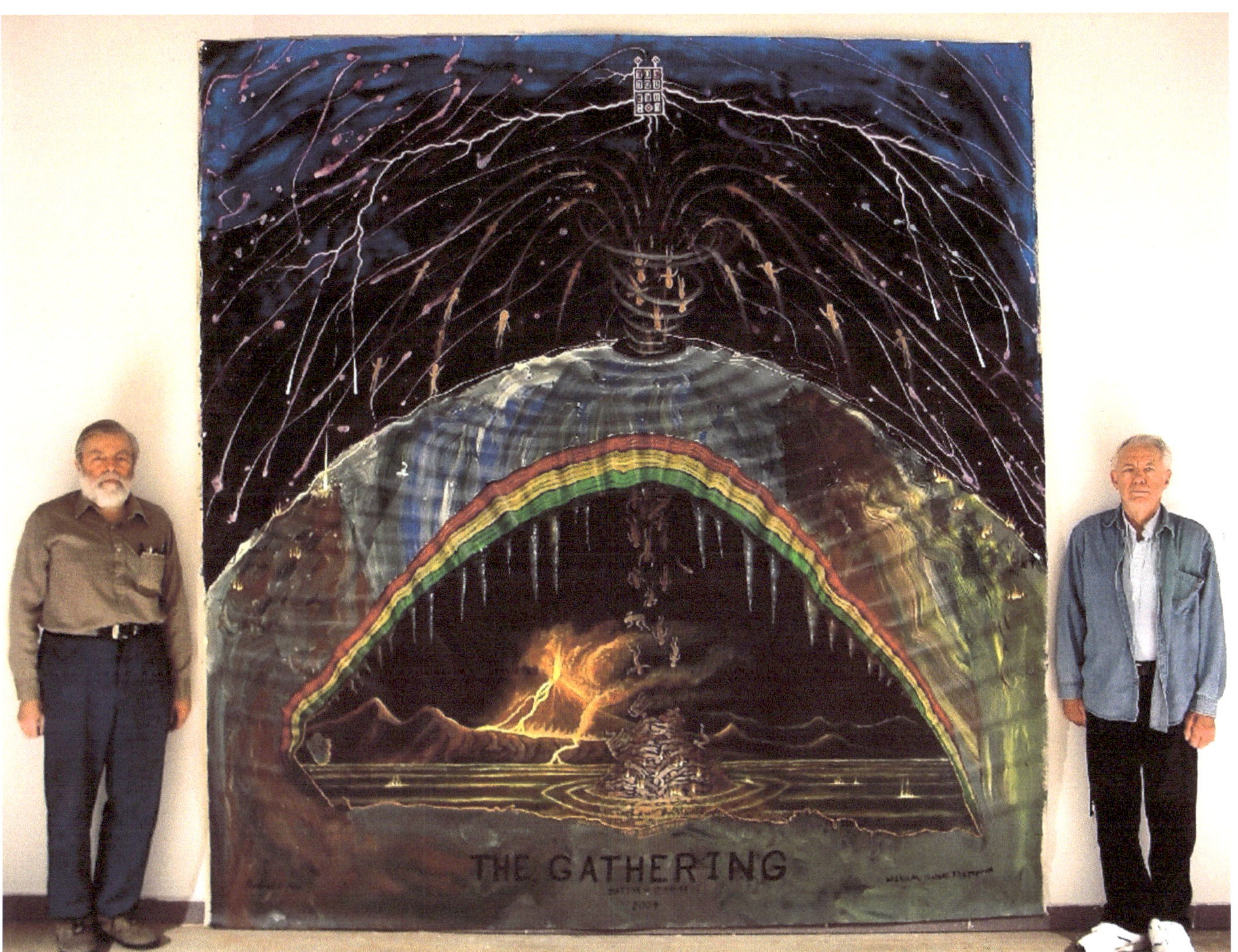

The Gathering, 2004, collaboration by Norbert Kox (left) and William Thompson (right), acrylic on canvas, 10' 6" x 10'

This was our fourth and most difficult collaboration, because it took an unexpected turn. The painting we had envisioned for almost a year was suddenly being steered in another direction. It was a real struggle, as we each had to let go of preconceived ideas. The painting took a turn; we let it happen letting the Holy Spirit move. We both feel that the Holy Spirit guided us to paint this final message to the people and to the church at large.

THE GATHERING

The Elohim exhibit included the painting titled, *The Gathering*, which is timely in its apocalyptic message. Most Biblical scholars agree that we are living in the "end times," when the judgment of God is about to culminate upon the earth and its inhabitants. The visible vibrations of the earth seen in this painting are both literal and symbolic, opening a portal simultaneously in time and space, to show the end of both the wicked and the deceived.

The breastplate of judgment (Exodus 28: 15-30) is unfolded at the top of the painting, illuminating the sky with lines of light and lightning, simulating the fire and light that was emitted when the fierce power of God electrically interacted with the frequencies in the "stones of fire."

The whole World is seen vibrating and quaking as the frequencies of Earth's harmonics open a portal to the nether world. Interestingly, in the Hebrew Language, "earthquake" spelled backward is "portal."

On top of the World, is pictured a "whirlwind of false doctrine" that sucks people up in its vacuum, and down through the portal into the heart of the earth. They are deposited onto a huge pile. An analogy in the Scripture says, "I will even make the pile for fire great. Heap on wood, kindle the fire, consume the flesh, and spice it well, and let the bones be burned." (Ezekiel 24: 9-10). It also says, "Tophet ['the fire place'] is ordained of old; yea, for the king it is prepared; he hath made it deep and large: the pile thereof is fire and much wood; the breath of Yahweh, like a stream of brimstone, doth kindle it." (Isaiah 30: 33). The painting shows the lake of fire burning with bodies piled high, and volcanoes erupting.

Isaiah said, that Yahweh, "bringeth the princes to nothing: he maketh the judges of the earth as vanity. Yea, they shall not be planted; yea, they shall not be sown: yea, their stock shall not take root in the earth: and he shall also blow upon them, and they shall wither, and the whirlwind shall take them away as stubble." (Isaiah 40: 23-24).

This painting depicts the fallacy and false hope of many believers in religion, psychology, occultism, psychic necromancy, numerology, and any other number of systems.

People living outside the will of God fear the site of true scripture and truth. The Bible contains the holy Word of God, the inspired Scriptures, but man has changed much of the Bible as time has passed. Even the King James version has been corrupted and contains many inherent mistakes. One being the name of Christ. In the first edition, published in 1611 AD, it began with an I as Iesus (original English pronunciation, yay-soo). The name Jesus is a modern invention that came to us through gradualism and first became commonly accepted only a few hundred years ago.

Many are falling away and only a few will be saved by recognizing the truth of God. The artificial Jesus image, "Head of Christ," painted in 1940 by Warner Sallman, has been a stumbling block for the church at large becoming an icon idol one-billion-strong. This painting was actually plagiarized from a little-known French artist who painted it in the late 1800's but did not claim it to be the true Christ. It is almost universally accepted. The Protestant Church especially has adopted it as their Christ or as "Jesus" (the artificial and counterfeit Christ). It is now known as "the Protestant Idol."

The Pentecostal's have a good doctrine of sanctification and the infilling of the Holy Spirit of God but it is rarely practiced. ...There is no future for those who dwell in their own righteousness and fail to yield to God's will and Spirit to dwell within their hearts, to change their lives to true Christian. Those who claim to have it do not have it and will be the first to be harvested off the face of the earth in the final hour at the end of the World, which is interpreted to be the end of God's day of grace. The devil seems to work the hardest among church folks to harden their hearts and to steal their victory. ...Those who harbor hate and unforgiveness for others bring death to themselves... (from text by William Thompson and Norbert Kox).

Negativity is a destructive force. Everything in the world has frequencies, i.e. vibratory rates. People have specific frequencies at which the body must harmonize for perfect health. Un-forgiveness and other negative thoughts and actions lower the body's frequency and bring sickness and death. A positive and loving attitude will raise one's frequency and ultimately encourage renewal and healing in the body. Just as our bodies need healing, the body of Christ ("church") needs healing. In the end, the unforgiving ones will be cut off so the whole body not perish (Matthew 5: 29-30). Yesu Christ said, "For if ye forgive men their trespasses, your heavenly Father will also forgive you: But if ye forgive not men their trespasses, neither will your Father forgive your trespasses." (Matthew 6: 14-15).

The Gathering depicts the cutting off and has several applications in meaning and fulfillment, with no chronological order in this painting, but all aspects are shown simultaneously as if being viewed from eternity in a moment of time. It appears as a virtual time machine.

The enemies of God are deceived by false miracles performed by demons and are gathered to Armageddon for destruction (Revelation 16: 12-16).

Those caught up in false doctrine... are "damned" [katakrino: down-judged]. ...The evil ones, tares, children of the wicked, are gathered for destruction by fire, "Gather ye together first the tares, and bind them in bundles to burn them: but gather the wheat into my barn." (Matthew 13: 29-43). ...

All the nations will be gathered before Christ for judgment (Matthew 25: 31-46). When he comes to judge the gathering, he says, "But those mine enemies, which would not that I should reign over them, bring hither, and slay them before me." (Luke 19: 12-27).

"And death and hell were cast into the lake of fire. This is the second death. And whosoever was not found written in the book of life was cast into the lake of fire" (Revelation 20:14-15).

"But the fearful, and unbelieving, and the abominable, and murderers, and whoremongers, and sorcerers, and idolaters, and all liars, shall have their part in the lake which burneth with fire and brimstone: which is the second death" (Revelation 21:8).

"And I beheld when he had opened the sixth seal, and, lo, there was a great earthquake; and the sun became black as sackcloth of hair, and the moon became as blood; And the stars of heaven fell unto the earth, even as a fig tree casteth her untimely figs, when she is shaken of a mighty wind. And the heaven departed as a scroll when it is rolled together; and every mountain and island were moved out of their places. And the kings of the earth, and the great men, and the rich men, and the chief captains, and the mighty men, and every bondman, and every free man, hid themselves in the dens and in the rocks of the mountains; And said to the mountains and rocks, Fall on us, and hide us from the face of him that sitteth on the throne, and from the wrath of the Lamb: For the great day of his wrath is come; and who shall be able to stand?" (Revelation 6: 12-17).

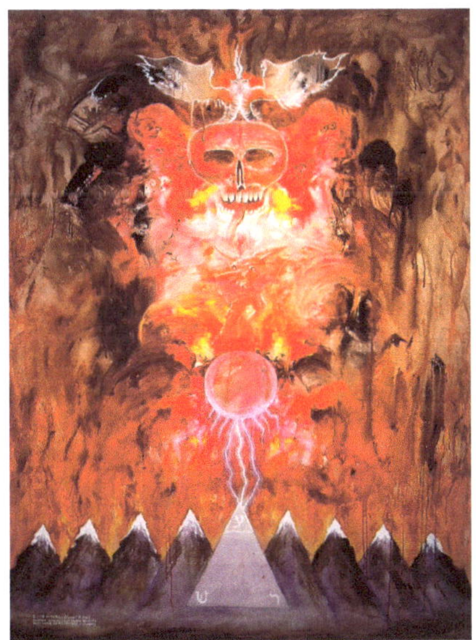

Portal of Doom, 2004-2005, acrylic on canvas, 64" x 47"
Painted in Bimini with coconut frond brushes made by Mr. Tommy Saunders.
(See larger image on page 97)

Armand Hein
and TOXIC Gallery
are pleased to invite
you to the opening
of the exhibition

"LAST CHANCE APOCALYPSE"

by
NORBERT H. KOX

Opening
september 18th, 2009
from 6 pm to 8 pm
in the presence
of the artist
Exhibition
september 18th through
november 21st, 2009

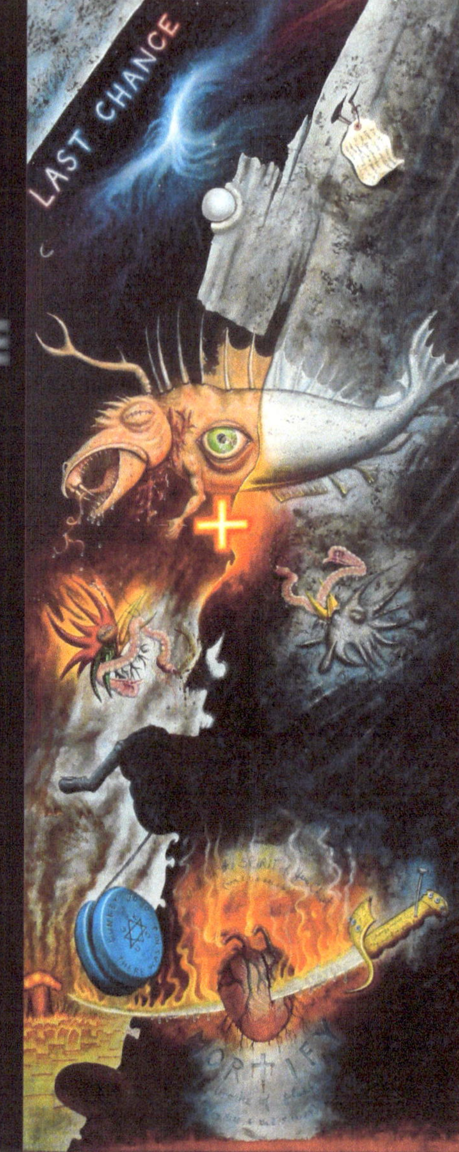

Armand Hein
et la Galerie TOXIC
ont le plaisir de vous inviter
au vernissage
de l'exposition

"LAST CHANCE APOCALYPSE"

de
NORBERT H. KOX

Vernissage
le 18 septembre 2009
de 18h à 20h
en présence
de l'artiste
Exposition
du 18 septembre
au 21 novembre 2009

Invitation card image: *Last Chance: Apocalypse in Blood and Flames*, 1995-1997, acrylic & oil on canvas, 75" x 30" (not painted in Bimini)

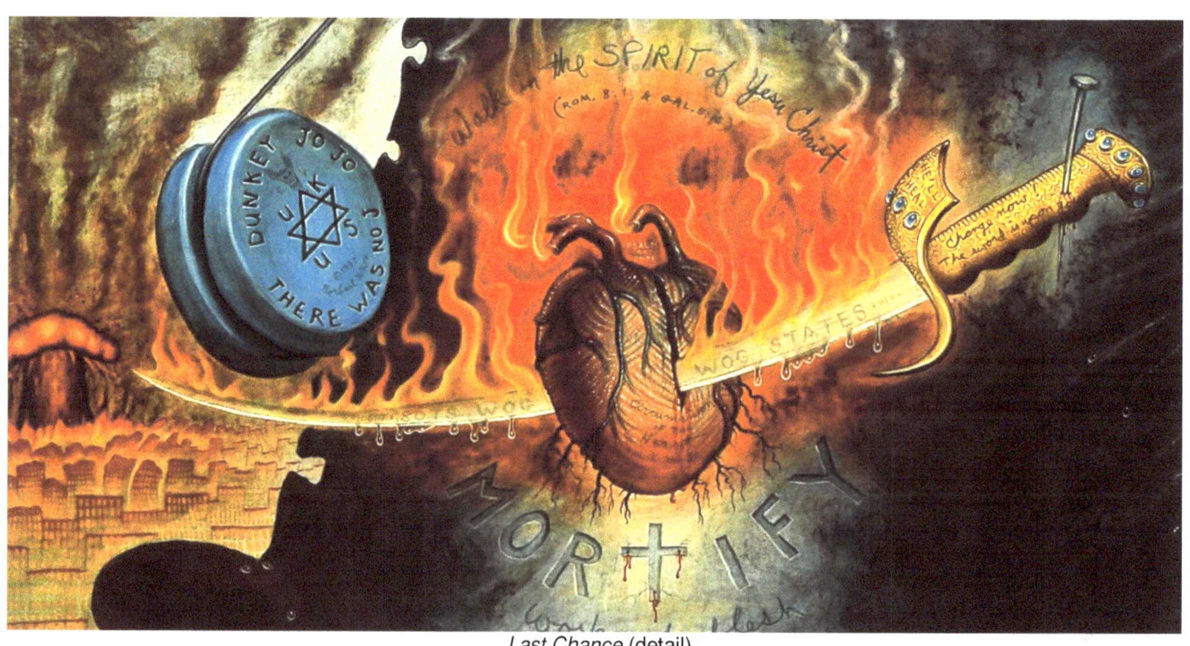

Last Chance (detail)

LAST CHANCE APOCALYPSE

In 2009, a number of the Bimini paintings were included in the solo exhibit, Last Chance Apocalypse, at Armand Hein's Galerie Toxic in Luxembourg, Europe, along with several other Apocalyptic Visual Parables. The Bimini works in the exhibition are shown here.

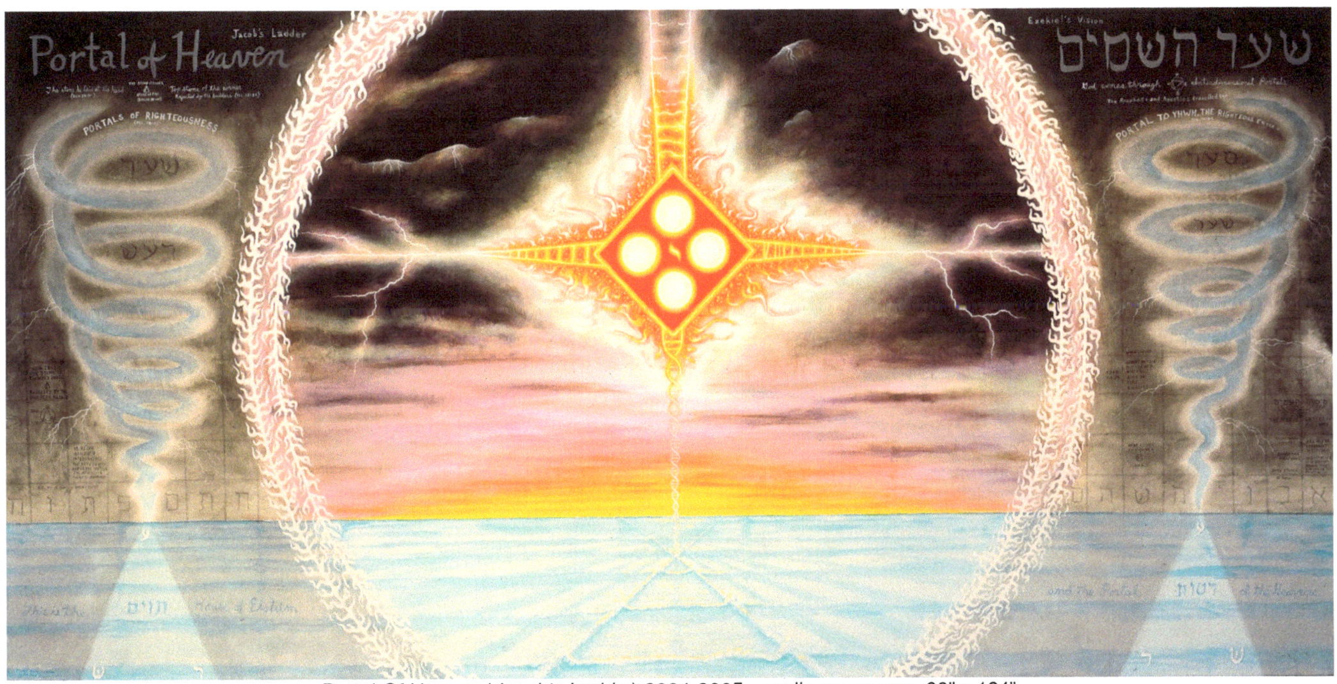

Portal Of Heaven (*Jacob's Ladder*) 2004-2005, acrylic on canvas, 60" x 124"

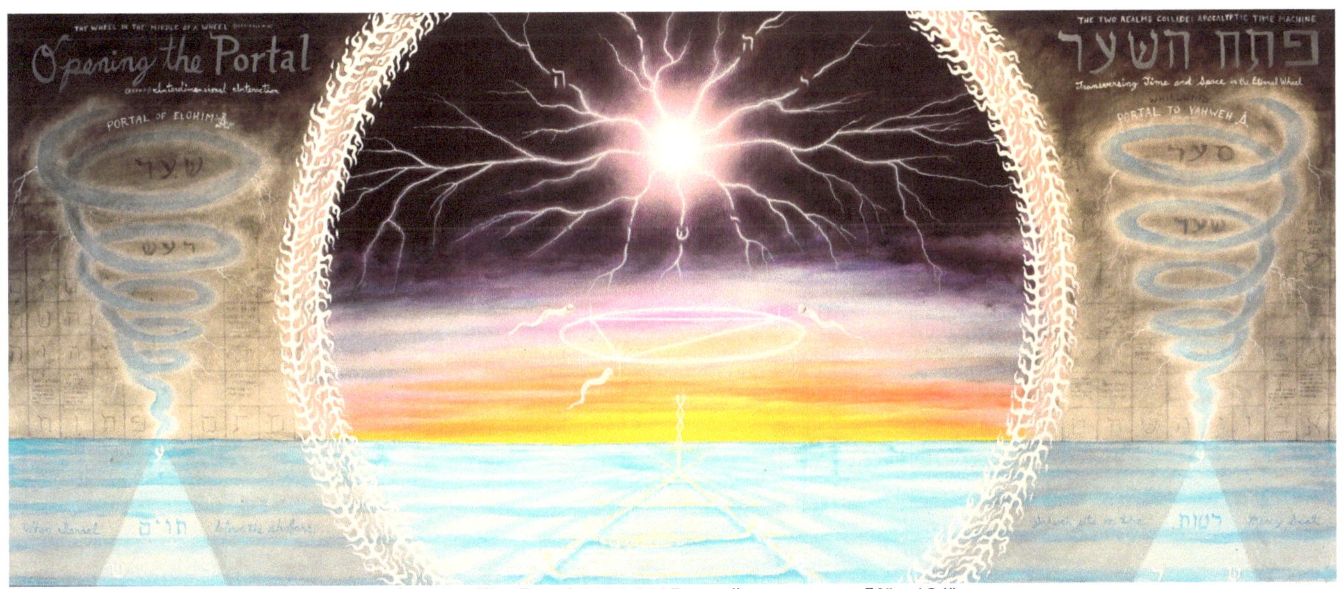

Opening The Portal, 2004-2005, acrylic on canvas, 50" x 124"

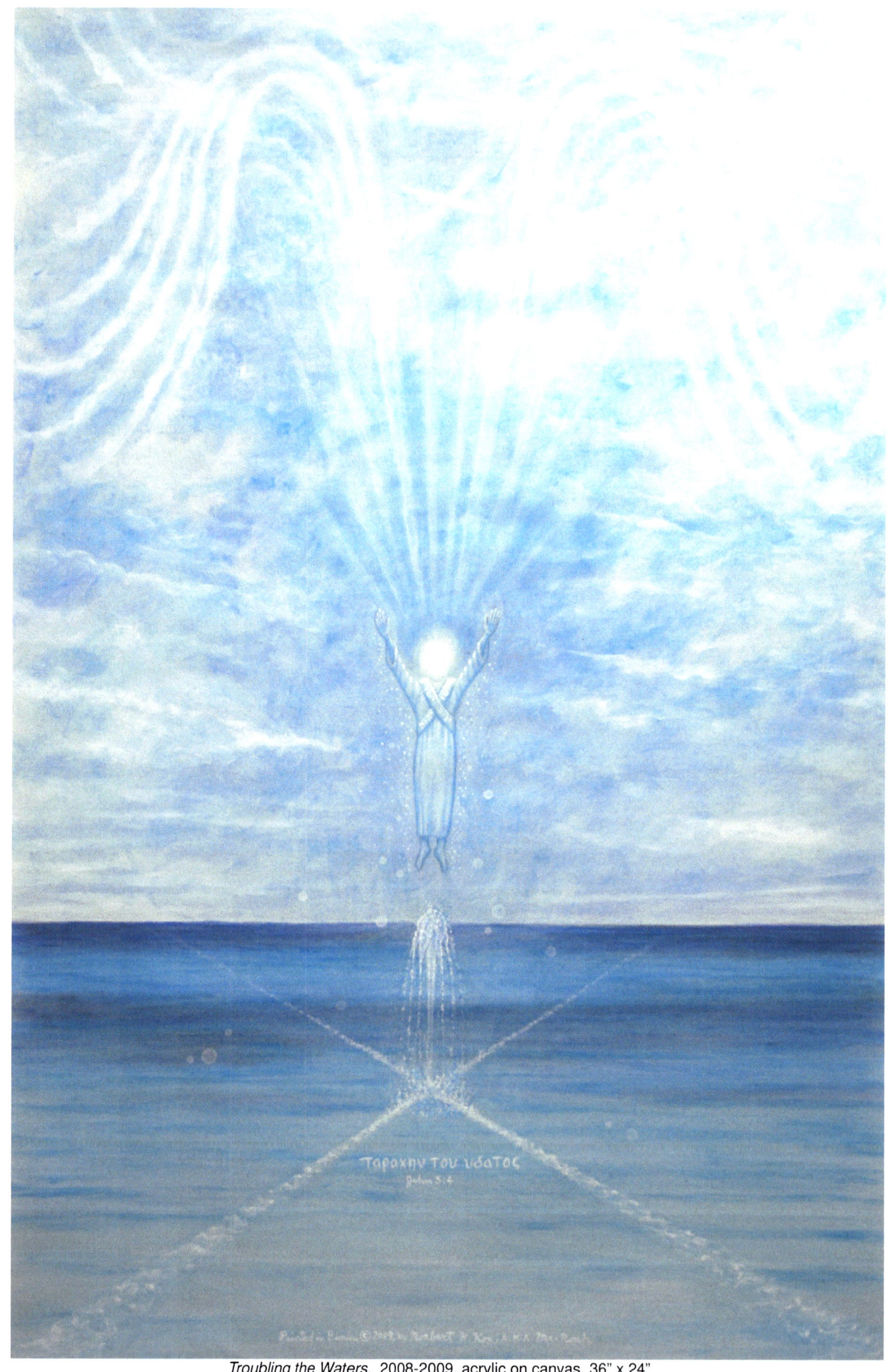

Troubling the Waters, 2008-2009, acrylic on canvas, 36" x 24"

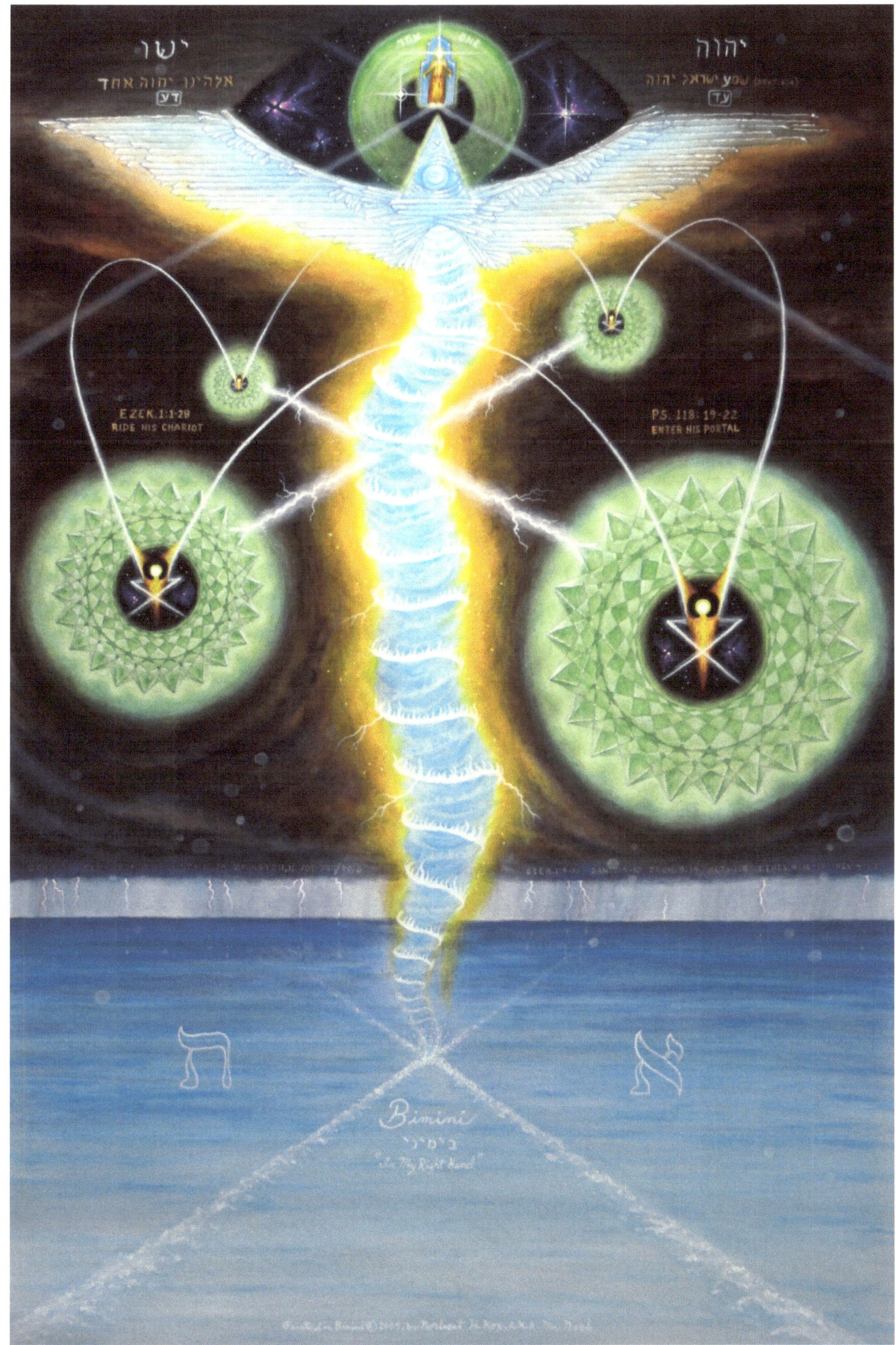

Celestial Chariot, 2008-2009, acrylic on canvas, 36" x 24"

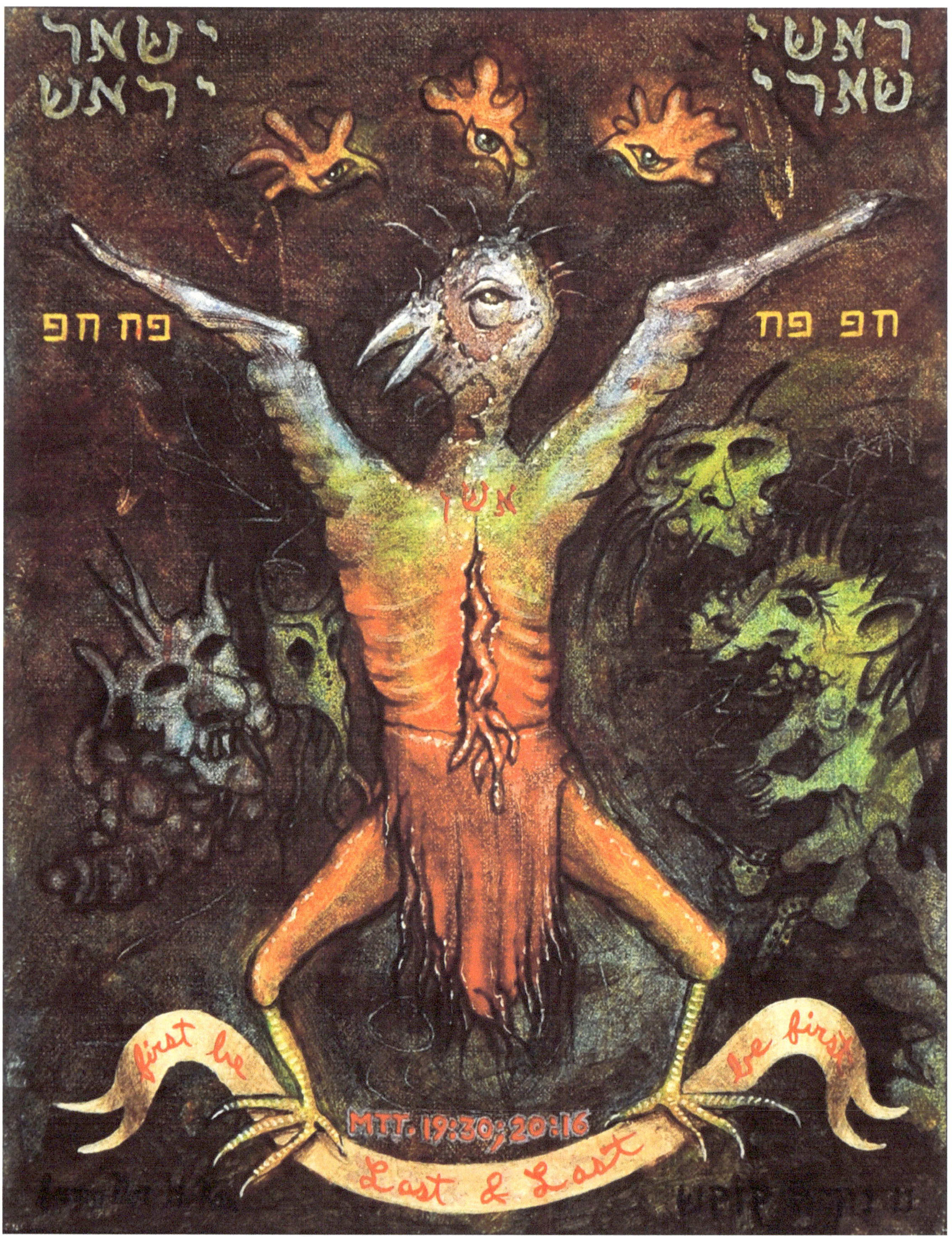

First and Last, 2000, acrylic on canvas panel, 10" x 8"

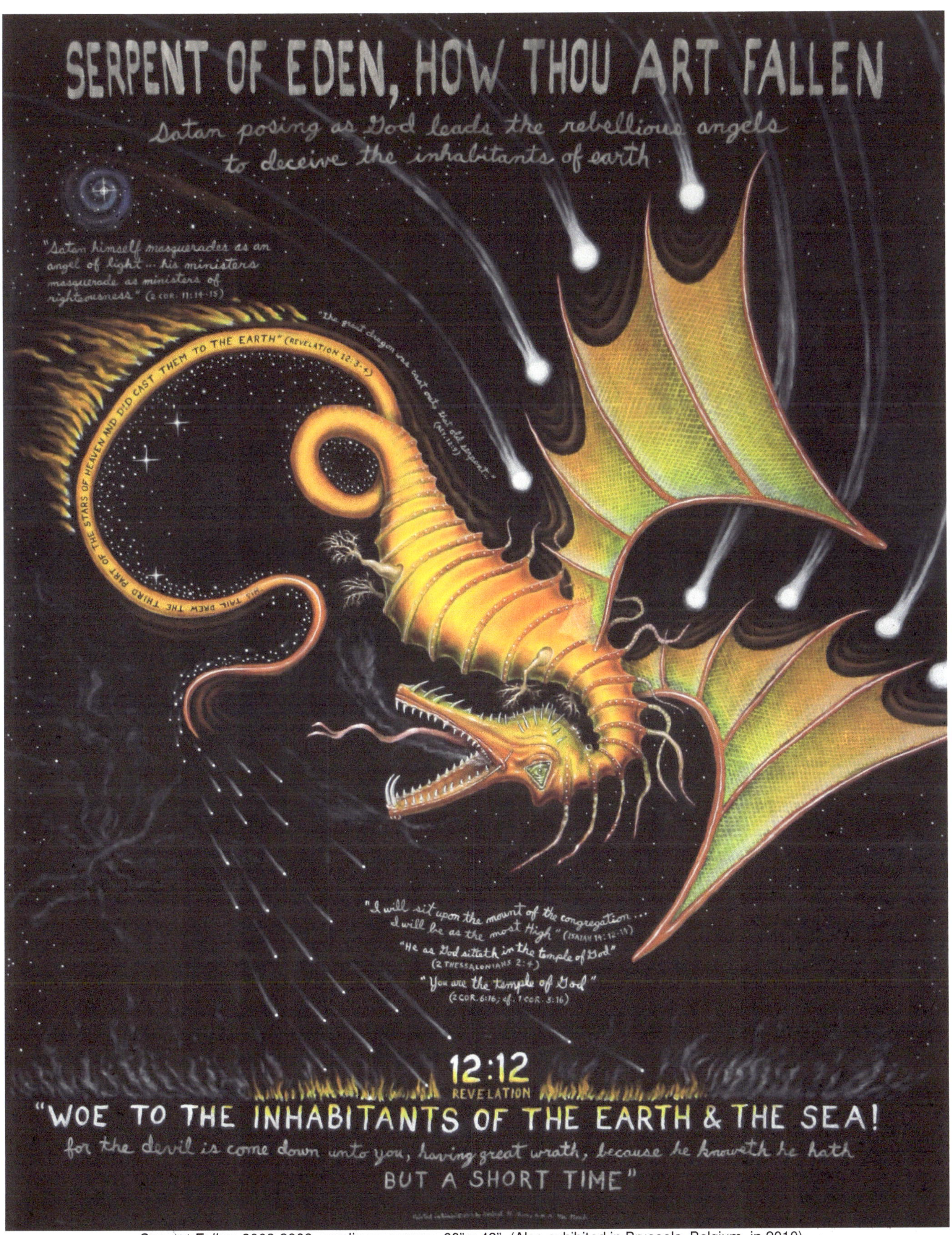

Serpent Fallen, 2008-2009, acrylic on canvas, 60" x 48" (Also exhibited in Brussels, Belgium, in 2010)

DIVINE SYSTEM OF SPONTANEOUS REGENERATION

In the winter of 2005-2006, came the inspiration to paint the symbolic image of God transmuted into the tree/plan of life and the blueprint of man. This is the same pattern of energy that is imprinted upon the beds we each sleep in. We each have our own pattern of positive or negative energy. The heavenly lines of energy from God that connect to this pattern actually recharge us as we sleep. It is the divine system of spontaneous regeneration. The energy of the universe will respond to our attitude and treat us accordingly. If we have imprinted negativity into our pattern we will have problem areas at the points where the bad energy is. This can even cause health problems for us, both physically and mentally. We can ask God to change negative or non-beneficial energy to beneficial and through prayer and attitude it will be done. This has nothing to do with spiritual salvation. It is all part of the laws of the universe laid out by the Creator to benefit all of mankind, "...he maketh his sun to rise on the evil and on the good, and sendeth rain on the just and on the unjust" (Matthew 5:45).

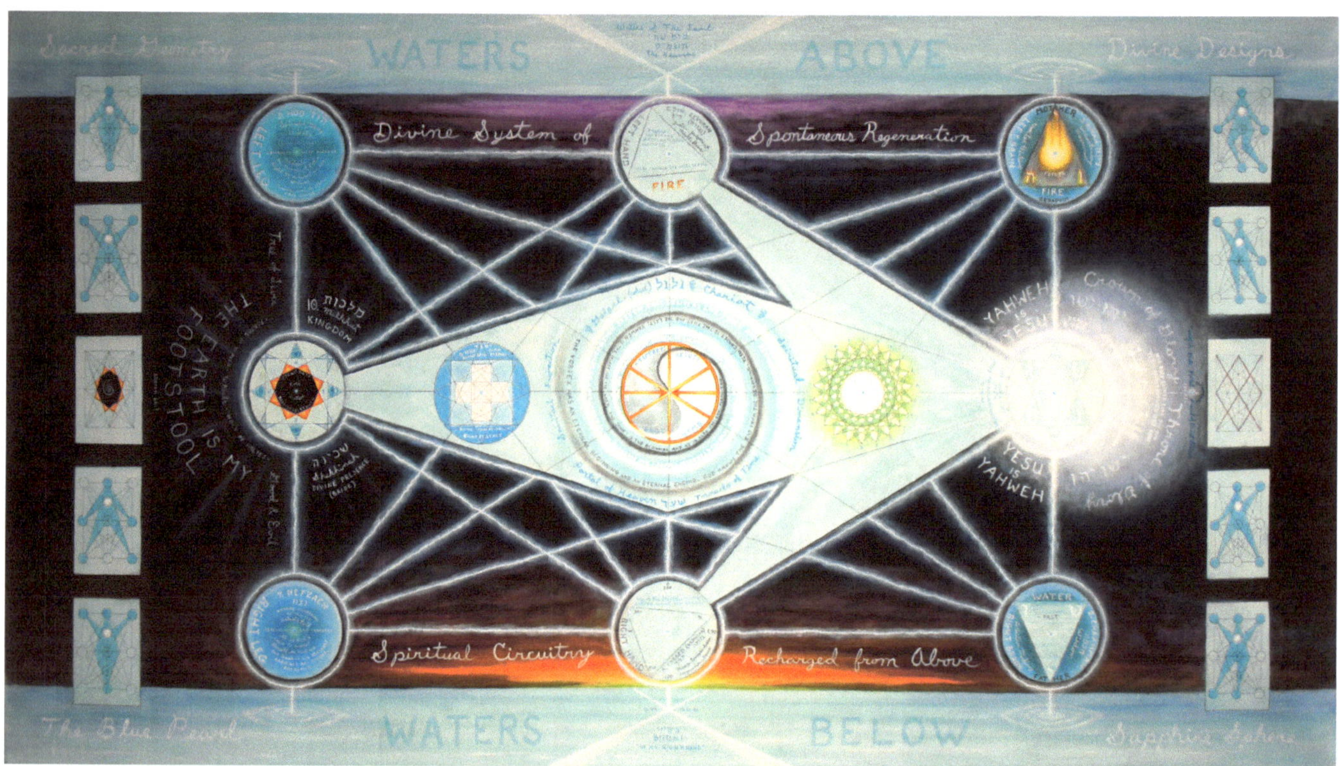

Divine System of Spontaneous Regeneration, 2005-2006, acrylic on canvas, 60" x 108"

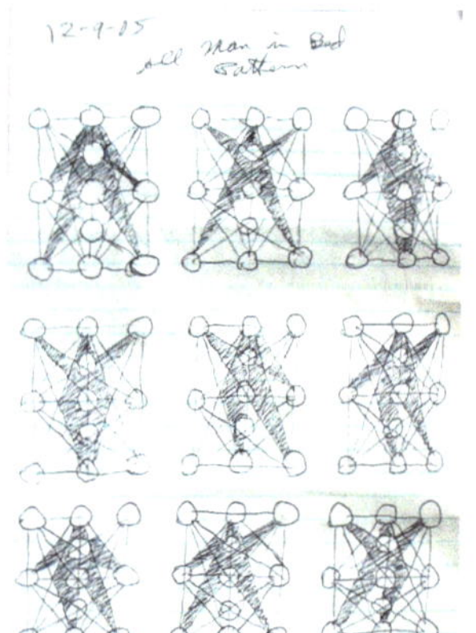

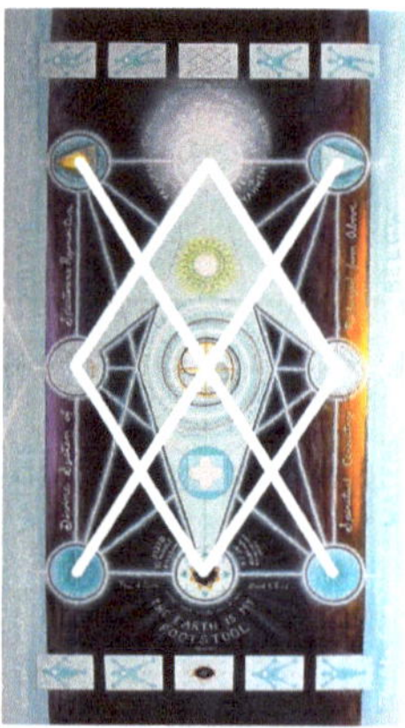

Left: Working sketches. The 11 main power spots in the tree of life are plotted by the paths of the energy lines forming the human image, as can be seen when the various intermediate spaces are shade-in. Right: A symbol of quintessence, the 5th element (ether) is revealed when lines are drawn connecting the nine primary spheres in the tree/plan.

A symbol of quintessence, or the fifth element, is present in the tree of life. Nine is the number of divine manifestation. The energy lines between the nine primary spheres in the pattern form two stacked tiers of double X's: two side-by-side X's are standing on top of two more. The four X's in that configuration actually create a fifth X at the center of a diamond shape that is made up of four smaller diamonds. The four X's and four diamonds represent the four elements, earth, fire, water,air, while the fifth X and the fifth diamond represent the fifth element, ether.

The four elements represent the physical world we live in, and the fifth element, the quintessence, is the ether, representing the spiritual realm of light and energy. The fifth element symbol is centered on the *sefirot* or sphere named Tiferet, which is at the exact middle of the tree and connects all the other spheres. It also represents a portal between the heavenly and earthly domains. *Tiferet*, תפארת, means adornment, beauty, glory. It is the sixth sphere and corresponds to the Hebrew letter *waw* (or, *vav*) which is another portal symbol linking heaven and earth.

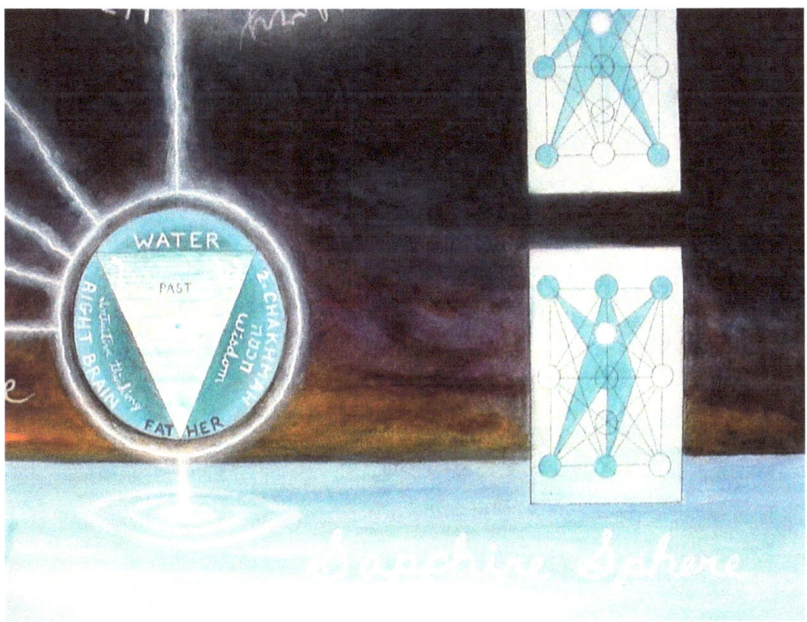

Divine System of Spontaneous Regeneration (detail)

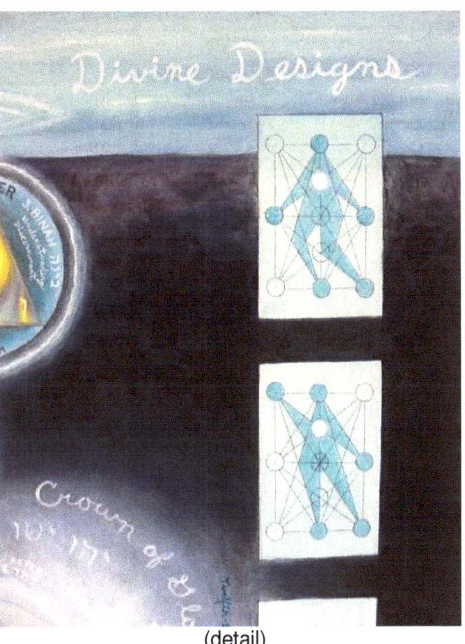

(detail)

The world we now see was first created of pure energy. According to ancient writings Adam and Eve were made of energy; they were beings of light. After the fall God made them coats of *skins* (Genesis 3:21). In the Hebrew text it is written in the singular, "skin." It is probably not referring to coats sewn together of animal skins, since skin is singular. It may be a reference to beings of light receiving actual skin. Yahweh evidently slowed down their frequencies so that they manifested as flesh and blood physical beings. Like Einstein once said, "What we have called matter is energy, whose vibration has been so lowered as to be perceptible to the senses."

After Adam and Eve had disobeyed God and realized what they had done, they were frightened, and the Bible says, "Adam and his wife hid themselves from the presence of Yahweh God amongst the trees of the garden" (Genesis 3:8). In the Hebrew text we immediately see that it does not say "trees." It is singular "tree" (עץ). They hid "in the middle of the tree of the garden" (בתוך עץ הגן). When we examine the tree of life plan, the *Tiferet* is directly "in the middle of the tree." The man and woman went into the *Tiferet*.

The beams of light from the entire tree all converge into the *Tiferet* possibly making it the brightest spot, a natural place for beings of light to attempt to hide. They unwittingly did exactly what God had planned for them. By going into the portal they were moved by God from the ethereal kingdom of spirit, light and energy into the physical realm of darkness and matter, where they were *coated with skin*. Essentially they had cut themselves off from God and the light, slowing their frequencies and becoming physical beings.

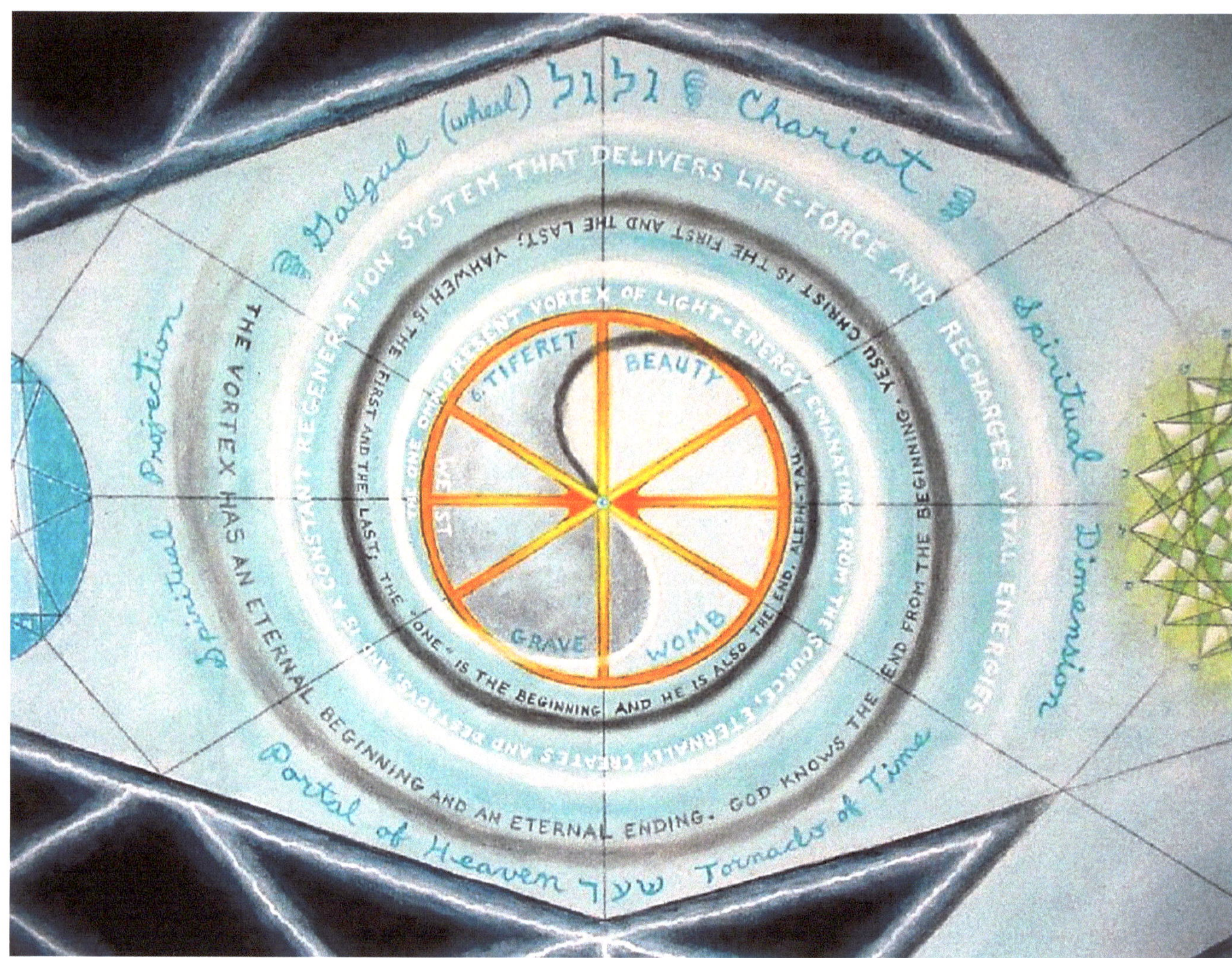

Divine System of Spontaneous Regeneration (detail)

At the Bimini art show reception in 2006, visitors were asked to comment on the artworks. Ms. Cotton Hanna pointed out the *Tiferet* portal wheel at the center of the regeneration painting, and said that she could feel the energy coming from it, and that it reminded her of a giant crystal that had washed up on South Bimini after the last hurricane. She described how she had been walking on the shore and saw a bright light sparkling in the distance. As she approached the dazzling light she could feel the energy coming from it and began to tingle all over. It was an enormous crystal structure approximately two feet in diameter. She felt inspired to sit on it and when she did the energy shot through her body so that she began to shake and tremble.

I would be leaving the Island the next day, and Ms. Cotton offered to show me the crystal.

Next morning I crossed the channel in the water taxi and met with Ms. Cotton and Pastor Angelo Rolle on South Bimini. They took me to the location of the crystal. It appeared as described, but sadly it had been damaged with chisel marks by souvenir hunters. Pastor Angelo recognized it as an aragonite crystal. I picked up several smaller crystal pieces that were laying there, about four inches in diameter, to take back to Wisconsin for experimentation with energy. The experiments culminating with the Van de Graaff generator proved very interesting and rewarding.

Aragonite is considered a Semi-precious gemstone, with a medium translucency that is believed to increase energy especially in prayer, and also to produce deep peaceful meditation. It boosts self-confidence and self-worth while bringing about a calming effect by diminishing anger and relieving stress.

"Aragonite's six-sided crystal forms symbolize the hexagram and the Star of David or Solomon's Seal" (http://www.shimmerlings.com/gemstones/aragonite.htm). Interestingly, the six-pointed star is another symbol of the fifth element, the ether. When the symbols of the four elements are overlaid on top of each other, a six-pointed star is created thus a fifth symbol representing the fifth element. So the Seal of Solomon is actually a symbol linked to the portal. Thus the aragonite crystals that are filled with energy and power are also a symbol of the invisible kingdom of heaven.

Research indicates that Bimini is surrounded by aragonite crystals. This is the substance that pearls are made of, and is what gives them their translucent concentric layering that produces a luster and an almost iridescent luminosity. In essence the term "blue pearl" is a fitting appellation when speaking of Bimini and its surrounding luminescent aqua-blue waters.

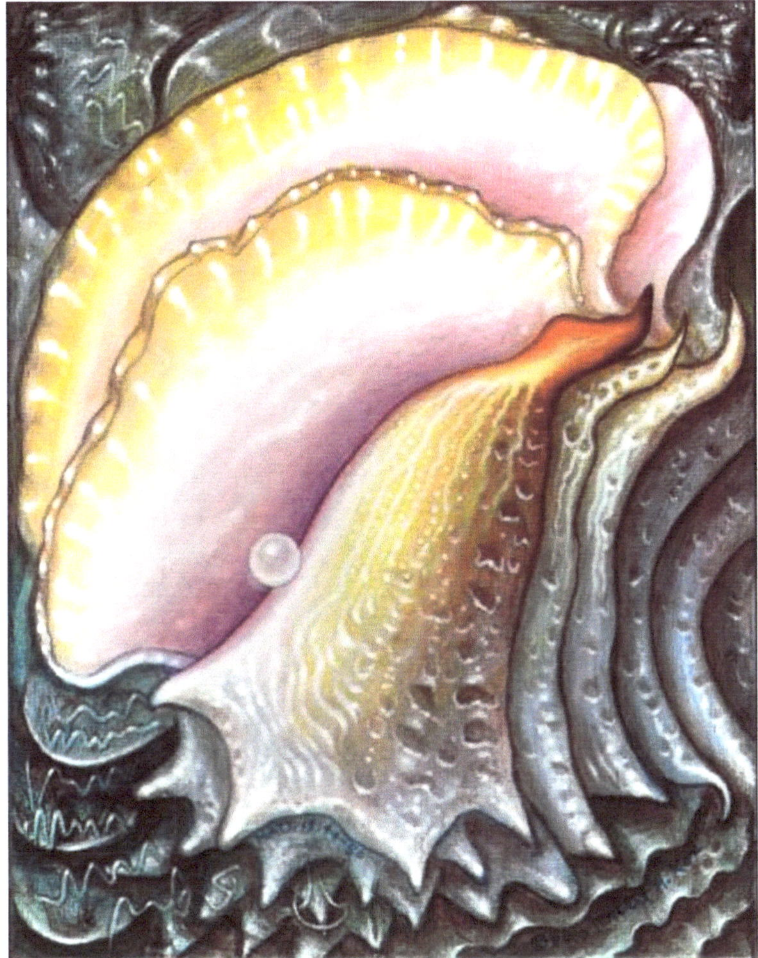

The Pearl of Great Price, 1999-2000, acrylic on canvas panel, 10" x 8"

PEARL OF GREAT PRICE

God has chosen to program unclean creatures of the sea to produce precious pearls, the very thing that the kingdom of God is likened unto in preciousness, "the pearl of great price" (Matthew 13:45-46).

Pearls are an analogy for holy things: "Give not that which is holy unto the dogs, neither cast ye your pearls before swine, lest they trample them under their feet, and turn again and rend you" (Matthew 7:6).

In the book of Revelation God took John through a portal and showed him the new Jerusalem with twelve pearls as twelve portals through which the righteous shall enter, "and the twelve portals were twelve pearls" (Revelation 21:21). Each pearl is a portal!

MORE BIMINI ART, SELECTED EXHIBITS, SELECTED WORKS

APOCALYPTIC VISUAL PARABLES (2000)

(Also shown at Dean Jensen Art Gallery, Milwaukee, Wisconsin)

Paints in this series were ground and mixed on the island of Bimini with elements local to the Island

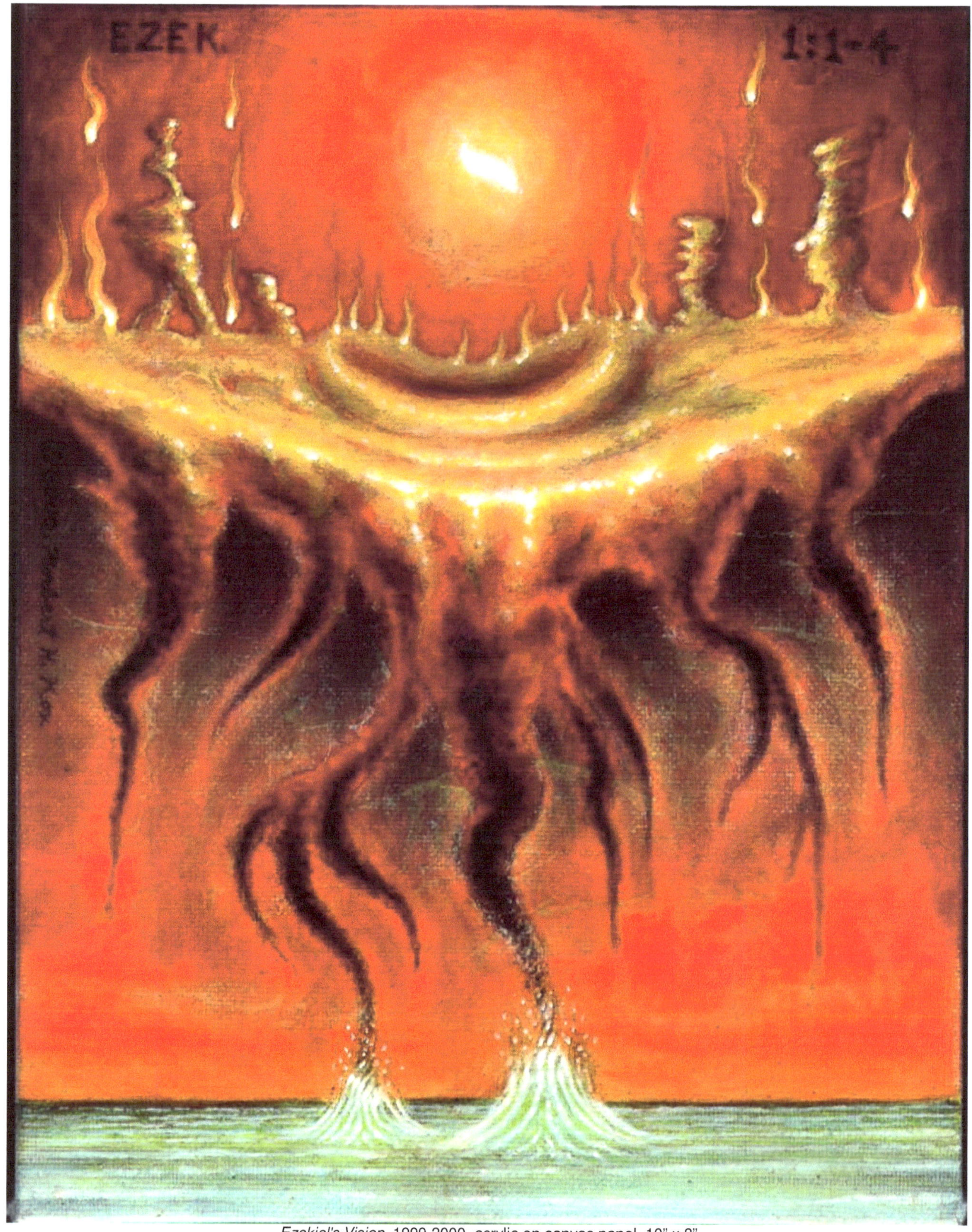

Ezekiel's Vision, 1999-2000, acrylic on canvas panel, 10" x 8"

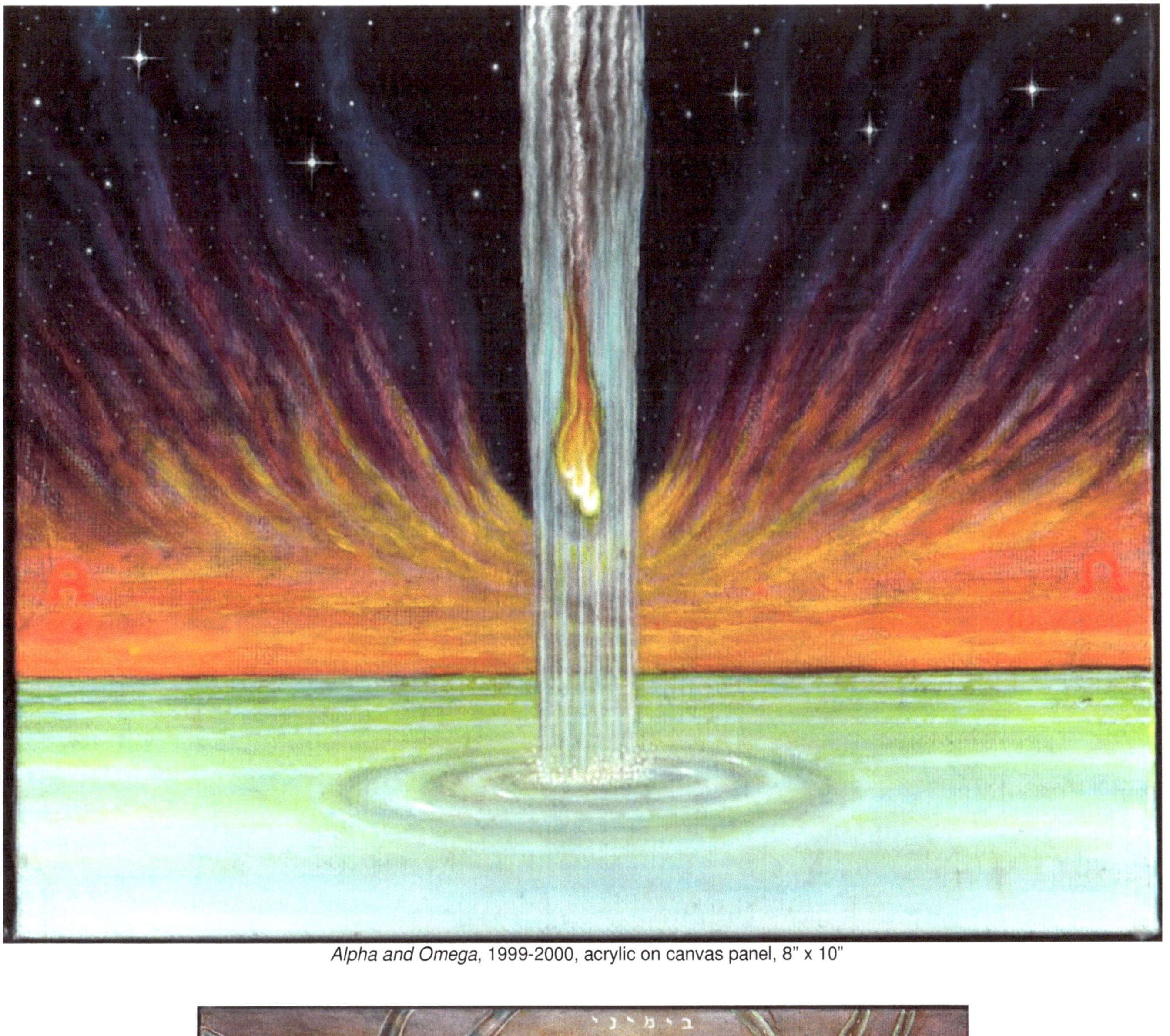

Alpha and Omega, 1999-2000, acrylic on canvas panel, 8" x 10"

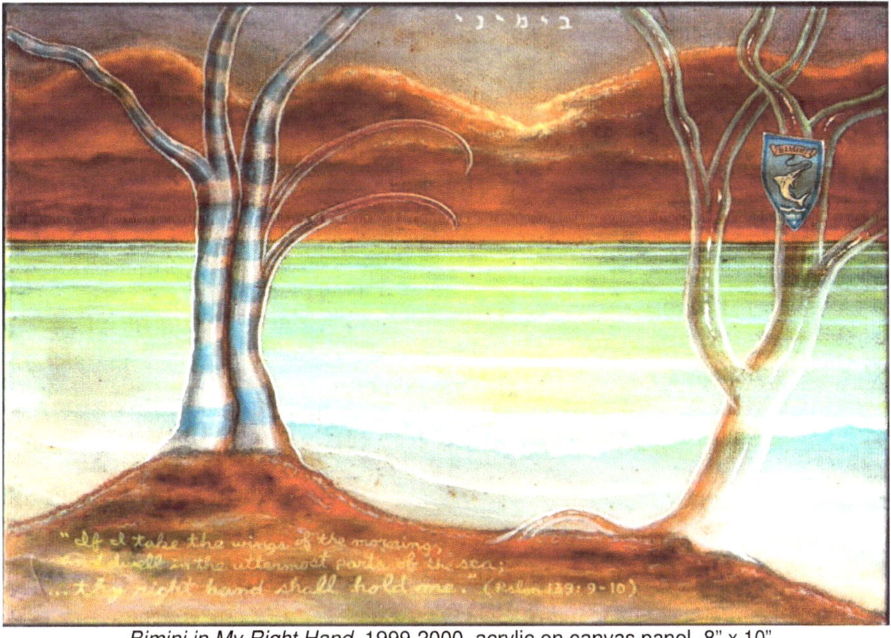

Bimini in My Right Hand, 1999-2000, acrylic on canvas panel, 8" x 10"

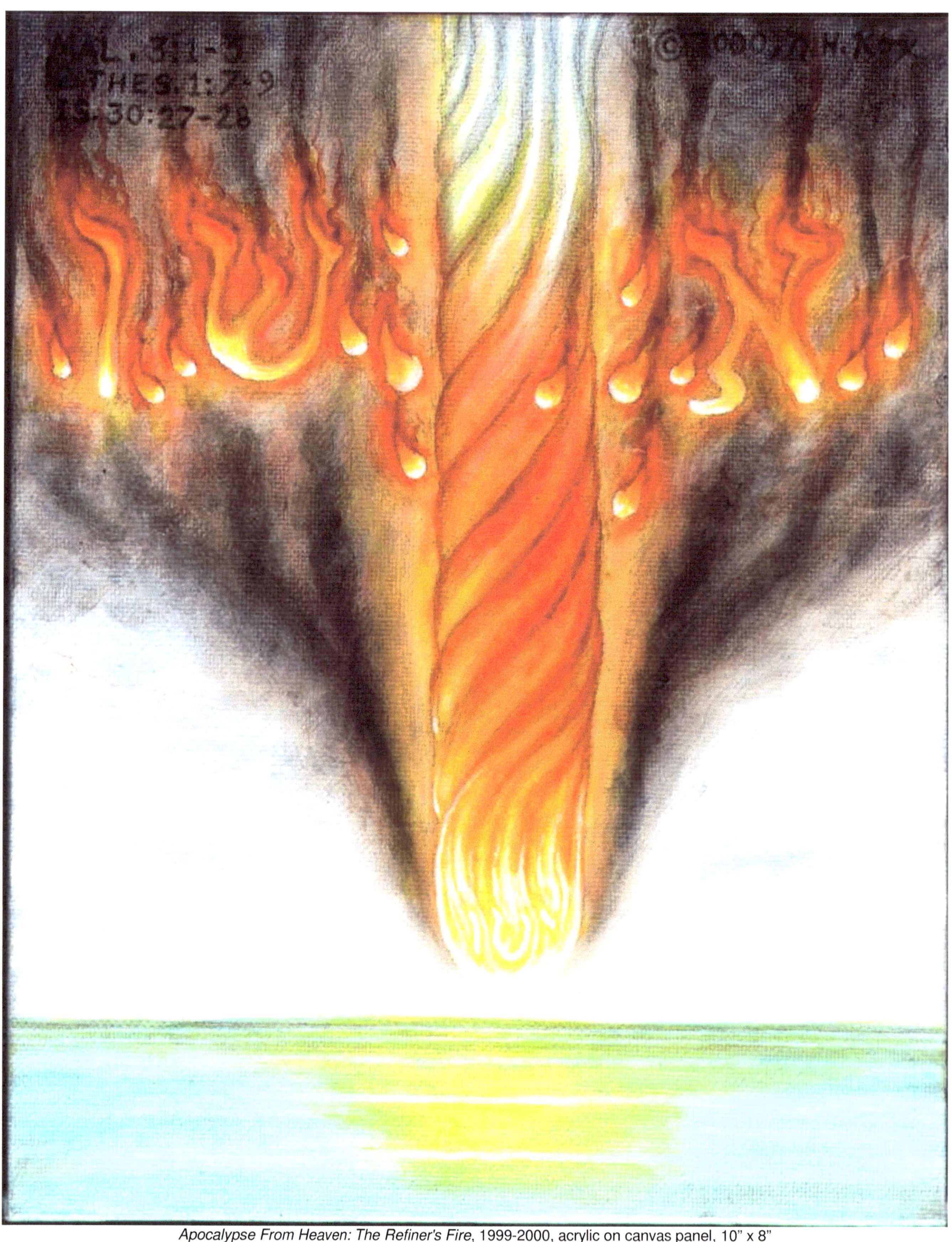

Apocalypse From Heaven: The Refiner's Fire, 1999-2000, acrylic on canvas panel, 10" x 8"

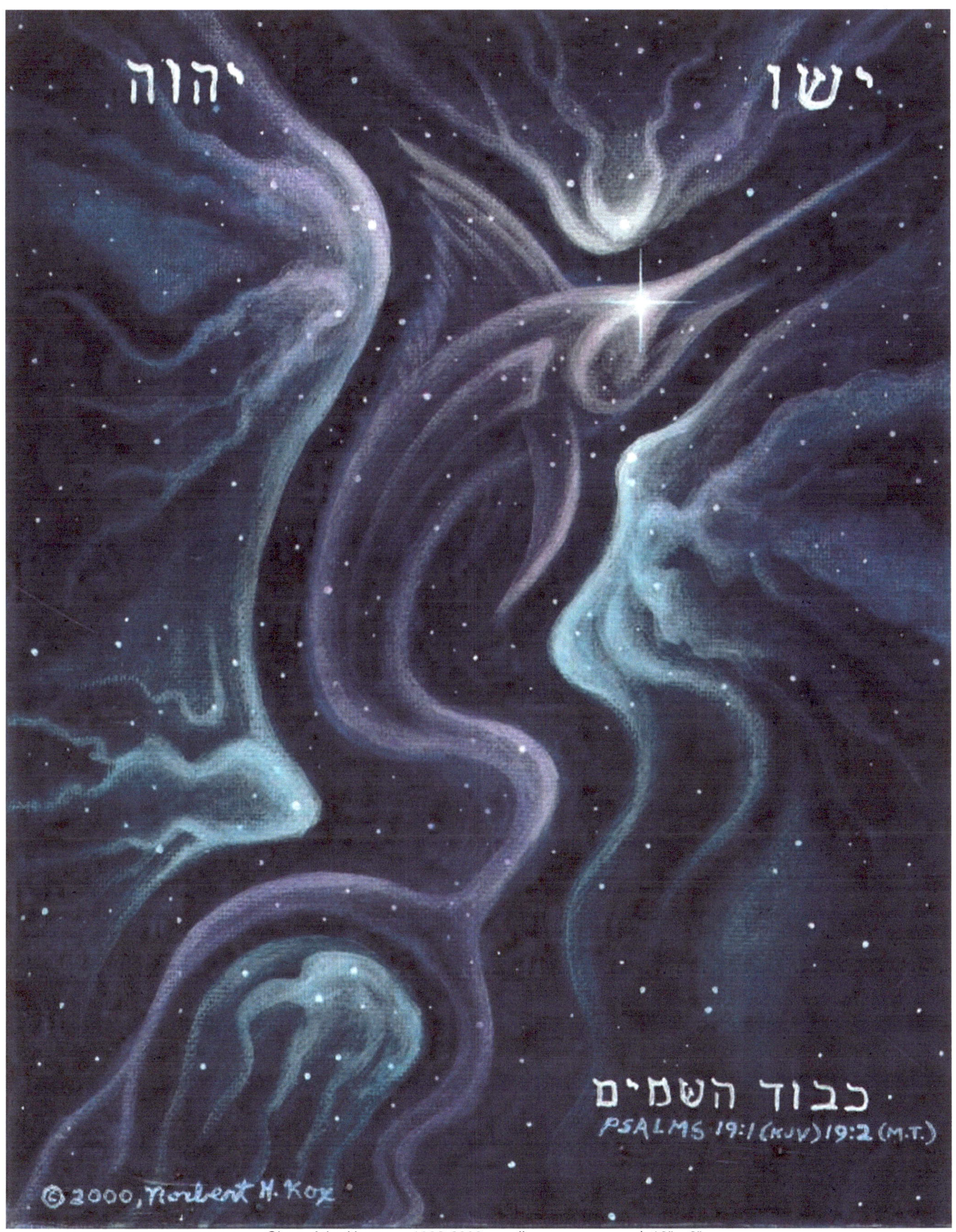

Glory of the Heavens, 1999-2000, acrylic on canvas panel, 10" x 8"

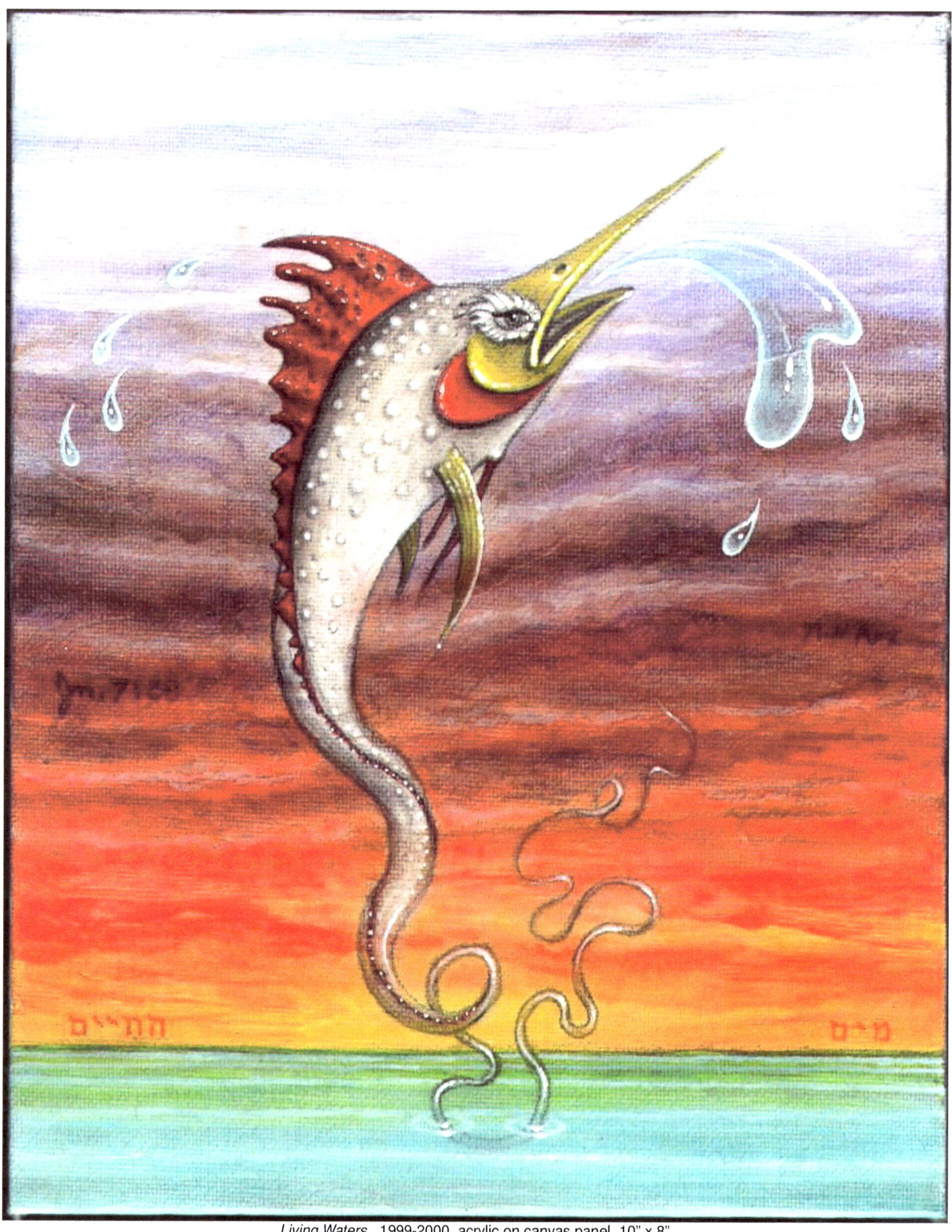

Living Waters, 1999-2000, acrylic on canvas panel, 10" x 8"

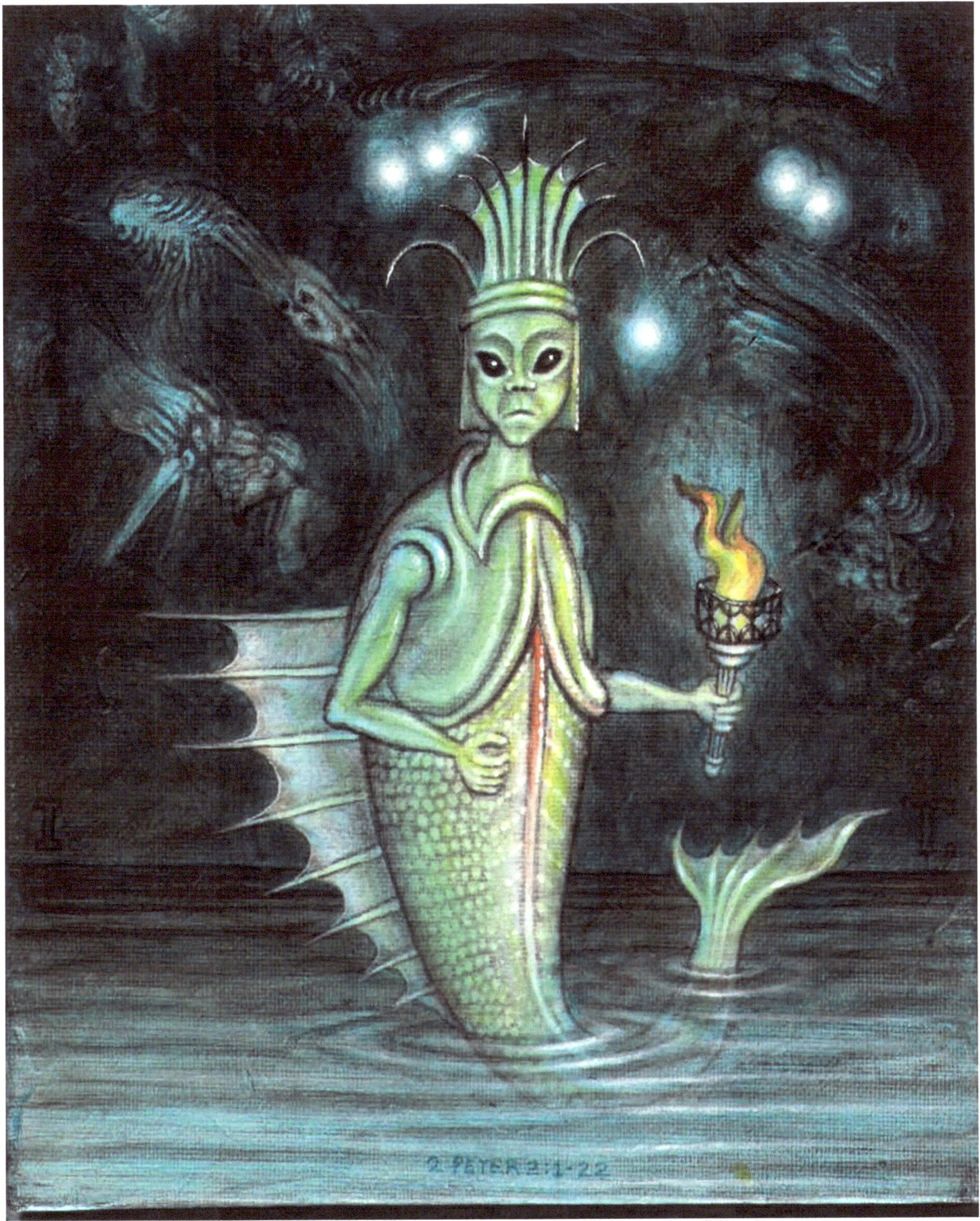

Dag-Aun I.T. They Promised Liberty, 1999-2000, acrylic on canvas panel, 10" x 8"

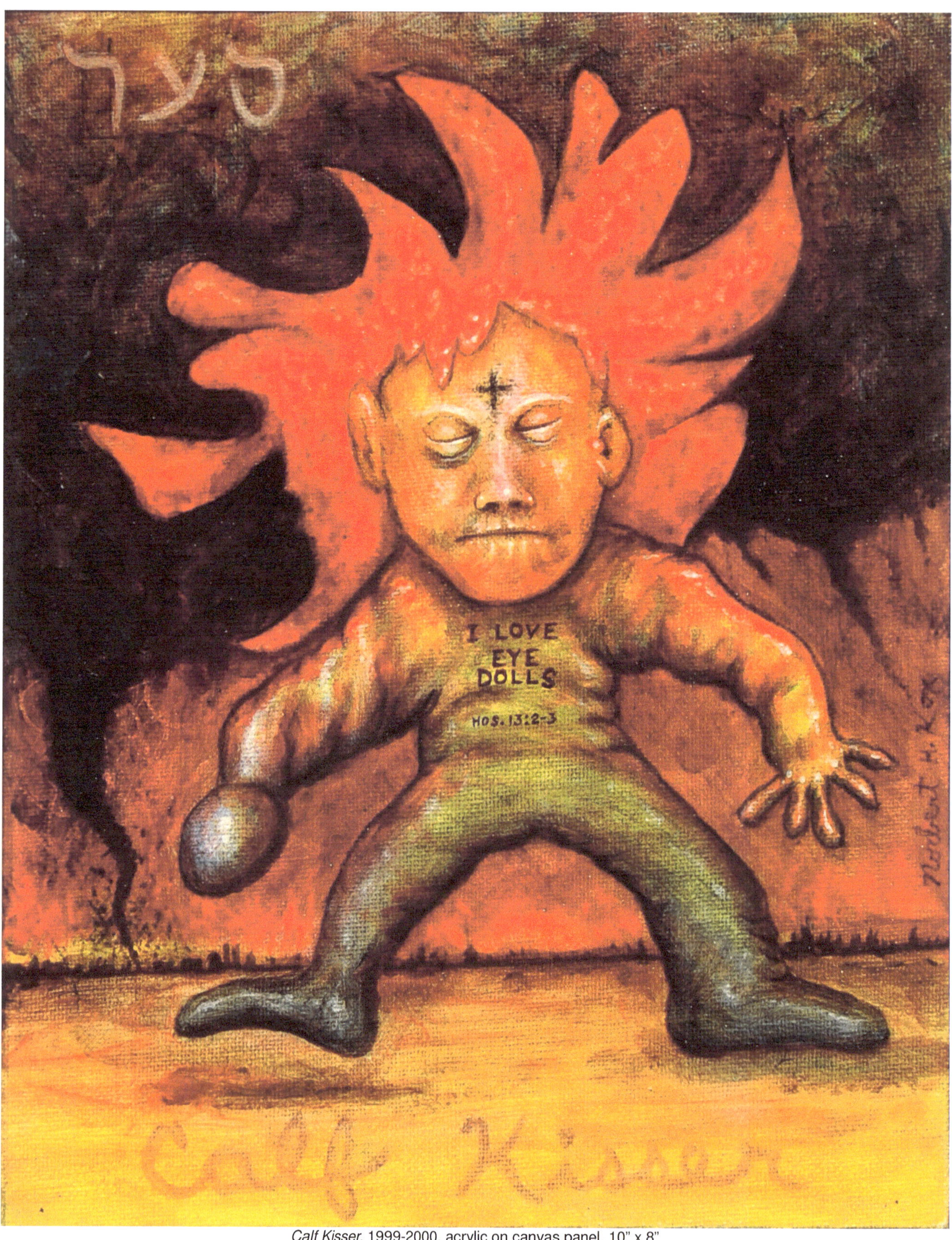

Calf Kisser, 1999-2000, acrylic on canvas panel, 10" x 8"

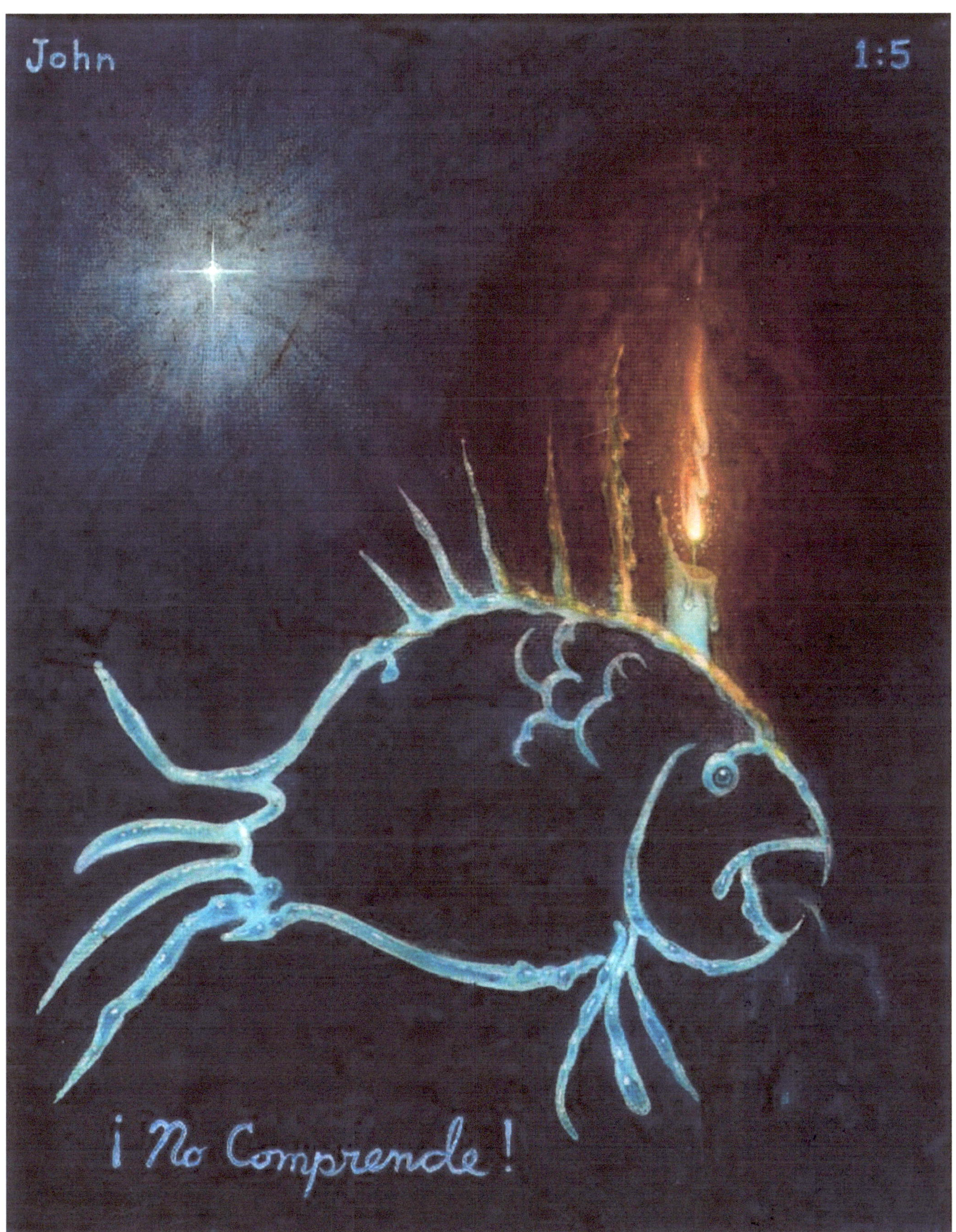

No Comprende, 1999-2000, acrylic on canvas panel, 10" x 8"

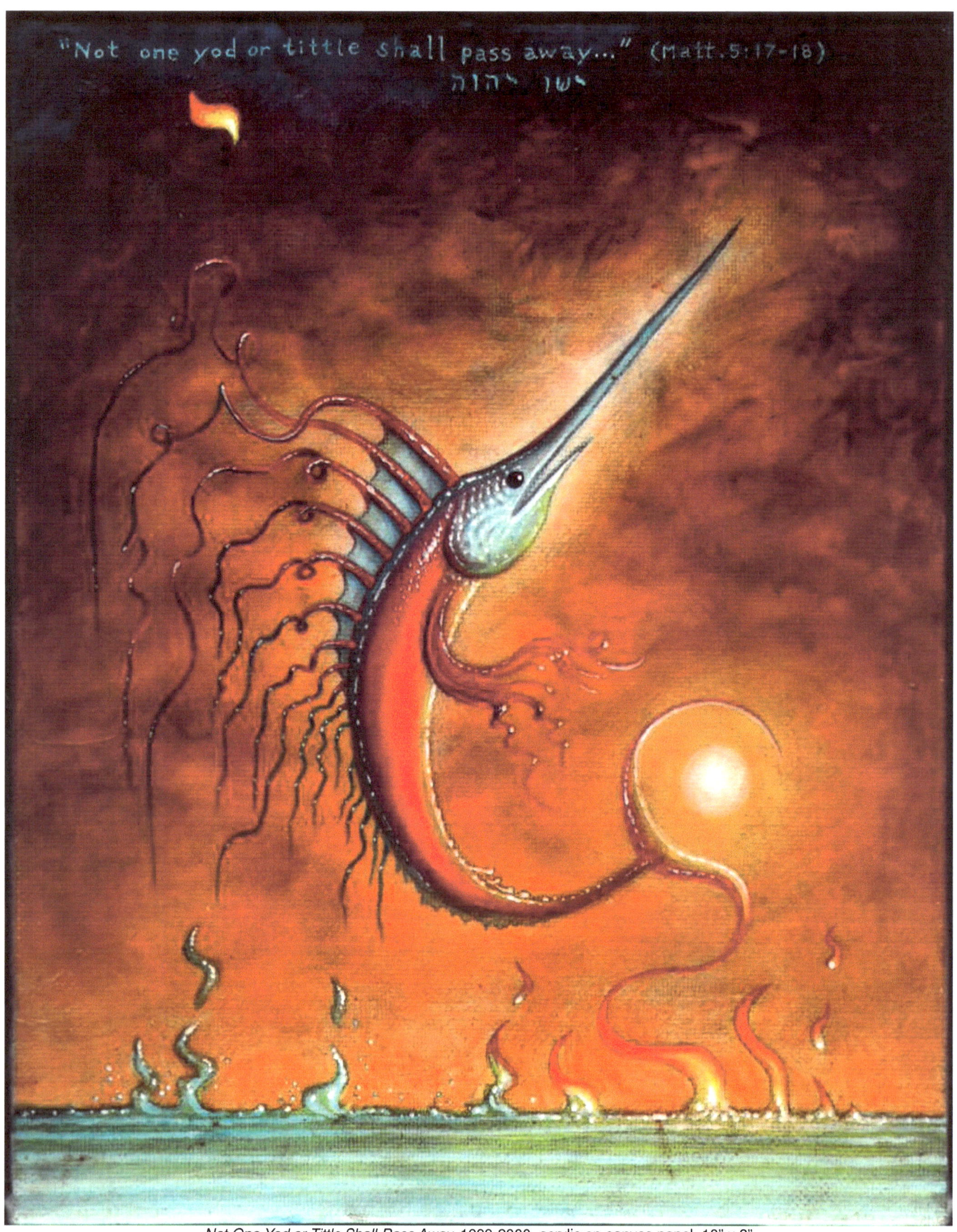

Not One Yod or Tittle Shall Pass Away, 1999-2000, acrylic on canvas panel, 10" x 8"

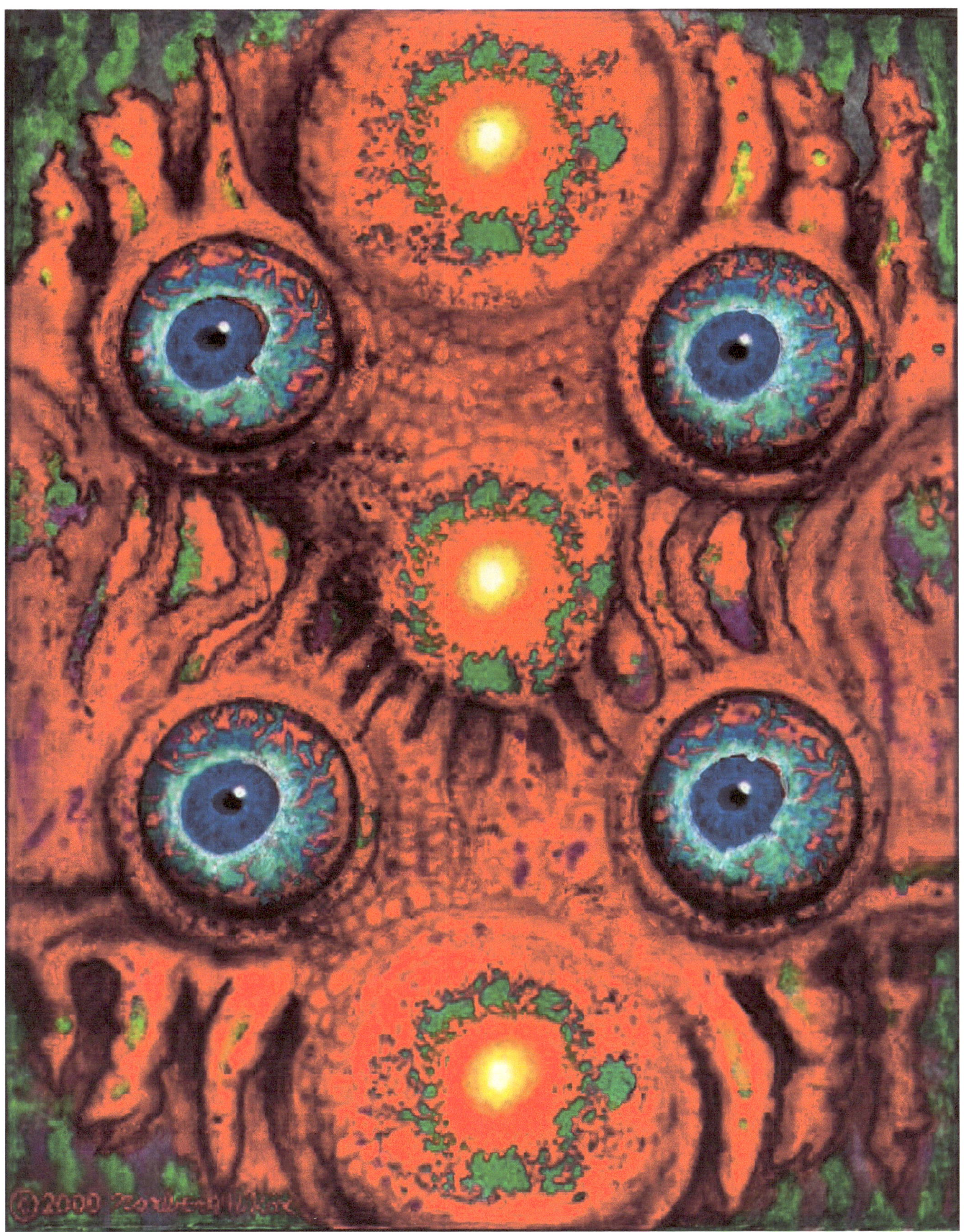

The Eighth Beast Awakens: He Was, and is Not, and Yet Is, 1999-2000, ink jet and acrylic on laminated panel, 10" x 8"

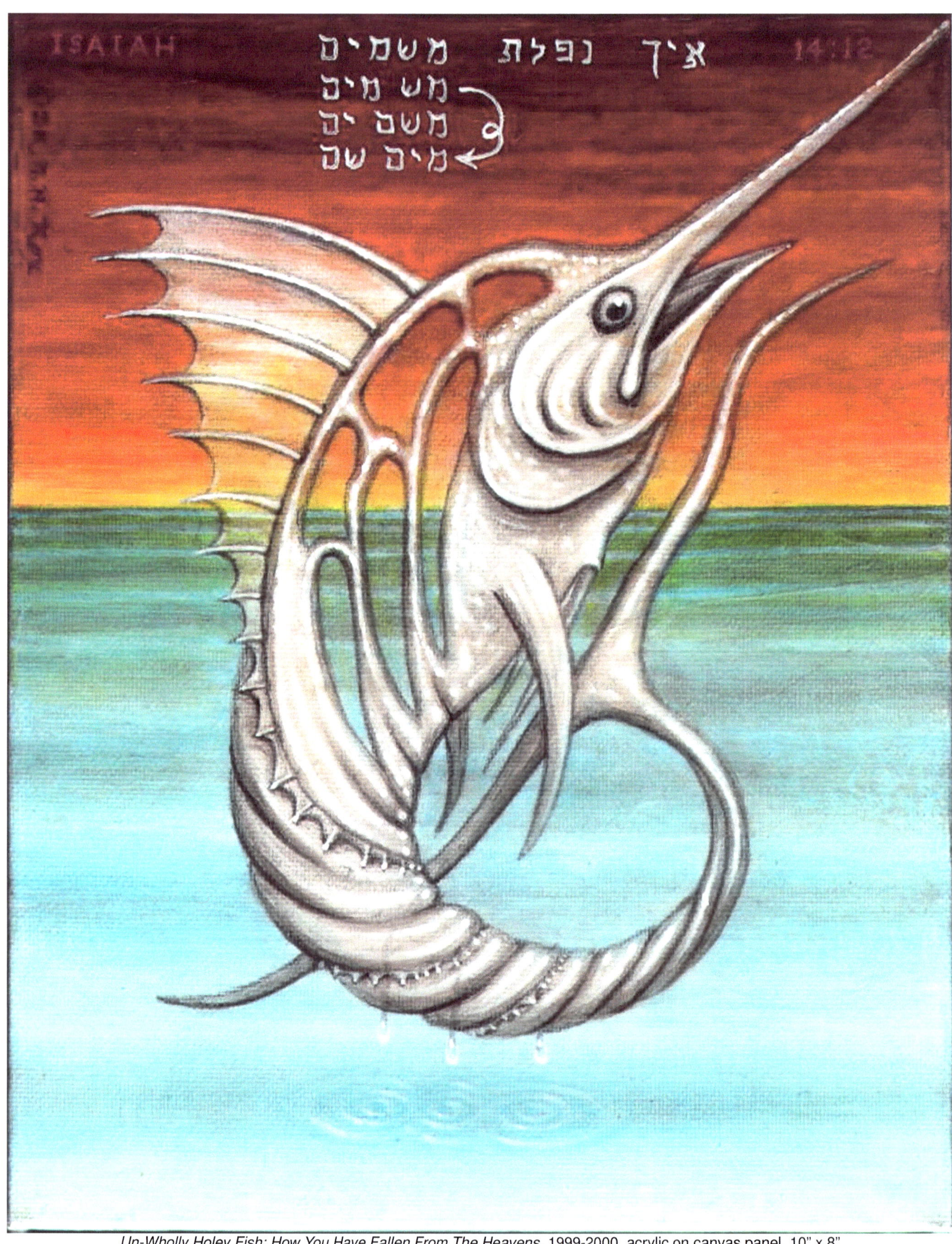

Un-Wholly Holey Fish: How You Have Fallen From The Heavens, 1999-2000, acrylic on canvas panel, 10” x 8”

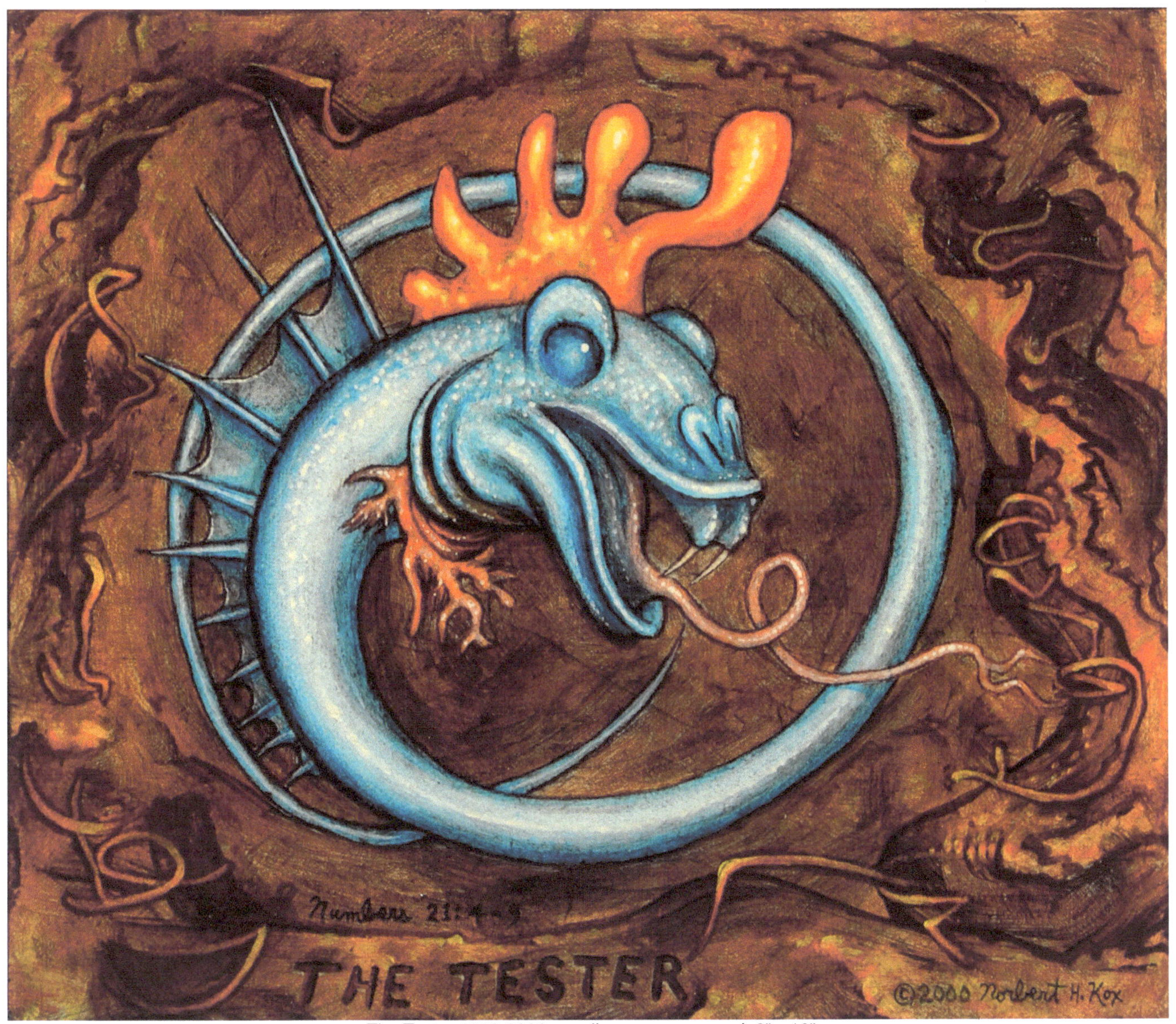

The Tester, 1999-2000, acrylic on canvas panel, 8" x 10"

DEEP WATERS: GLORY AND SHAME (2001)

2001, Bimini Art Exhibition
2001, Laluz de Jesus, Los Angeles
2003 TAG Art Gallery, Nashville

This exhibit [has] introduced Norbert's new image revealing process called "spontaneous symmetrical surrealism". It is a spontaneous process in which the pictures reveal themselves. They already exist and through a process of exploration Kox discovers a key to open the portal to these magnificent visual displays, which are present all around us every day. Our natural eyes do not allow us to see them but nonetheless they are right in front of us at all times. The intricate, sometimes very complex designs and patterns are reflections and enhancements of nature itself. God's inkblot, if you please. (Laluz de Jesus Gallery, and TAG Art Gallery).

Norbert Kox premiered a new series of paintings entitled DEEP WATERS: GLORY AND SHAME. This series is perhaps the first work ever produced by a visionary painter with images originating from a toy digital camera. The 34 paintings were created by Kox on the island of Bimini [and exhibited there] earlier in the year, and premiered [in the United States] on April 6, 2001 at La Luz de Jesus Gallery in Los Angeles. [Following] is a peek at these new images and statements from Kox describing the basis and technique of "Spontaneous Symmetrical Surrealism" (Dilettante Press, Los Angeles, CA).

Artist's Statement: Spontaneous Symmetrical Surrealism
"With this process images beyond the artist's control appear in the work. They are not placed there by the artist, but discovered. The images are revealed through completely natural means. There is no automatic writing, no trance state, nor spirit medium. In a sense, it is just like turning over a stone to see what is on the other side. Whatever you find, good or evil, it was there before you turned the stone. If you see something disturbing you wonder if you should turn over any more stones. Turning over these images is actually a little bit scary. Like, where are these pictures coming from. How do these things exist on so many different levels? And should we keep moving into these new areas? Are we actually eating the forbidden fruit? Perhaps we begin to eat of it the moment we are born, and we can not stop." Norbert Kox

Concept
The concept of "Deep Waters: Glory and Shame" is derived from the tree of knowledge of good and evil (and tree of life) being the book of knowledge of good and evil (and the book of life) i.e. the Bible. Open the Word and see good and evil, light and dark. Scripturally, deep water is an analogy to the WORD. Open the Word and see life and death, good and evil, glory and shame.

Medium
The images were originally captured [with a toy digital camera, and printed on Kodak photo paper] as digital Ink jet images sealed with acrylic polymer emulsion [and laminated onto Masonite panels]; Details and color reinforced with acrylic paint.

Process
Many of the images in this exhibit have been "created" through a new image revealing process which I call "spontaneous symmetrical surrealism". It is a visual response to the tree of knowledge of good and evil, having the elements of both light and darkness. It is a process which I discovered as the result of my investigation and constant search of the Bible Codes (Torah Codes). One of the keys to the Bible Code is symmetry. Symmetry is a key to unlocking the mysteries of God. The most powerful and impressive code matrices in the Bible often have several symmetrical features. The awareness of symmetry is important in searching for and on unlocking the inner codes, which are the second witness, the Bible within the Bible.

My research of the symmetrical aspects and tendencies of the spoken (English) language (1980-1983) which I termed "hypostrephonic echo" has carried over into my research of the symmetrical aspects and tendencies of the written languages as related to the Hebrew Language and the Bible code (1997-2001). This has led to my recent discovery of spontaneous symmetrical surrealism (February 2001). These new symmetrical pictures that I have stumbled upon are created through a very spontaneous process in which they almost create themselves, or should I say reveal themselves. They seem to already exist, and through a process of exploration I am discovering a key to open the portal to these magnificent visual displays which are present all around us every day of our lives. Our natural eyes just do not allow us to see them but nonetheless they are right in front of us at all times. The intricate sometimes very complex designs and patterns are reflections and enhancements of nature itself. God's inkblot, if you please.

In certain cases I have combined two photographs to make one picture. In other works I have added elements from some of my previous paintings. In some pieces only a portion of the painting has been interpreted symmetrically. But, in the many cases of the extremely symmetrical patterns nothing is added (save possible text). I do not create or invent these images as with typical image making.

I feel led to photograph certain things which others would probably overlook. In these photographs I see things which lead me to open them up, so to speak. The investigation of these elements initiates a process of revelation which grows like a flower. This process can reveal literally hundreds of different images from a single snapshot. Each image is a unique picture which is simply a magnification of God's wonderful creation.

This process involves seeing symmetrically, as if everything has a mirrored reflection, like an inkblot. The image changes as the mirror is moved about within it. The resulting image is then passed through the color spectrum at various levels of contrast and brightness. Thus each image that is discovered is a revelation of pre-existing elements, and not a creation or invention of an imaginative mind. What it does take is an intuitive mind to unlock the images. The artist becomes a pioneer penetrating a new frontier. He is the scout; to go forth exploring the outer realms and to bring back the report of what he sees.

Spontaneous symmetrical surrealism appears to hinge the duality of good and evil, glory and shame. It is a folding and mirroring of the universe into an infinite series of magnificent unearthly inkblots waiting to be deciphered.

I am not always sure how to literally interpret these images. Usually my artwork has a very specific message, often in the form of a warning, which is clear to me and intentionally placed there as a didactic reference. This new symmetrical series seems to be much more obscure. It is hard to tell whether the works are representing good or evil. Evidently because both aspects are present, as they are in everyday life. God is light. Yesu Christ is the light of the world. But, also remember, Satan appears (disguises/masquerades) as an angel of light.

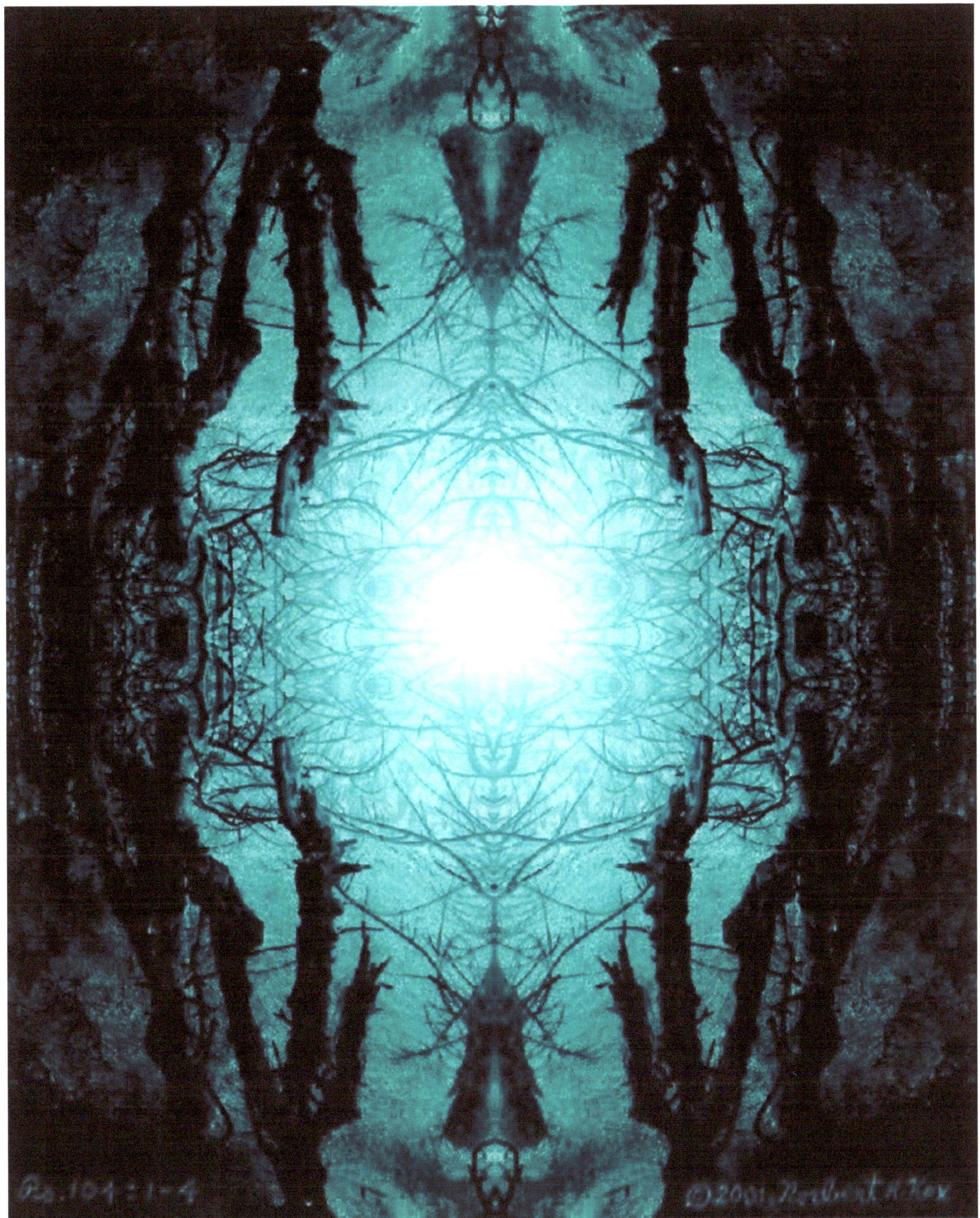

His Beams In The Waters Of His Upper Chambers, 2000-2001, ink jet and acrylic on laminated panel, 10" x 8" study

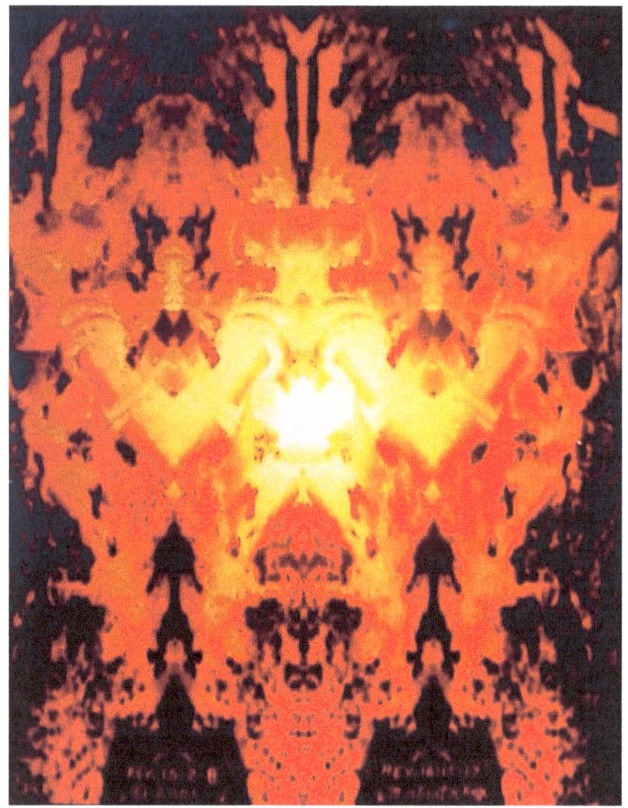

Glory and Shame I, 2000-2001, 10" x 8"

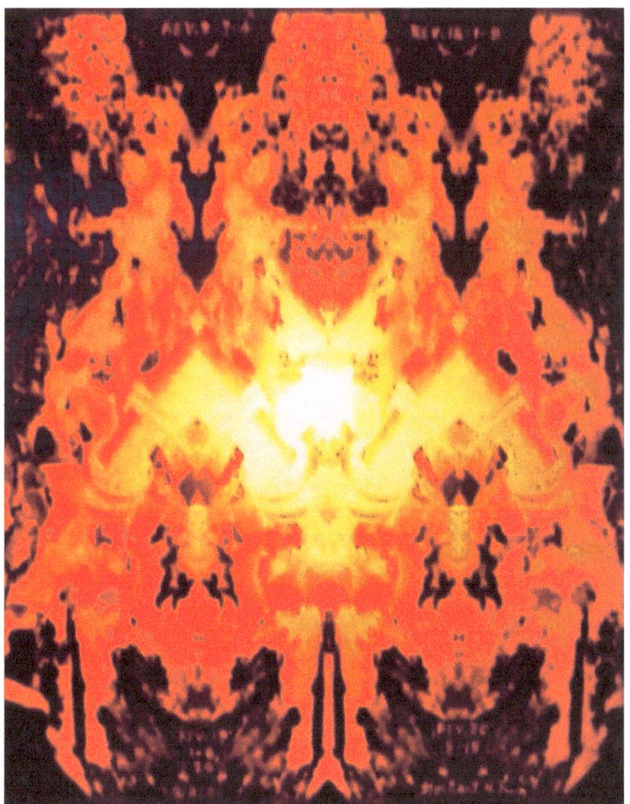

Glory and Shame II, 2000-2001, 10" x 8"

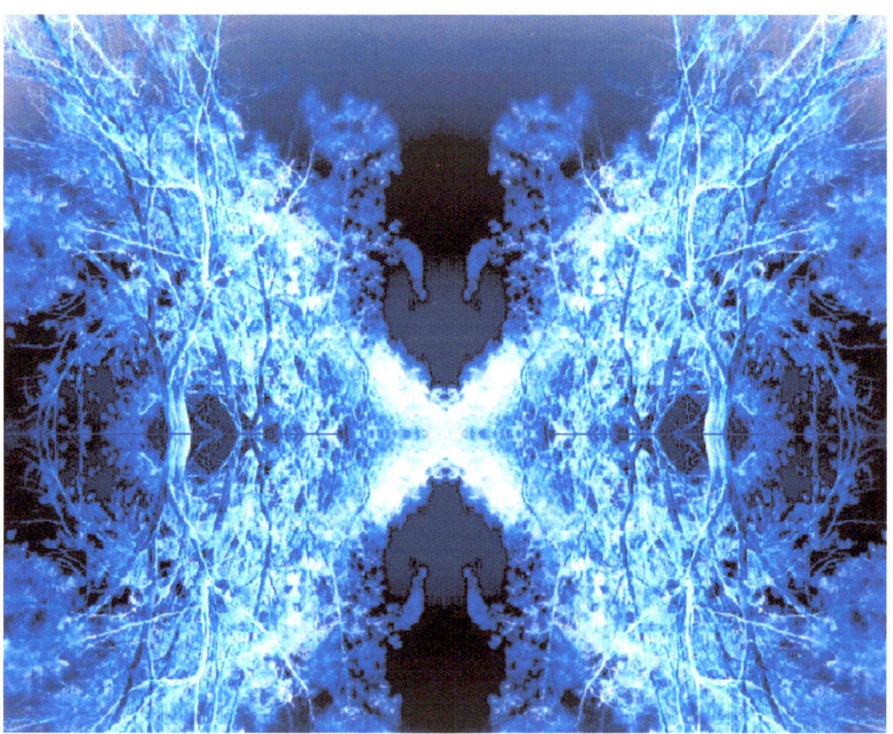

X: Path On The Water (By Him Were All Things Made), 2000-2001, 8" x 10"

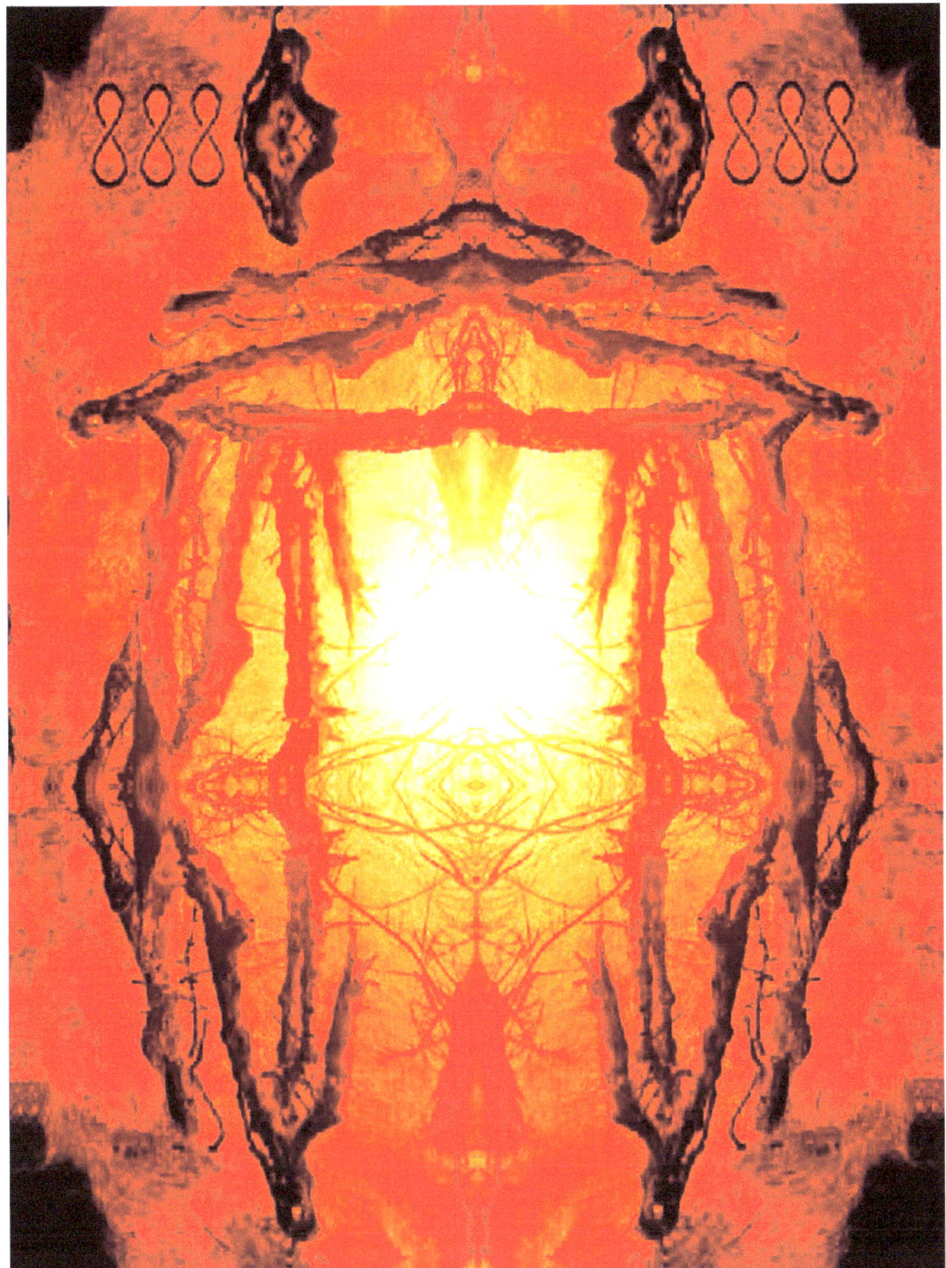

Burning Of The Branches, 2000-2001, ink jet and acrylic on laminated panel, 10" x 8"

Burning Of The Branches was also exhibited in 2002, at the Raw Vision show in London, and again at The Horse Hospital in Unquiet Voices, 2004.

Unquiet Voices was an exhibition to celebrate 10 years of The Chamber Of Pop Culture at the Horse Hospital, London. It featured a century of English and American Visionary art covering art brut, outsider and visionary art....

Norbert H. Kox is one of the few visionary artists who proffers a viewpoint clearly at odds with the mainstream.... His life in various notorious biker gangs is well documented in *Apocalypse Culture II*. At the age of 30, after a life of drugs and violence on the road, Kox had reached a dead-end and spent the decade from 1975 onwards as a recluse contemplating the bible. Kox's interpretation of the bible was outlined in his Apocalyptic Visual Parables; prophetic revelations consisting of painting, poetry and bible codes.... Kox's paintings are by far the most controversial on display here. The Catholic Church has described Kox's work as blasphemous. Kox is a devout follower of Christ and regards himself as a prophet. The word of God, as Kox provides, isn't necessarily palatable to organized religion but Kox is aware of this and knowingly accepts it. His research has found inconsistencies and falsehoods [*mistranslations*] in the bible which Kox feels he must reveal.... Freemasonry, the Illuminati and Satanism are recurring motifs in the work of Kox.

(*Unquiet Voices: Horse Hospital, London*, http://www.compulsiononline.com/unquiet.htm)

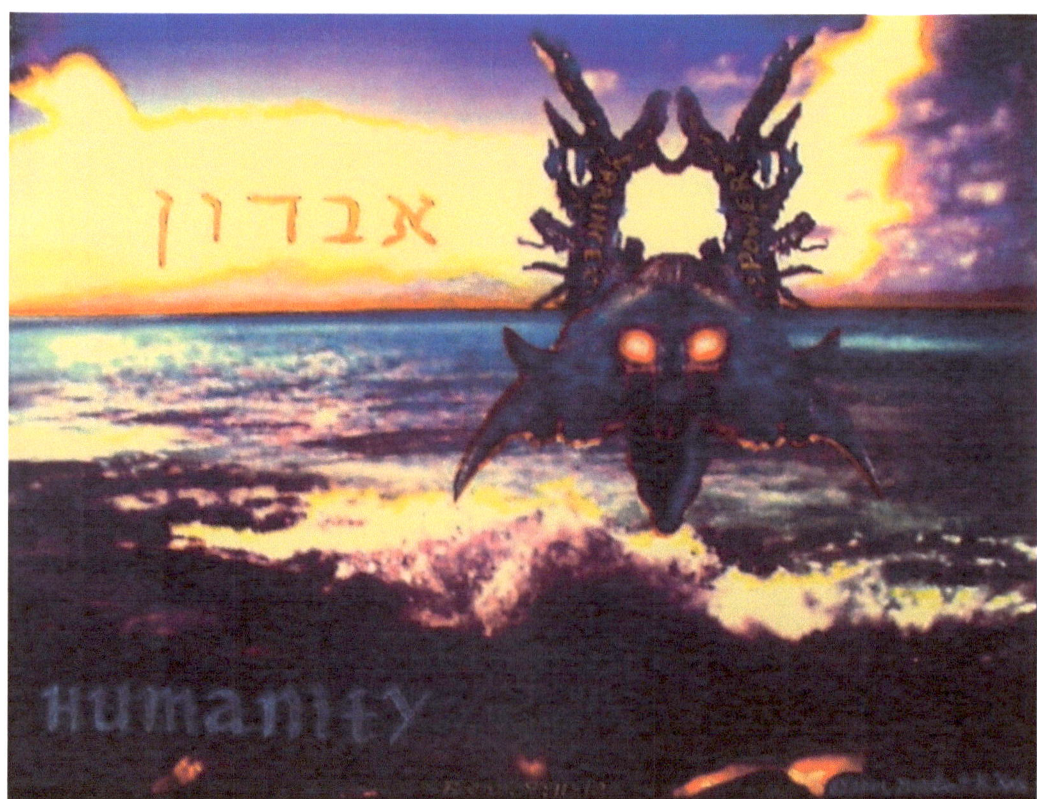

Abbadon I: Royal Destroyer on the Sea of Humanity, 2000-2001, ink jet and acrylic on laminated panel, 8" x 10"

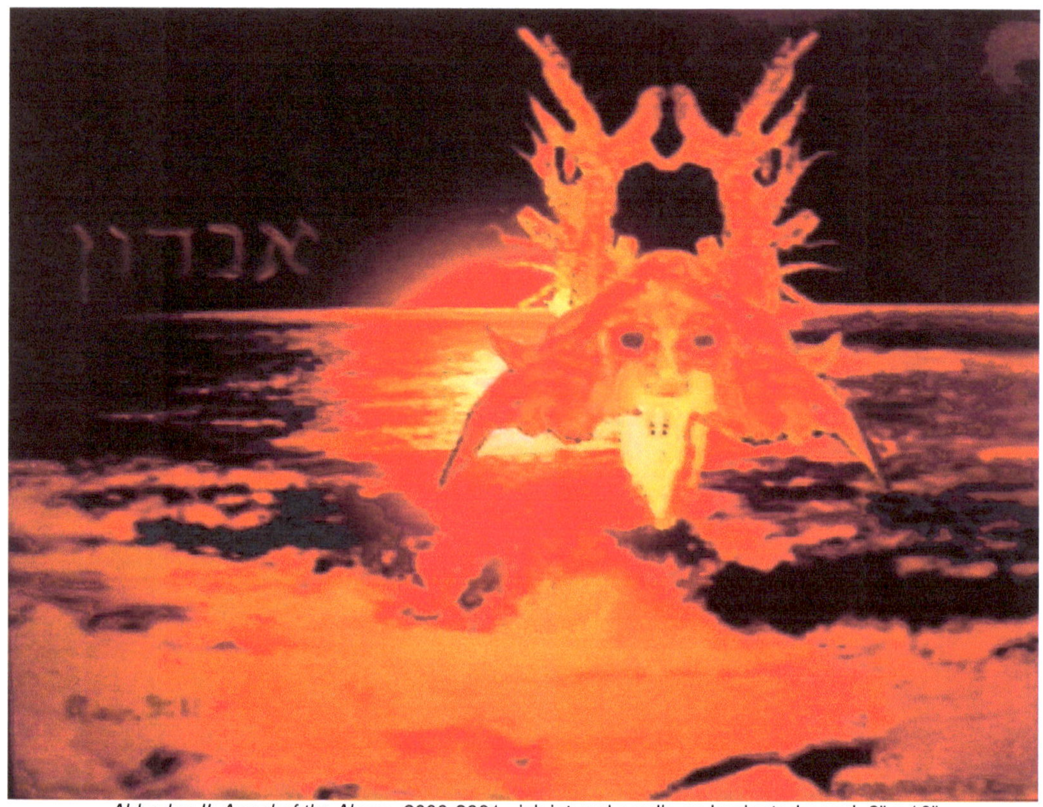

Abbadon II: Angel of the Abyss, 2000-2001, ink jet and acrylic on laminated panel, 8" x 10"

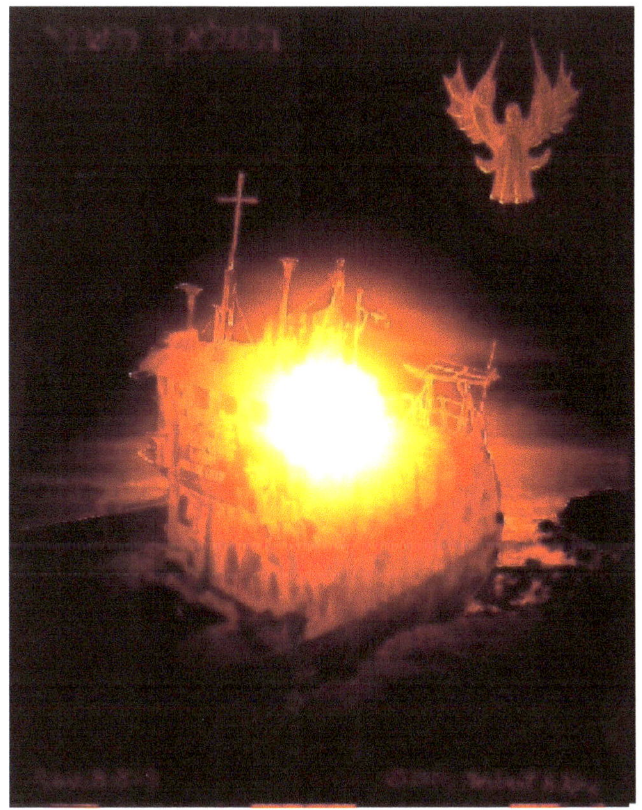

The Second Angel, 2000-2001, 10" x 8"

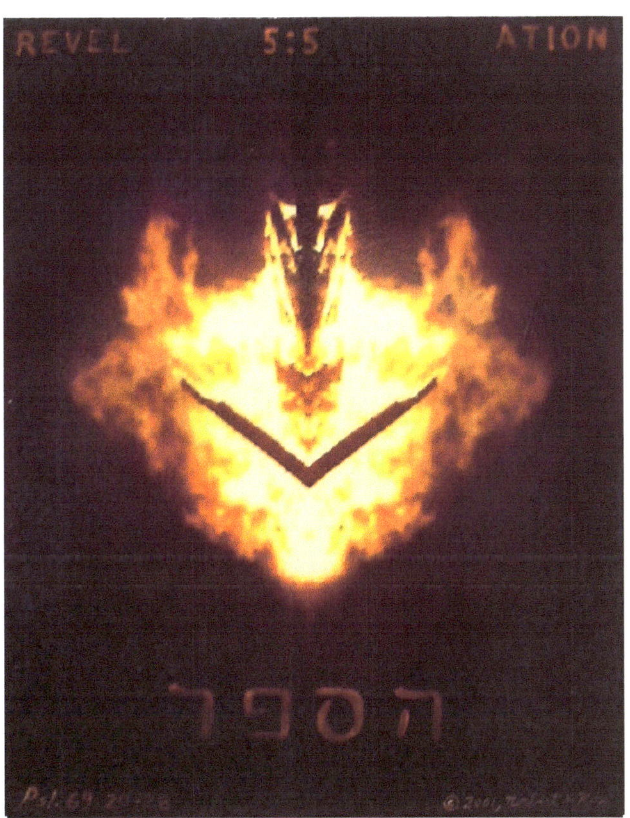

Cipher Of The Plagues, 2000-2001, 10" x 8"

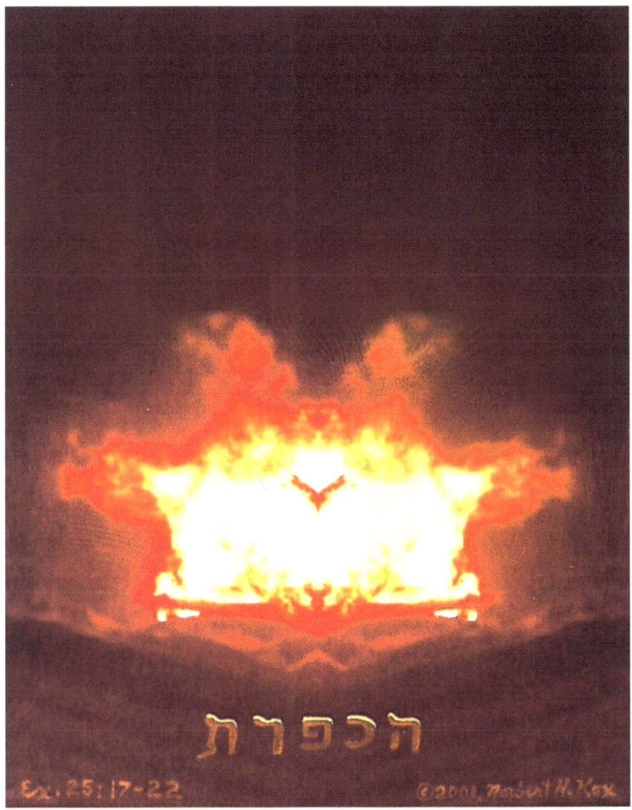

The Mercy Seat: The End Of Time, 2000-2001, 10" x 8"

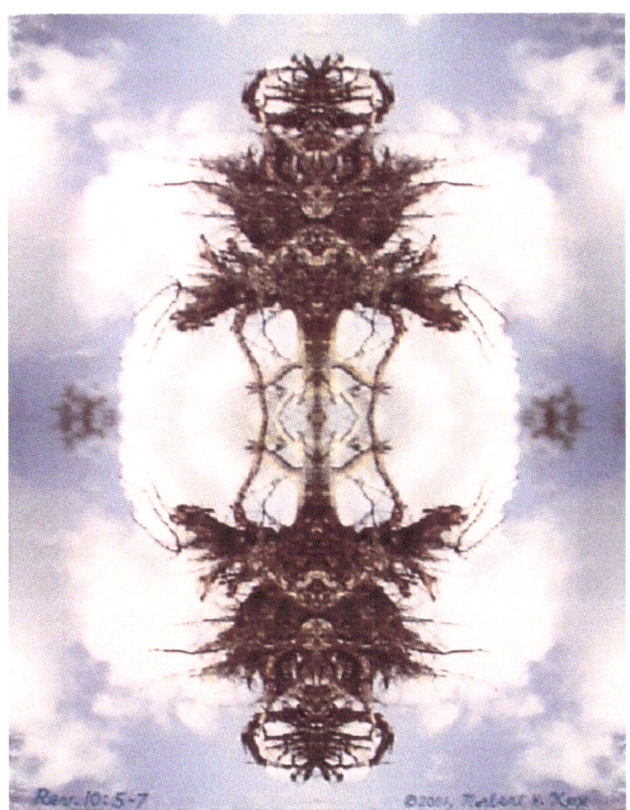

Omega Hourglass: The End Of Time, 2000-2001, 10" x 8"

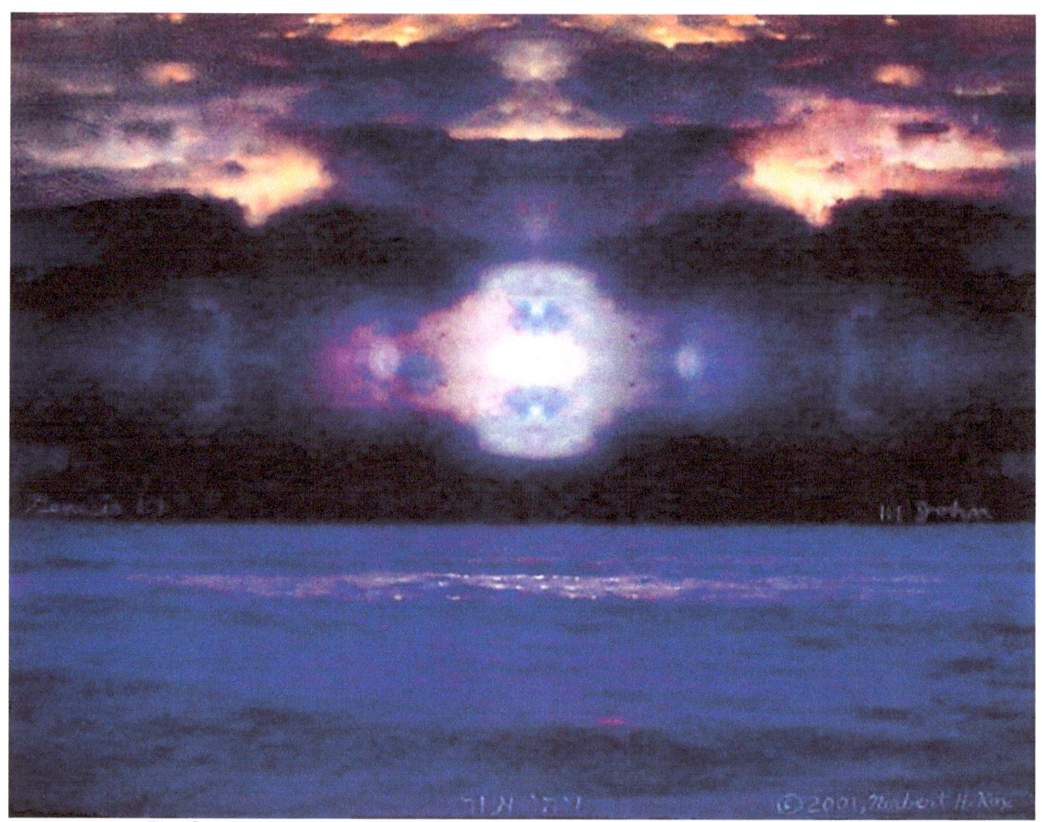

The Source (John 1-1), 2000-2001, ink jet and acrylic on laminated panel, 8" x 10"

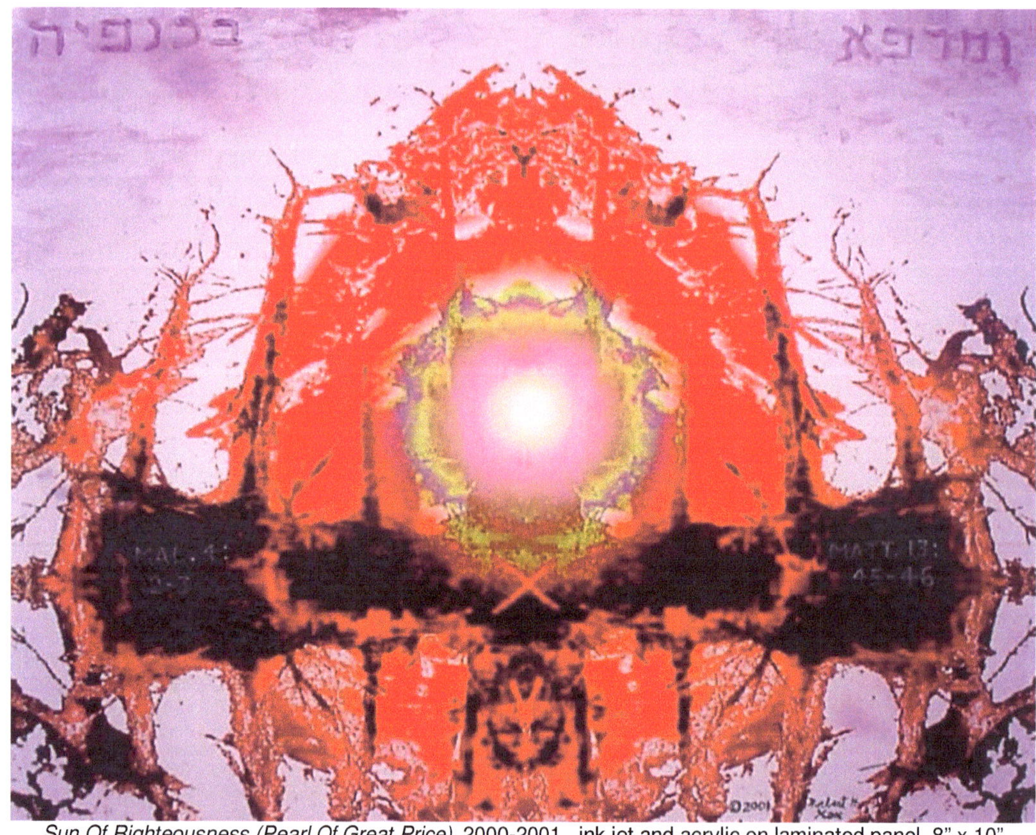

Sun Of Righteousness (Pearl Of Great Price), 2000-2001, ink jet and acrylic on laminated panel, 8" x 10"

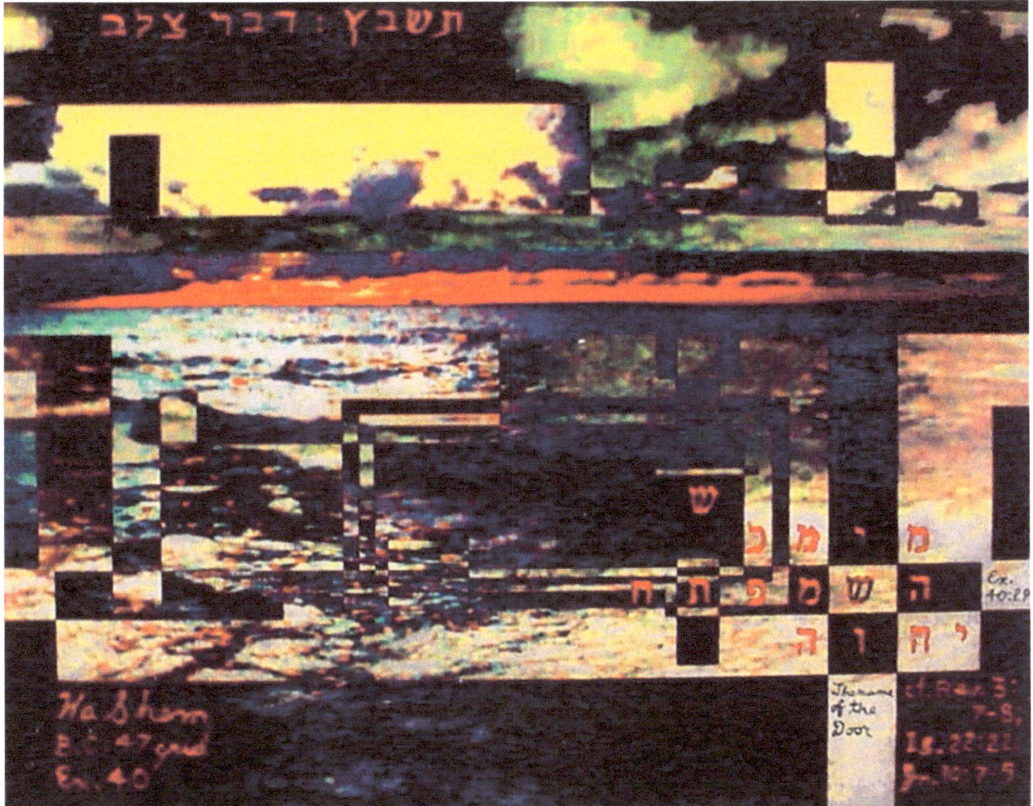

In The Beginning Was The Cross Word, 2000-2001, ink jet and acrylic on laminated panel, 8" x 10"

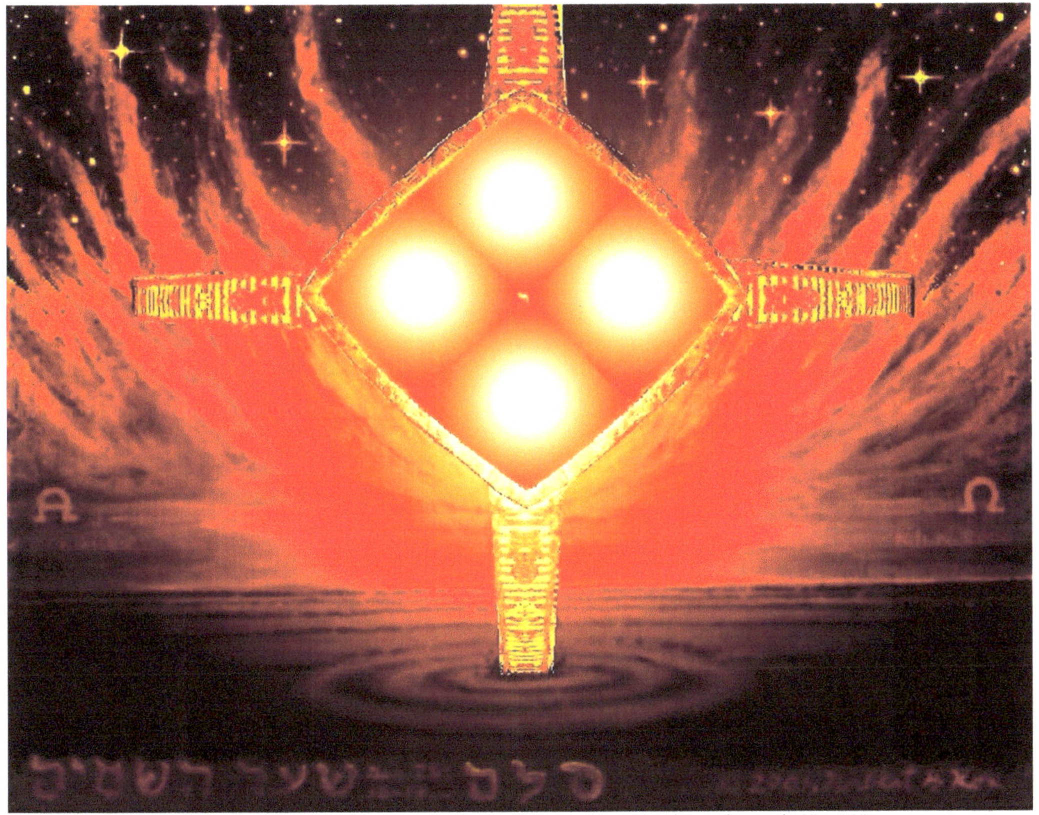

Jacob's Ladder, 2000-2001, ink jet and acrylic on laminated panel, 8" x 10"

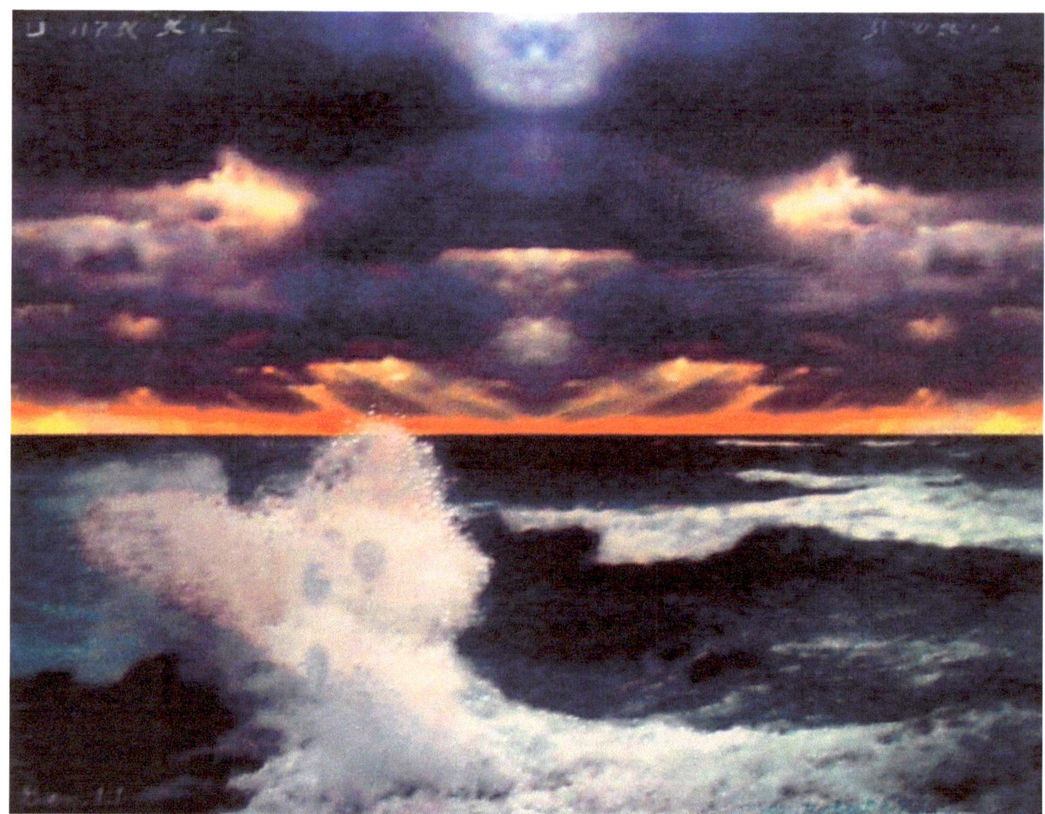

Primordial Waters, 2000-2001, ink jet and acrylic on laminated panel, 8" x 10"

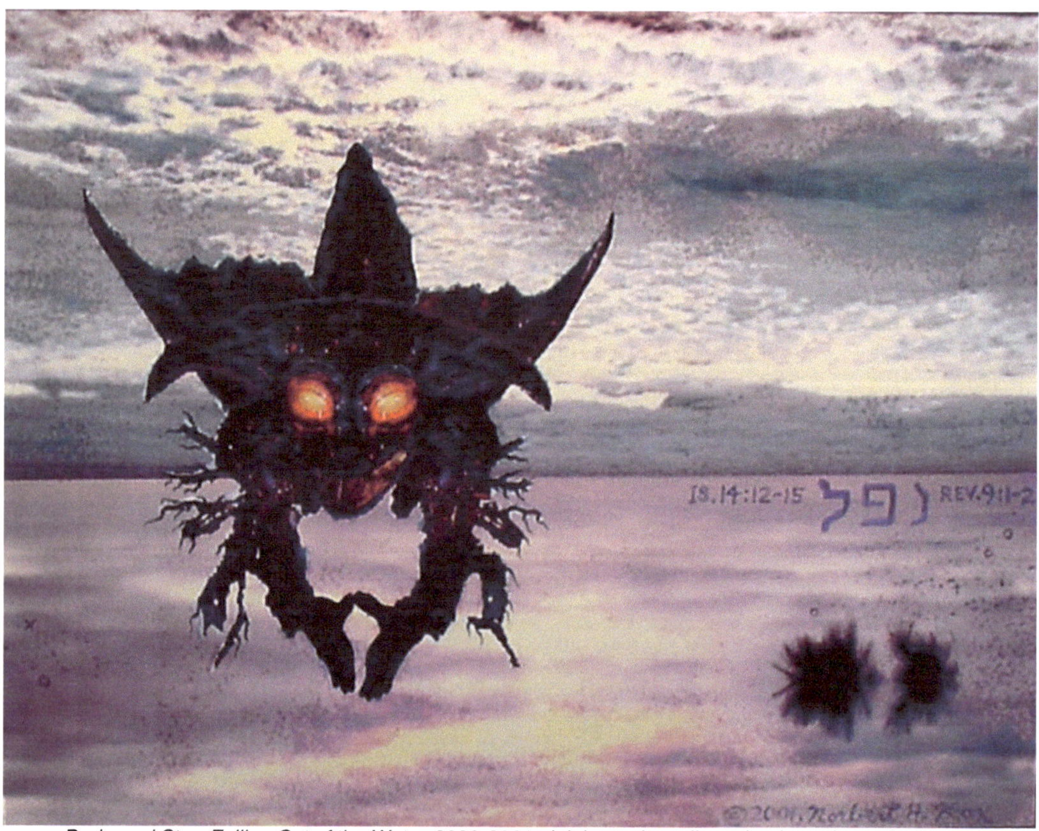

Darkened Star: Falling Out of the Water, 2000-2001, ink jet and acrylic on laminated panel, 8" x 10"

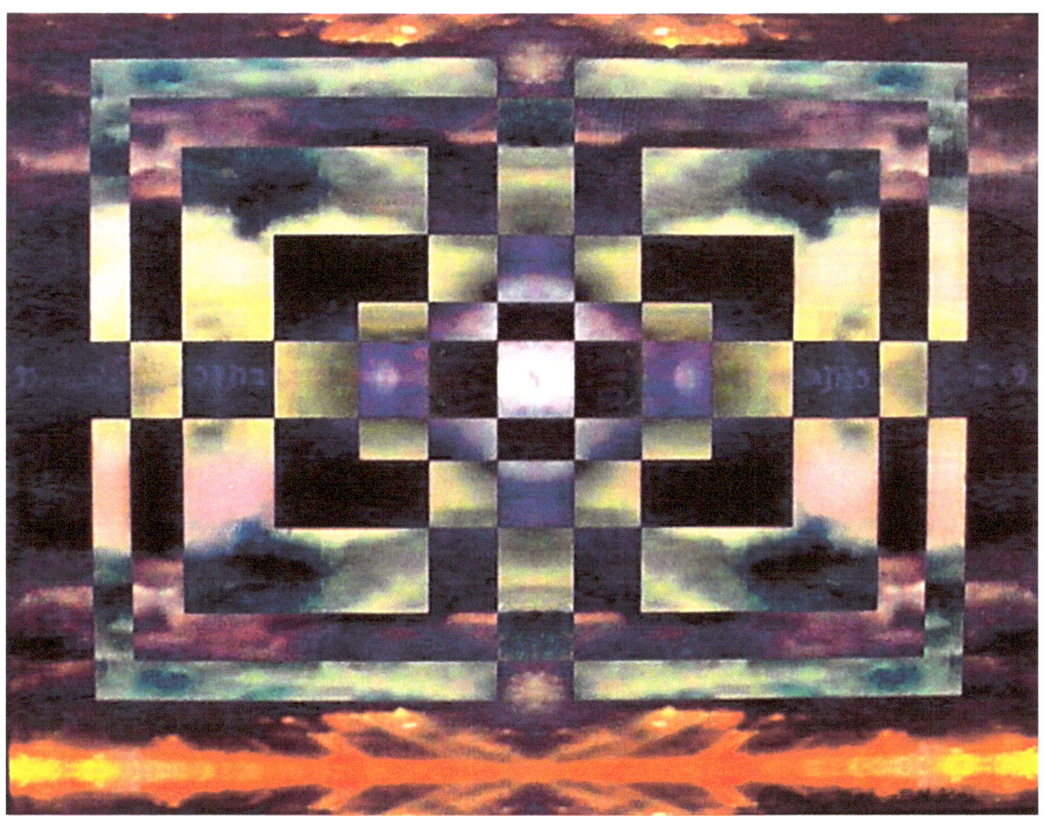

Mediator, 2000-2001, ink jet and acrylic on laminated panel, 8" x 10"

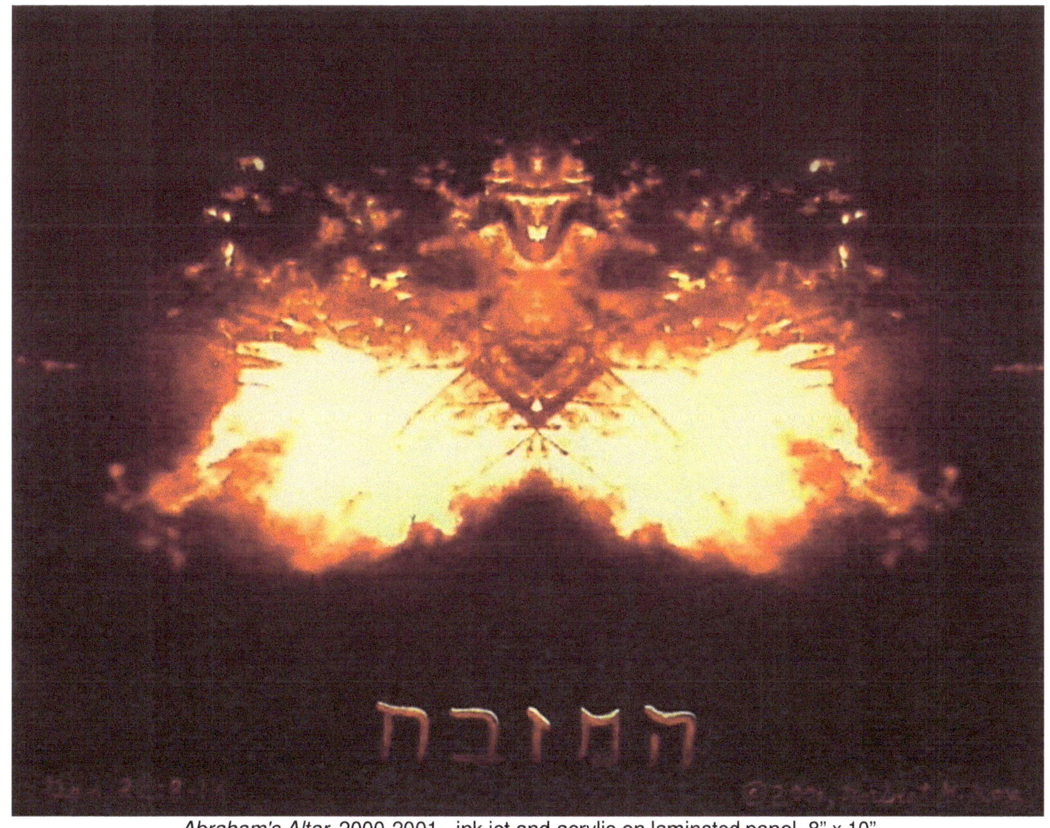

Abraham's Altar, 2000-2001, ink jet and acrylic on laminated panel, 8" x 10"

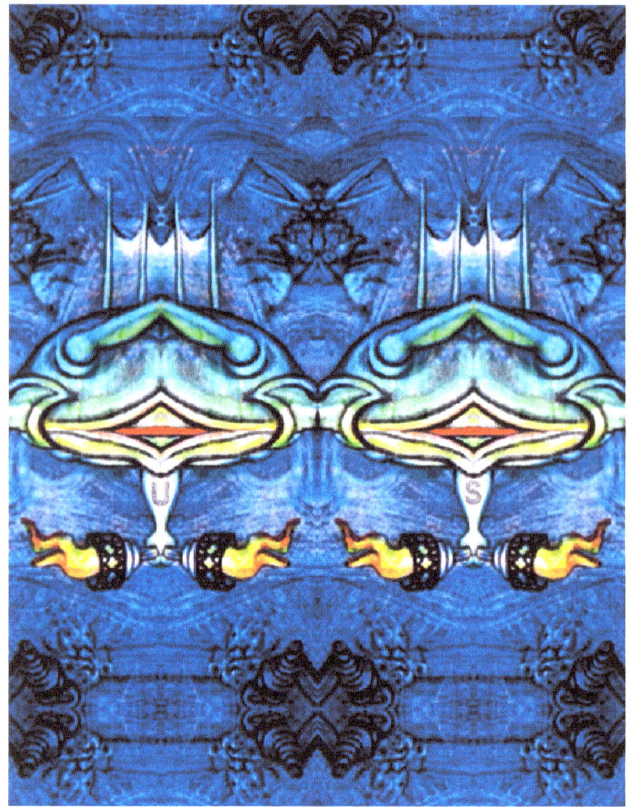

Frog Spears: Blind Leading, 2000-2001, 10" x 8"

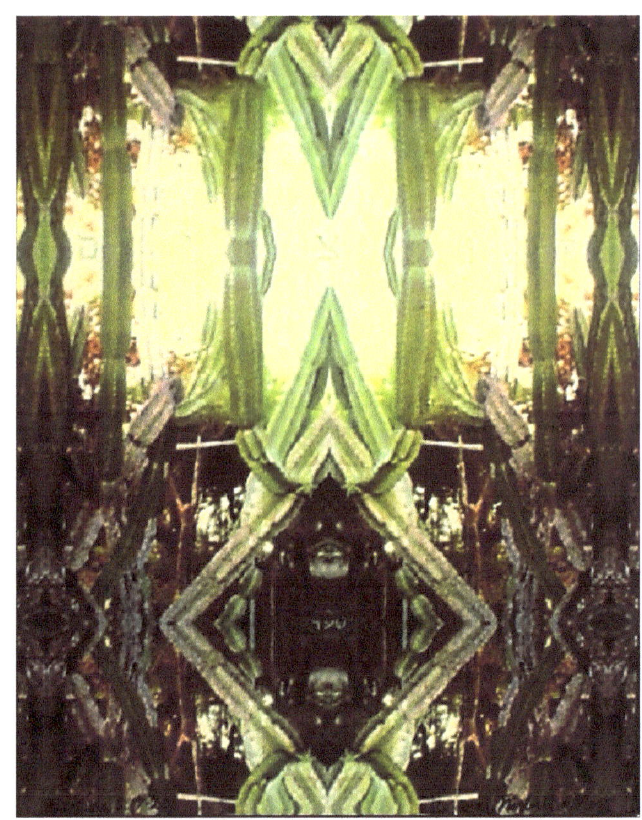

Gate of Thorns: Portal of the righteous, 2000-2001, 10" x 8"

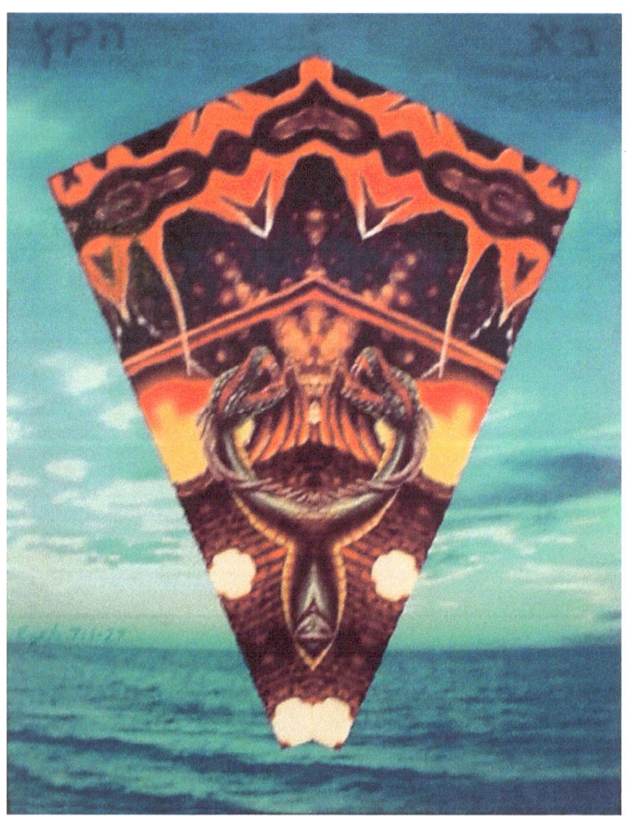

The End Is Come, 2000-2001, 10" x 8"

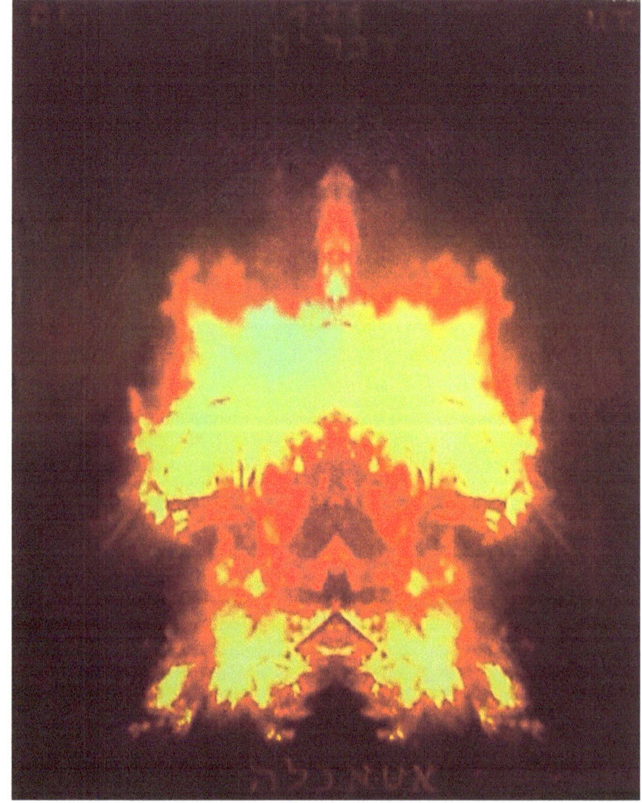

Consuming Fire, 2000-2001, 10" x 8"

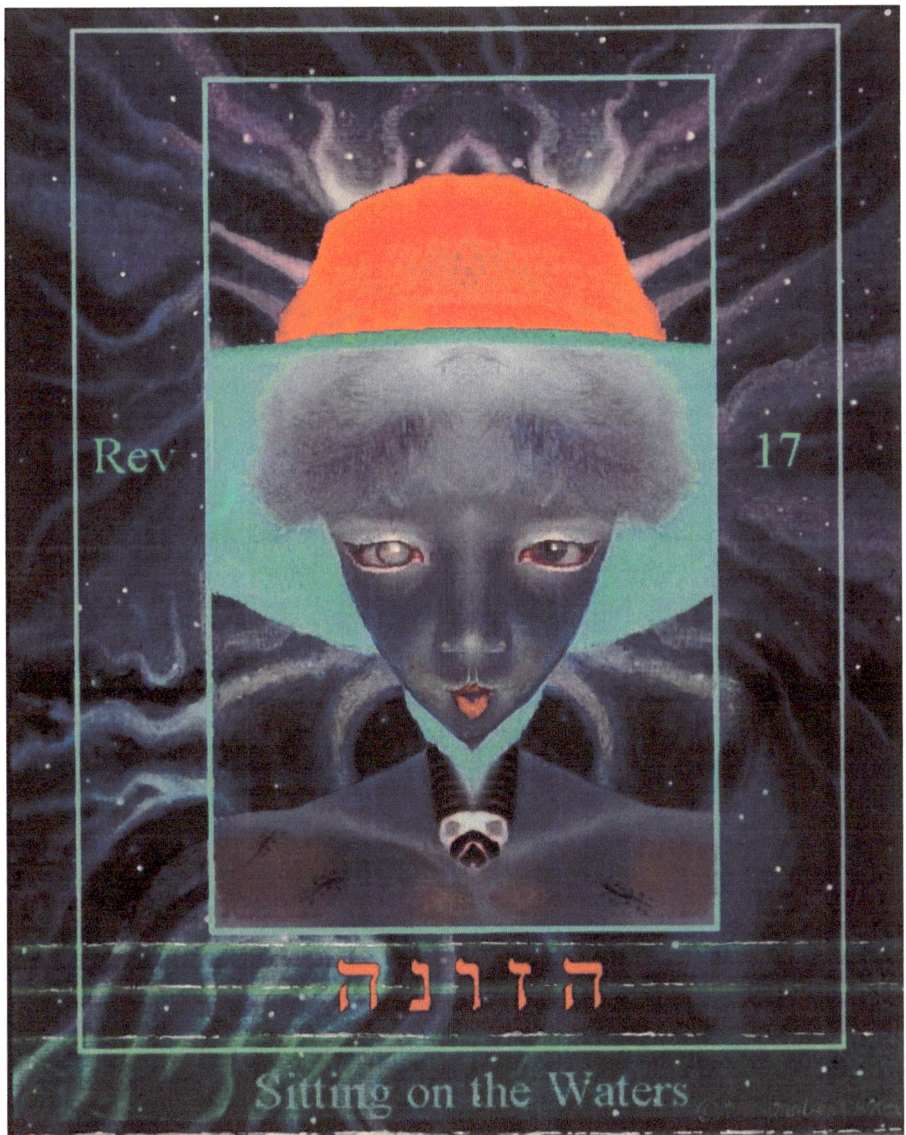

The Harlot: Sitting on the Waters, 2000-2001, ink jet and acrylic on laminated panel, 10" x 8"

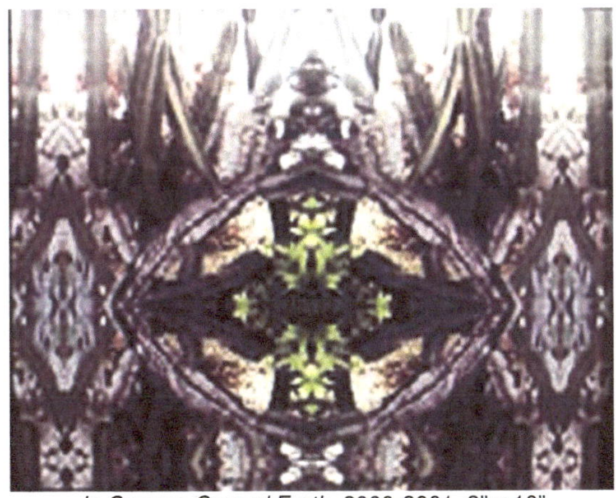

In Sorrow: Cursed Earth, 2000-2001, 8" x 10"

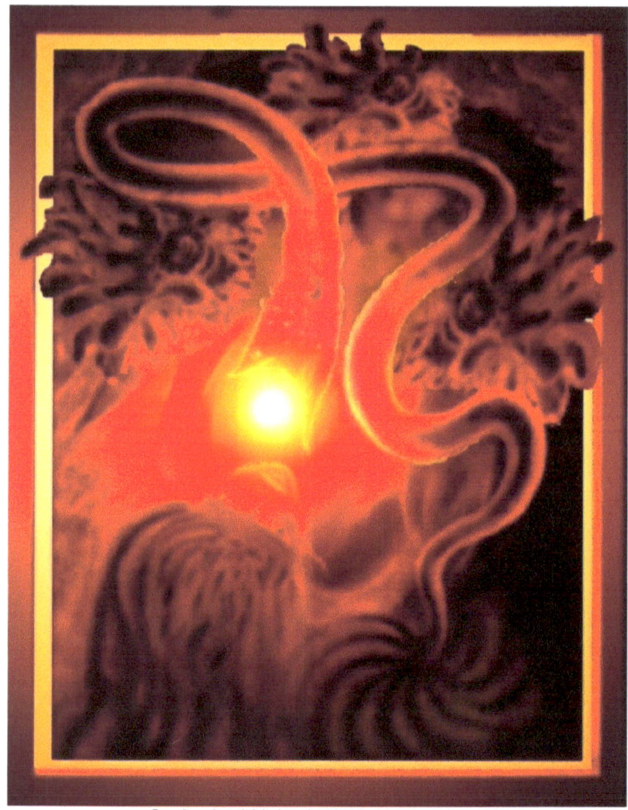

Crafty And Naked, 2000-2001, 10" x 8"

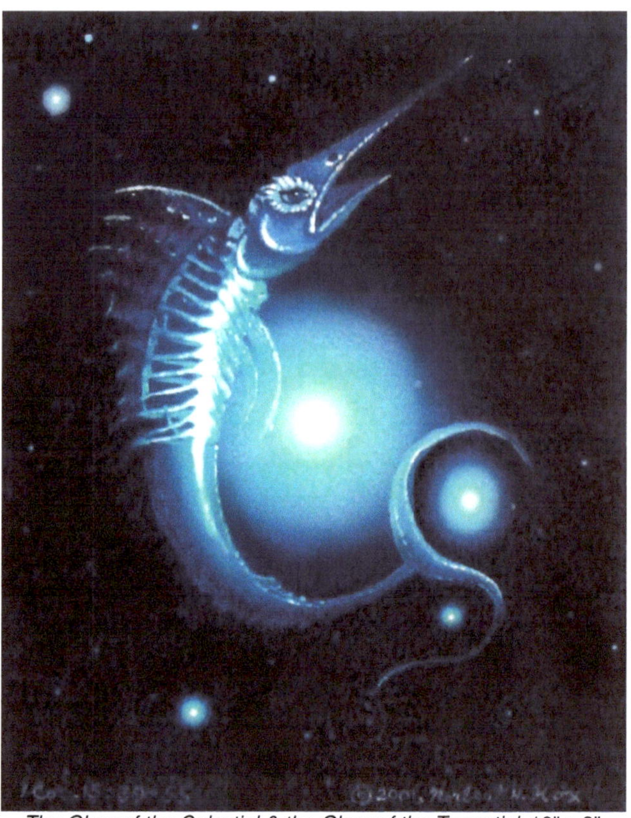

The Glory of the Celestial & the Glory of the Terrestial, 10" x 8"

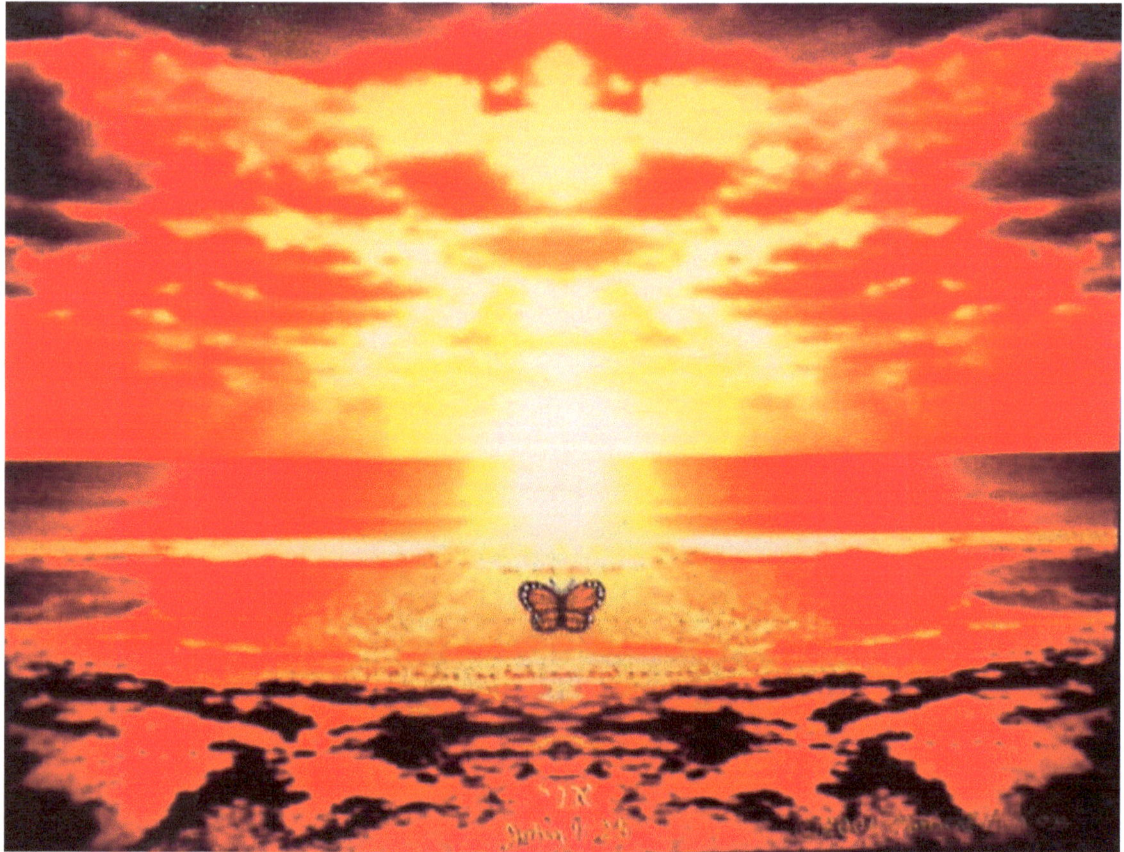

Resurrection, 2000-2001, ink jet and acrylic on laminated panel, 8" x 10"

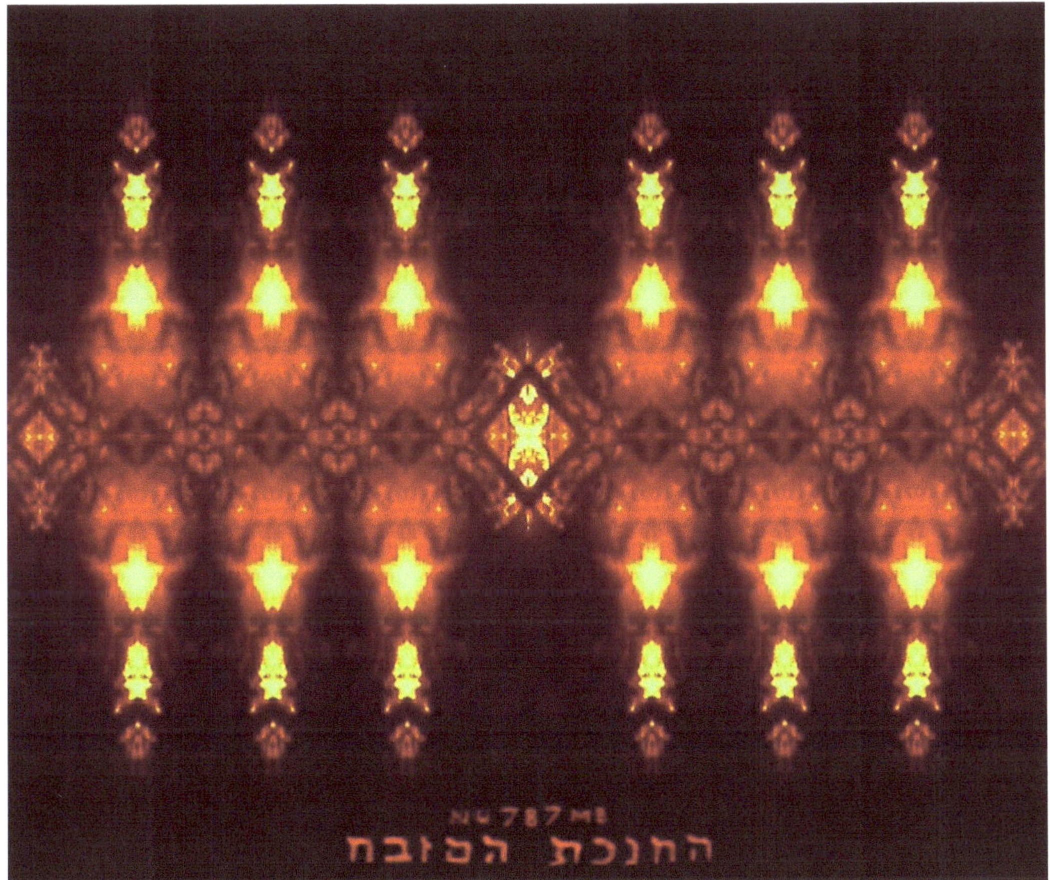

Dedication Of The Altar, 2000-2001, ink jet and acrylic on laminated panel, 8" x 10"

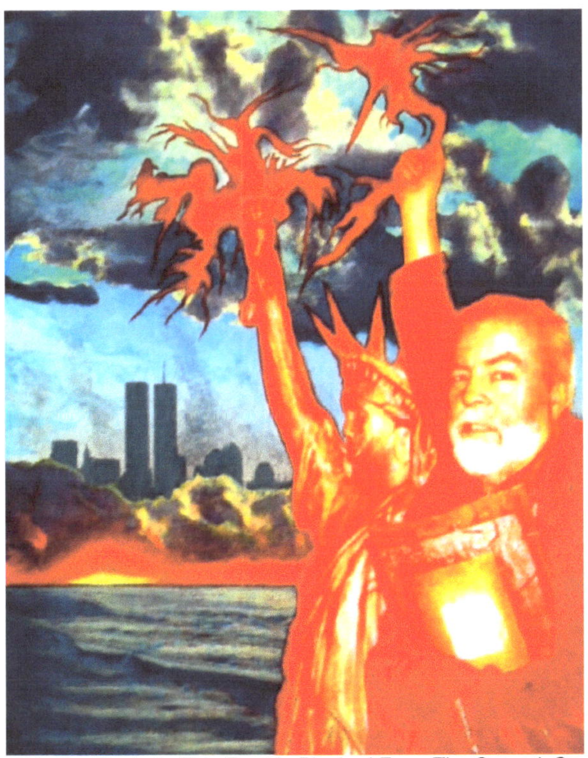

This Dry Root: As This Root Is Plucked From The Ground, So Shall Your Heart Be Plucked From The Midst Of You, 1/28/01, digital collage, ink jet and acrylic on laminated panel, 10" x 8"
(This was a 9-11 warning, painted 12/15/2000-1/28/2001, eight months before the Trade Center disaster.)

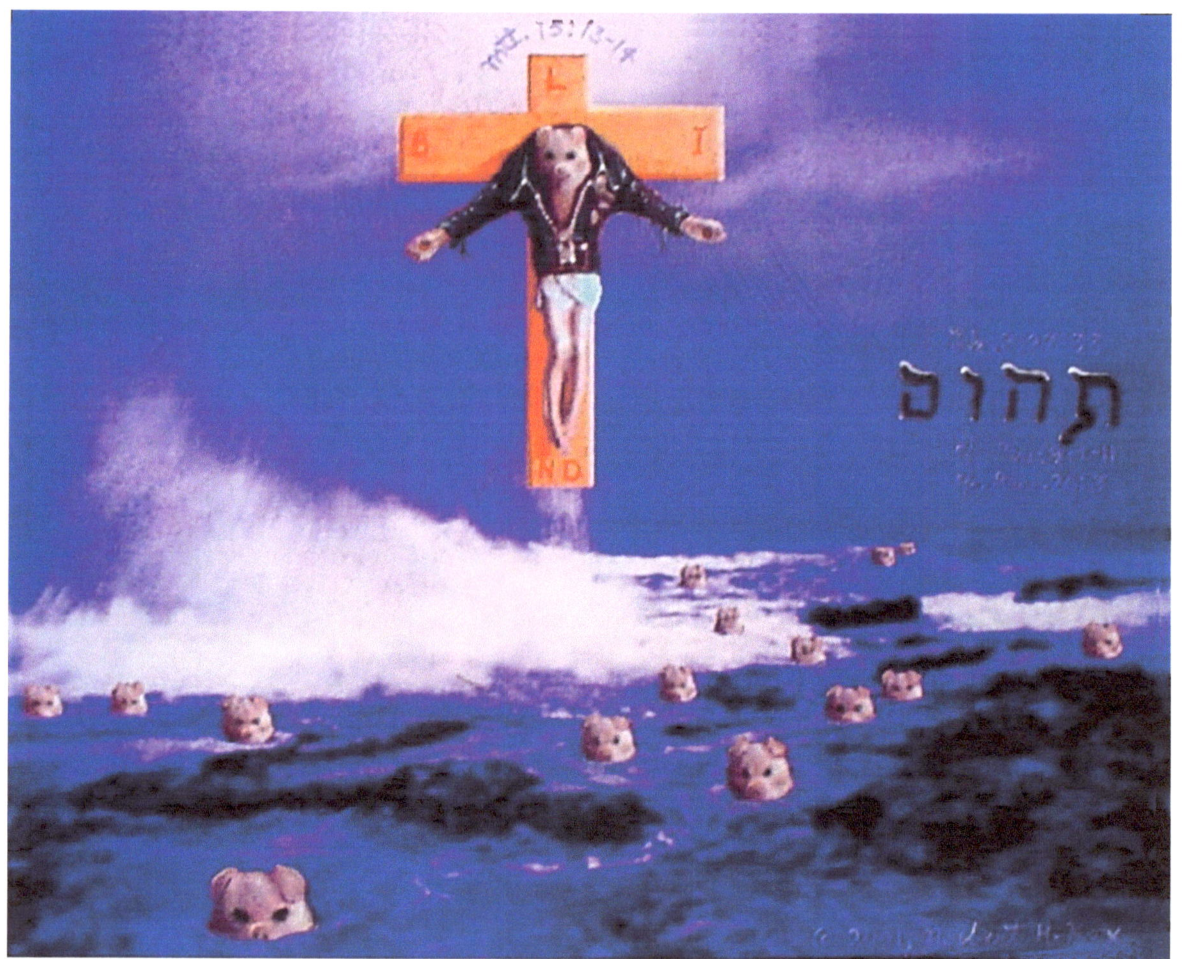

Up From The Deep: Return of the Legion, 2000-2001, ink jet and acrylic on laminated panel, 8" x 10"

2000 PIGS

The beast relies on pride of man, To work his evil deeds
He turns of their hearts to love of self, And hedonistic needs

With necks so stiff and hearts of stone, The children lose their sight
Their fathers teach them lies so bold, And turn their day to night

They love a lie, deceive themselves, Create a god their own
The number six is stamped three times, Right through their flesh and bone

Deceived by Dragon dressed in light, To kneel before his throne
And make amends to Satan-god, The way they have been shown

Most Christians worship image made, A god to fit their mold
They seek not truth, delusion find, Believe what they've been told

False saviour in the temple now, And no one wants to know
Their lies are precious gems so black, They'll never let them go

Religious people, pious ones, Are calling to the deep
The spirit-guides they trust upon, Speak demon-talk and peep

The serpent rises from the depths, Awakened from its sleep
She strikes her fangs into the brains, Of ever hapless sheep

2000 pigs now splash and choke, Arising from the sea
They come to join the Man of Sin, Blaspheme and snort with glee

But time is short for Devil's reign, He's falling from his place
Beelzebub, the Lord of flies, With dung upon his face

The evil angels, Satan to, Will burn when it's all o're
Lost ones sad, dissolve in flames, Beyond the glassy shore

The life they only thought they had, is lost forevermore
Because they turned from Yesu Christ, and closed the only door

Remove the number, mark and name, The Lord of Babel Gate
And turn to Yesu-Yahweh God, Before it is too late

(*circa* 2000, N. H. Kox)

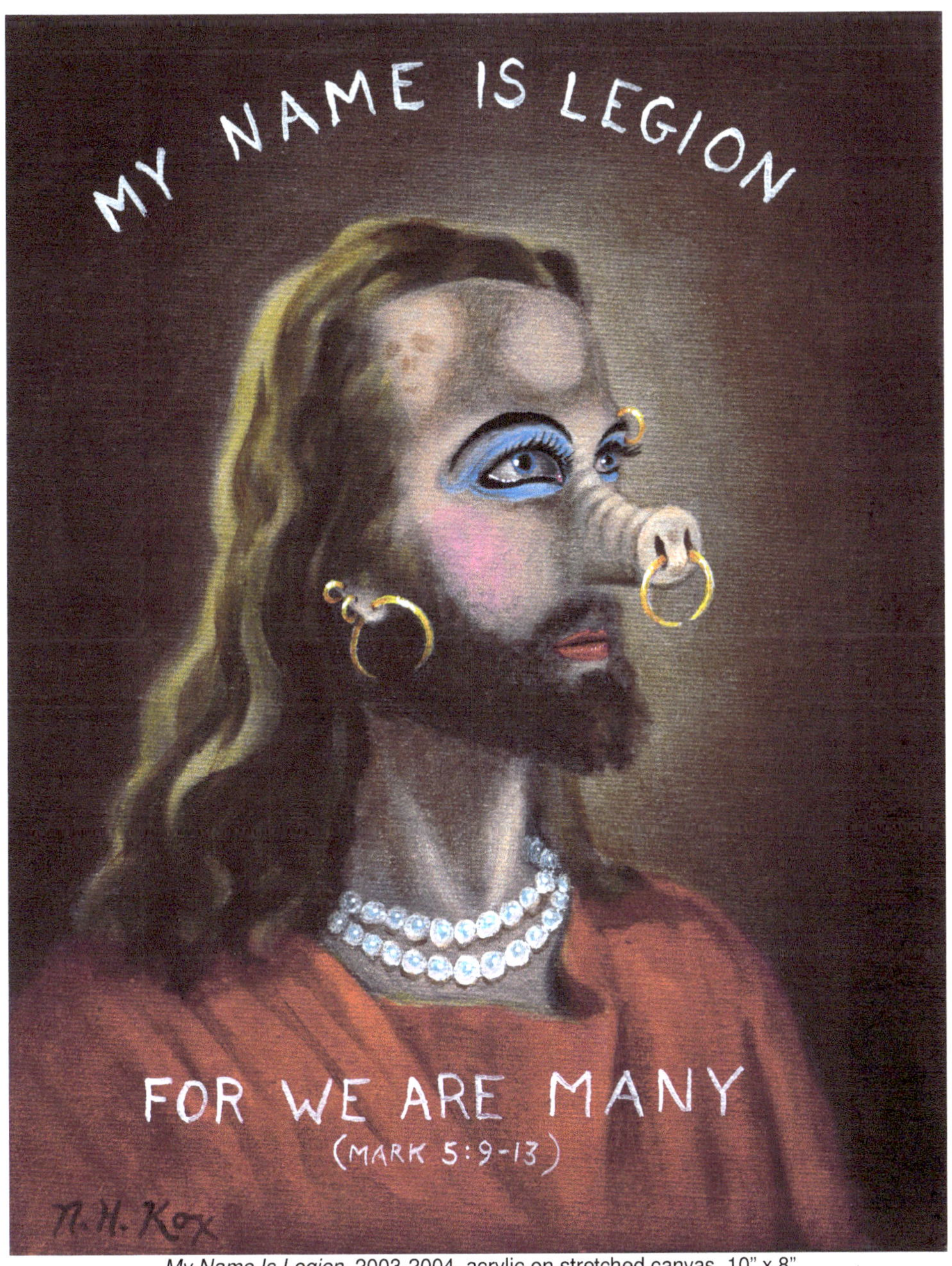

My Name Is Legion, 2003-2004, acrylic on stretched canvas, 10" x 8"

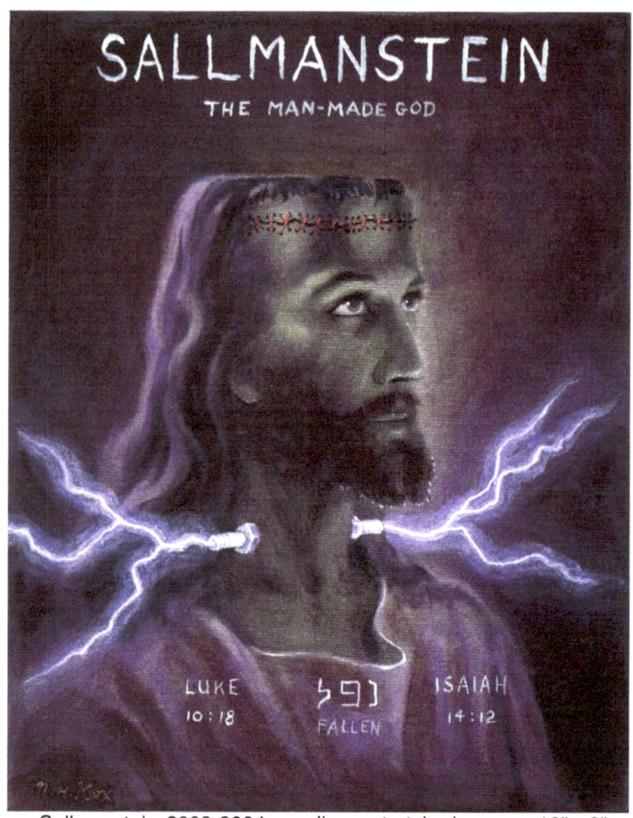

Sallmanstein, 2003-2004, acrylic on stretched canvas, 10" x 8"

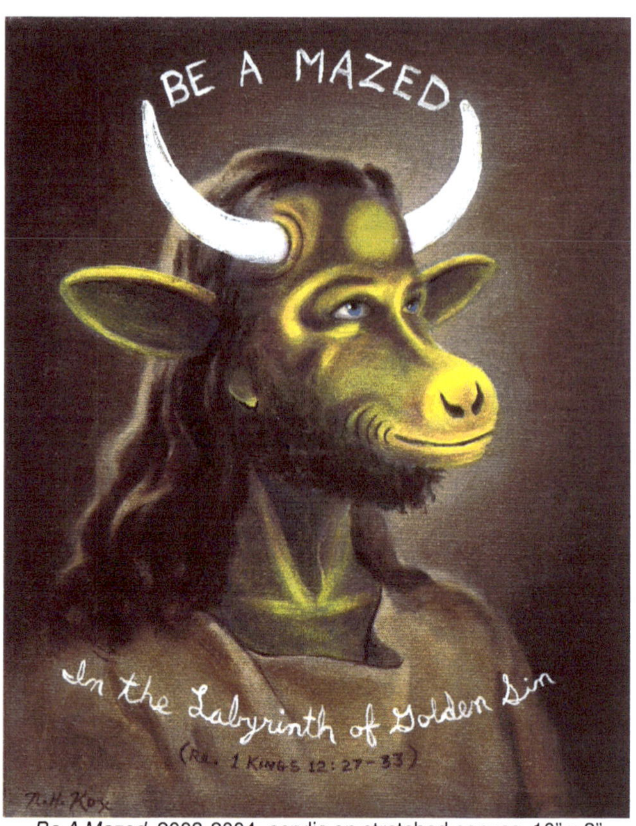

Be A Mazed, 2003-2004, acrylic on stretched canvas, 10" x 8"

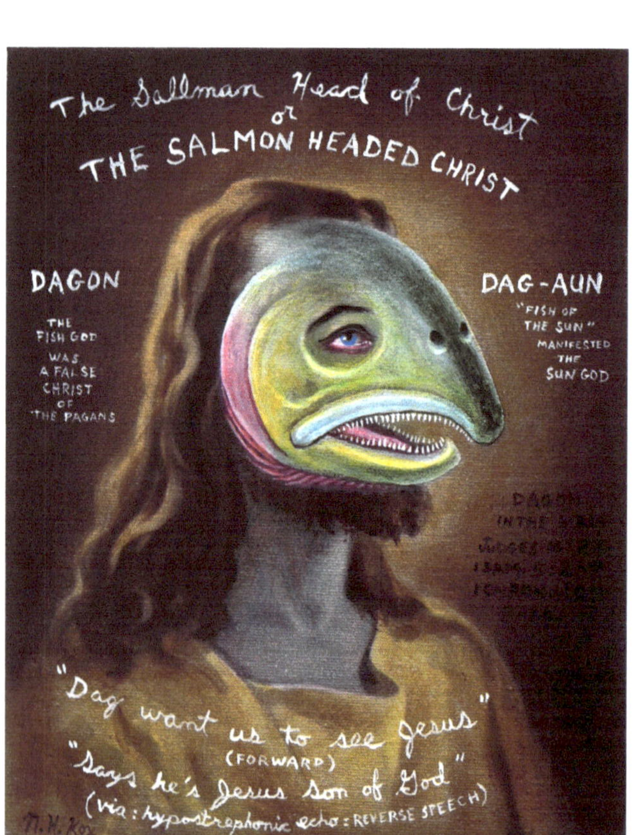

The Salmon Headed Christ, 2003-2004, acrylic on canvas, 10" x 8"

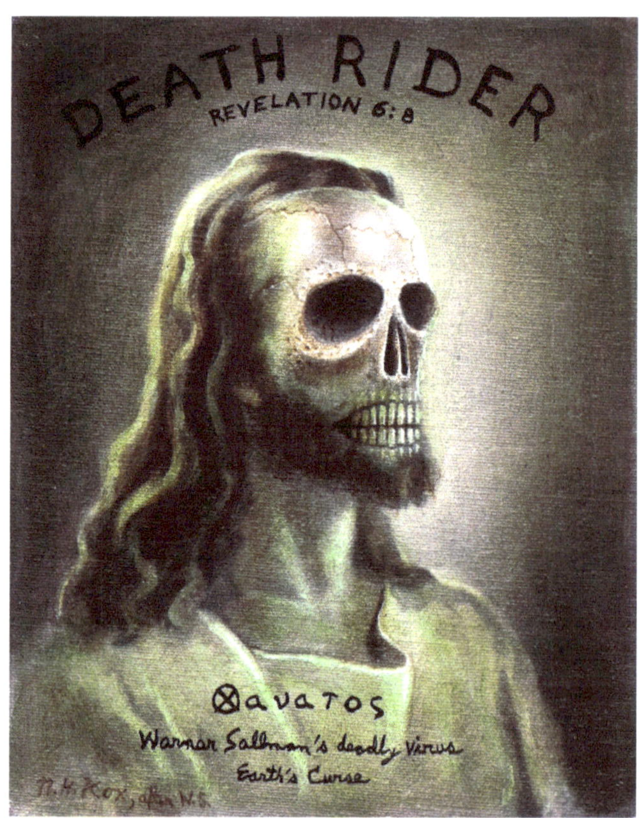

Death Rider, 2003-2004, acrylic on stretched canvas, 10" x 8"

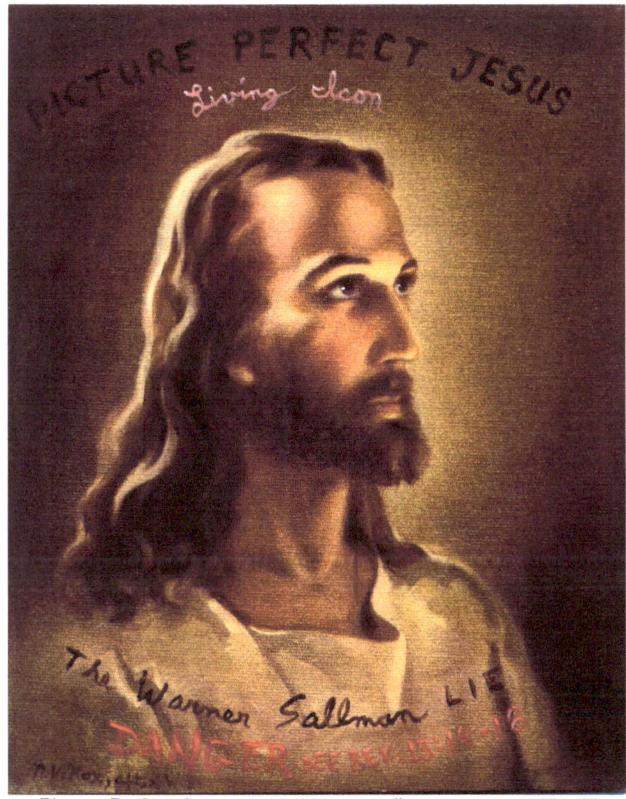

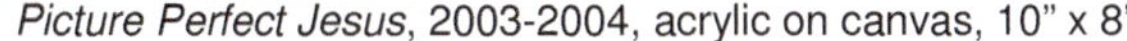
Picture Perfect Jesus, 2003-2004, acrylic on canvas, 10" x 8"

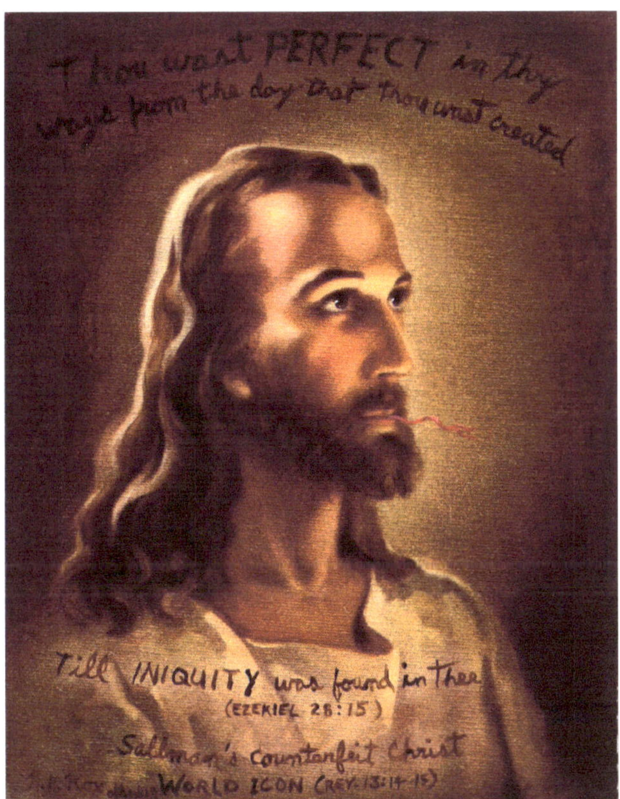

Till Iniquity Was Found In Thee, 2003-2004, acrylic, 10" x 8"

PICTURE PERFECT JESUS: THE GLAMOROUS FRAUD (2004)

(included more than 20 images created in Bimini)

2004, Bimini Art Exhibition
2004, America Oh Yes Art Gallery, Washington, D.C.
2005, Lawton Gallery, University of Wisconsin–Green Bay
2008-2009, Raw Vision (Winter Issue) pp. 30-35

The ridicule of Warner Sallman's Head of Christ focused upon in this exhibit is not a derision of the Saviour, but an exposé of Sallman's devious painting, with the intentions of revealing it as a counterfeit. Many people seem to think these images are making fun of Christ, when the opposite is true. These paintings, along with historic and Scriptural references, are actually indicating the characteristics of an idol and false image in such a contemptible manor, as to cause the viewer to be shaken out of complacency and obliged to investigate what is being presented.

ARTIST STATEMENT

The intention of my artwork is to cause people to think, to research and investigate, rather than accept the blind traditions of men. The ultimate goal is to entice people to search the Scriptures on their own. The usual focus of my work is to target specific errors and idolatries of Humanity, revealing their fallacies through Scriptural references. I also try to point out areas of interest that need further investigation, in hopes that someone will be able to carry it to the next level.

I have appropriated the Warner Sallman *Head of Christ* (1940) for the purpose of exposing it as a plagiarized fraud and not the Divine Image it is claimed to be.

Scripture warns against a false Christ image that becomes a living icon, and an object of worship (Revelation 13:14-15). Satan's plan is to be worshipped as God and Saviour (Isaiah 14:13-14; II Thessalonians 2:3-4; II Corinthians 11:14).

The Warner Sallman *Head of Christ* has become the accepted authentic portrait of Christ, having been reproduced over a billion times since 1940.

Sallman was a shrewd advertising marketer. He had a ploy to mass-market his art to the world. He found a painting [an artist's interpretation] of Christ that would be the perfect image to glamorize and sell to the world. It was the creation of French artist, Leon Lhermitte (lare-meet). The painting titled *Emmaus*, also known as *Friend of the Humble*, is a backlit Christ at a supper table (1892).

Being a graphic artist, Sallman was skilled in copy work. He simply copied the bust of *Christ* from Lhermitte's oil painting, transforming it into a charcoal drawing which he titled *Son of Man* [1924]. He never told anyone that he copied the image. There would have been no shame in copying (graphic artists do it all the time) if he had credited the original artist. But what glory is there in a copied image? Yet, if the drawing were original, received in a Divine Vision from God, it would be considered spectacular. So Sallman concocted an awesome story of a vision of light and an apparition of the Head of Christ.

By claiming the image as his own, Warner Sallman became a plagiarist, something he never admitted to.

The *Son of Man* charcoal drawing was first published in black and white on a magazine cover . Later it was mass-produced as a sepia print and sold to the people of America. In 1940, Sallman painted a full-color oil of his *Son of Man*, and renamed it *Head of Christ*. His colors, shading, highlighting, lay of the hair, folds of the robe, all matching the Lhermitte painting perfectly. The only difference, Sallman, being familiar with the glamor photographs of Hollywood movie stars, added the same type of backdrop to his *Head of Christ*. The result was the "Picture Perfect Jesus".

Accompanied with the story of its Divine origin, Sallman's *Head of Christ* met with mass-approval. Over 4,000,000 prints were sold in the first two years. By 1985 more than 500,000,000 copies had been sold, and by, 2004, the *Head of Christ* had been reproduced well over a billion times. It is the universally recognized portrait of Christ. This idol came with the stamp of authenticity. Who could doubt that this was the face of Christ when it *came from God in a heavenly vision*? Many revere it as a picture of God. It is the God and Saviour prayed to by the majority of the world's Christian population. It has been warned against throughout Scripture. It is all part of Satan's plan to rob glory from Yahweh.

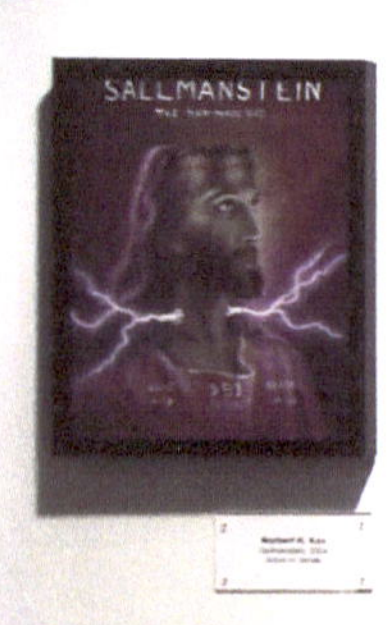

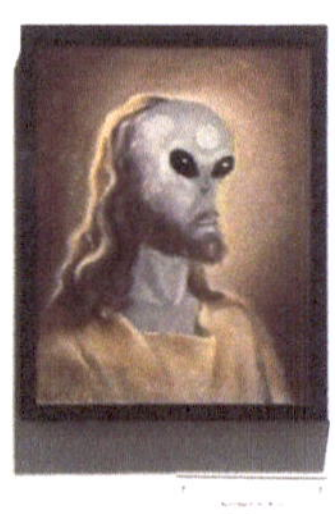
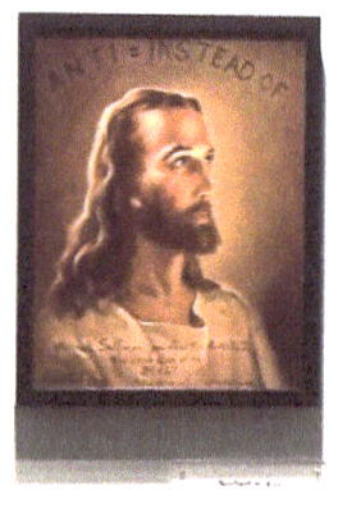
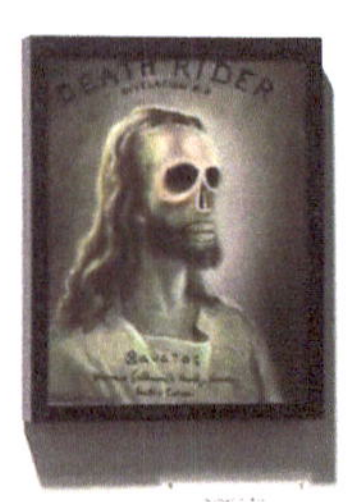
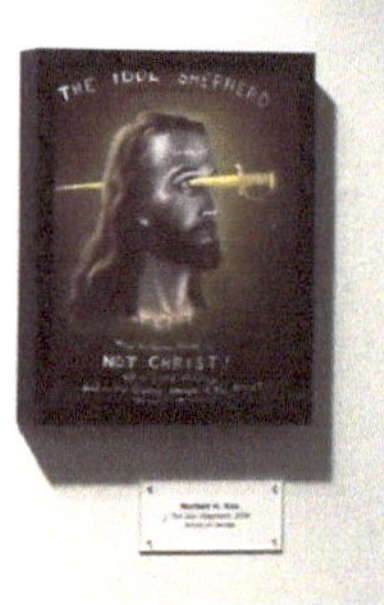

Picture Perfect Jesus, 2005 exhibition, Elohim The Apocalyptic Time Machine, Lawton Gallery, University of Wisconsin–Green Bay

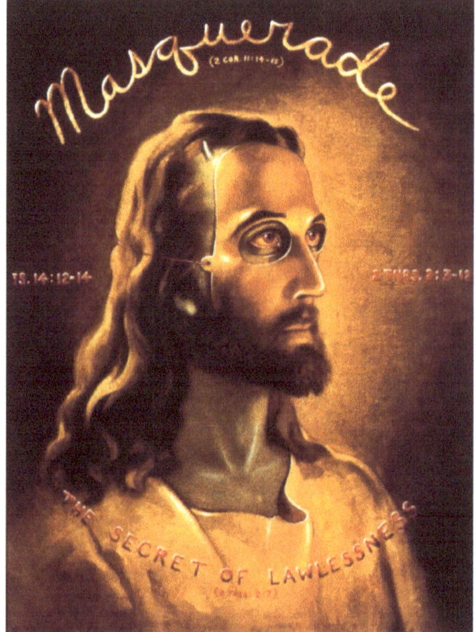

Masquerade, 1997, oil on lithograph, 24" x 18"
(not painted in Bimini)

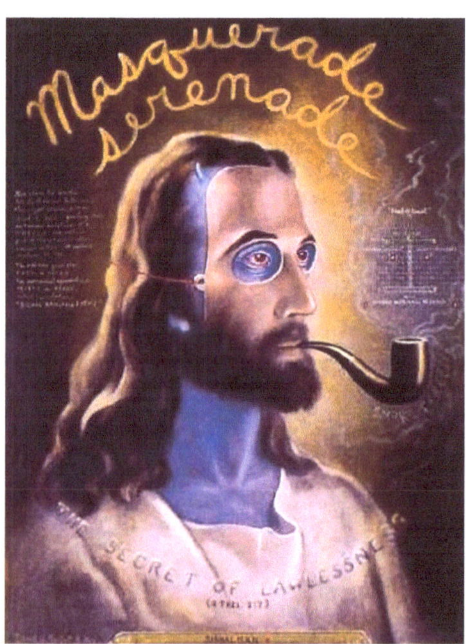

Masquerade Seranade, 2003, acrylic on canvas, 37" x 37.5"
(not painted in Bimini)

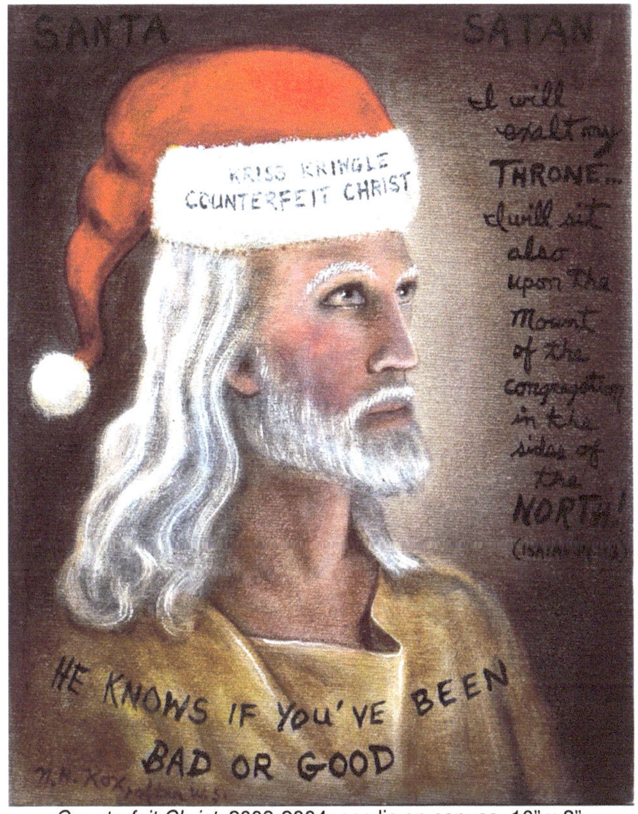

Counterfeit Christ, 2003-2004, acrylic on canvas, 10" x 8"

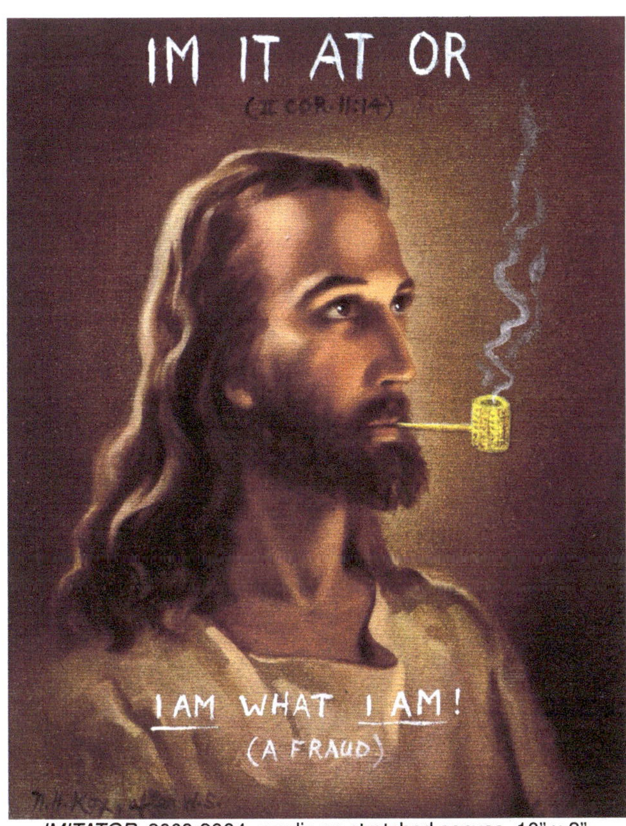

IMITATOR, 2003-2004, acrylic on stretched canvas, 10" x 8"

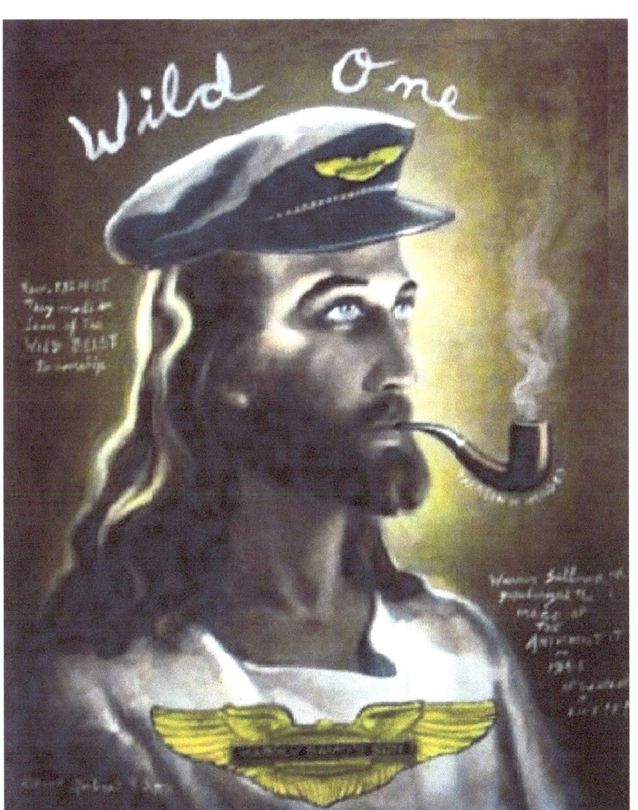

Wild One, 2003-2004, acrylic on stretched canvas, 20" x 16"

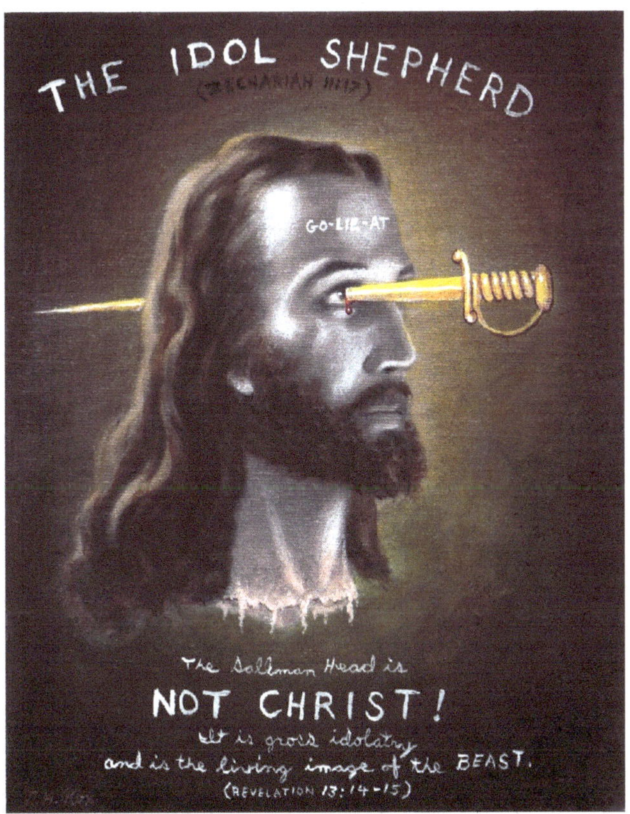

The Idol Shepherd, 2003-2004, acrylic on canvas, 10" x 8"

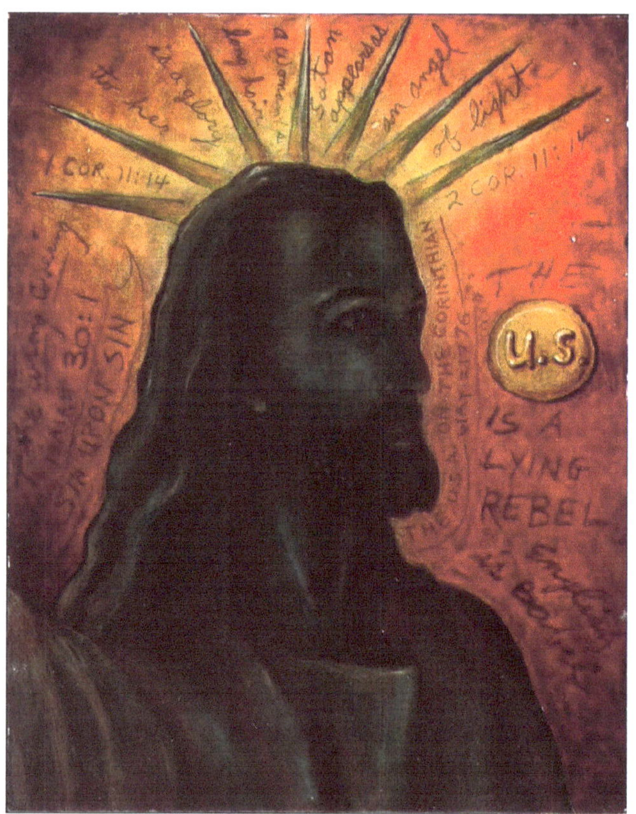

The Wrong Covering, 1993-1998, acrylic on canvas panel, 10" x 8"
(not painted in Bimini)

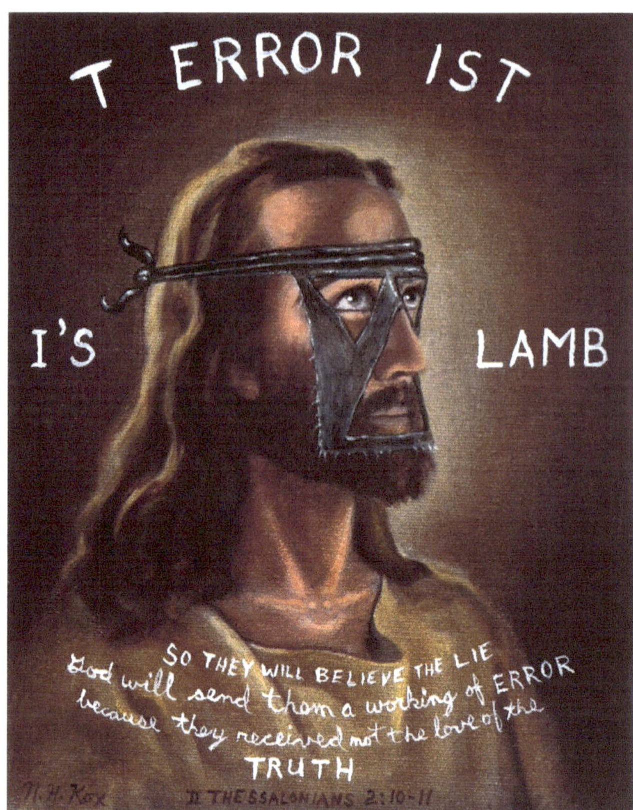

Terrorist, 2003-2004, acrylic on stretched canvas, 10" x 8"

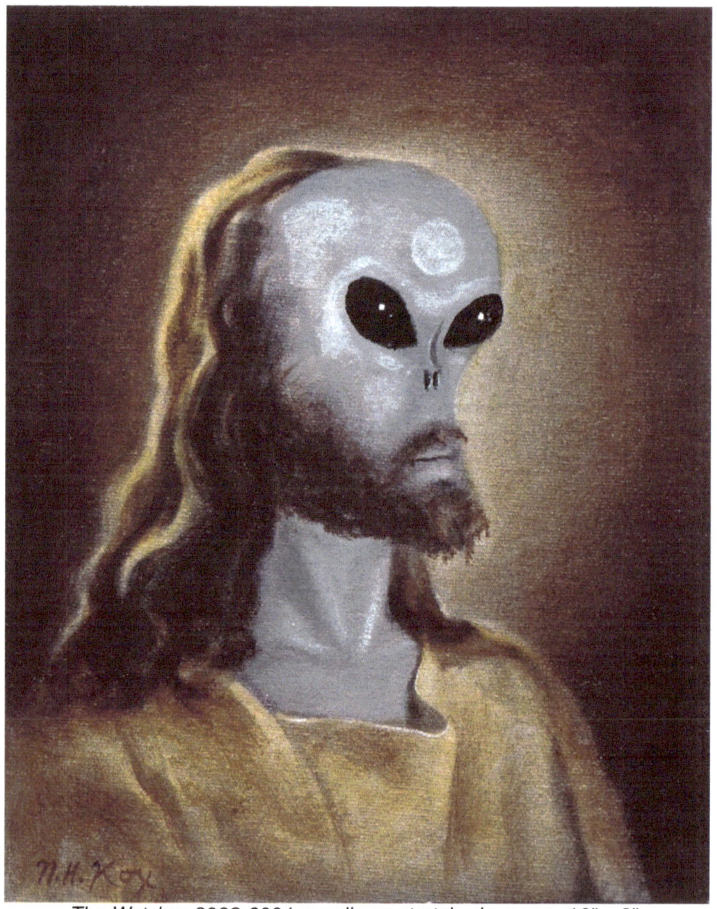

The Watcher, 2003-2004, acrylic on stretched canvas, 10" x 8"

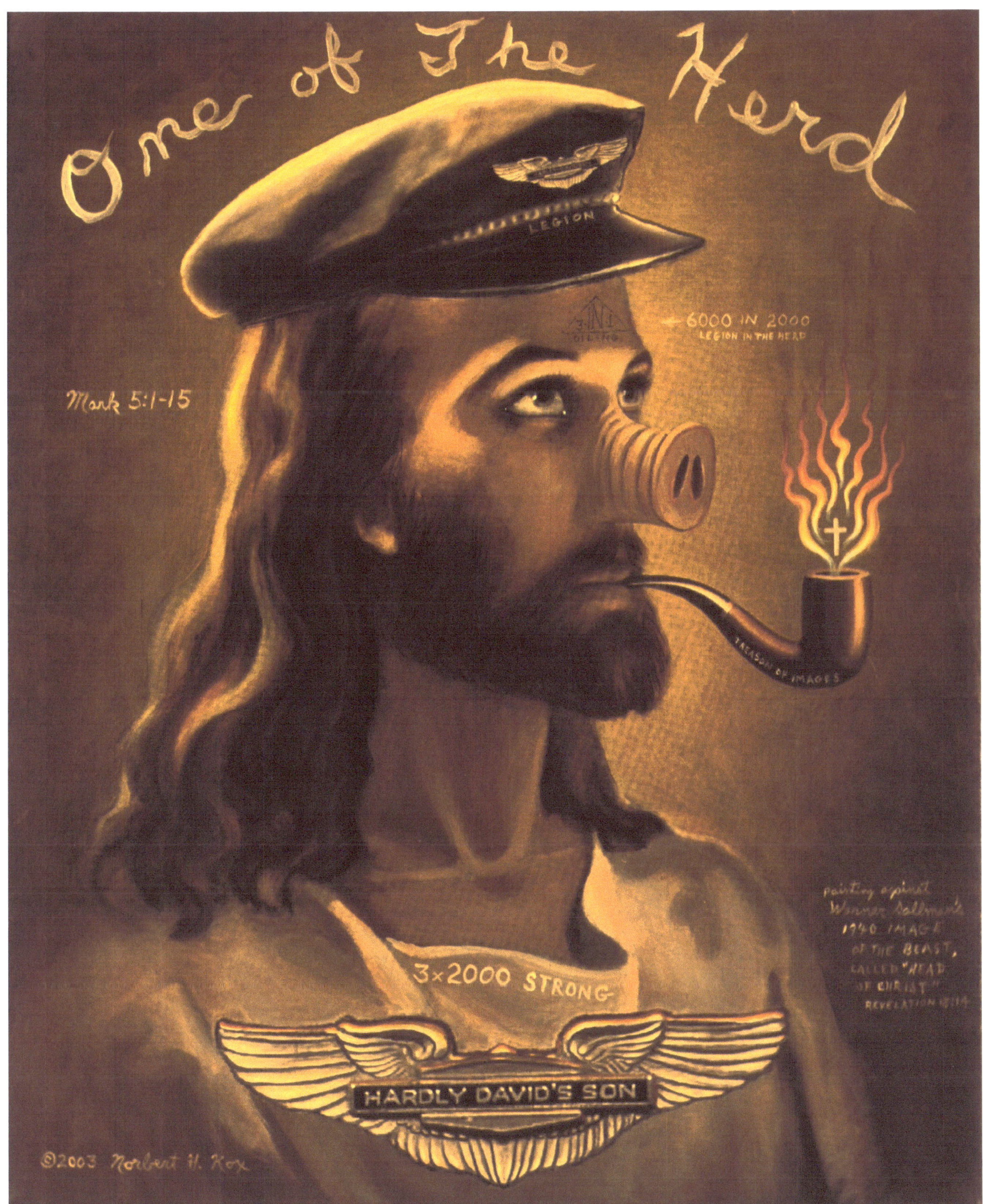

One Of The Herd, 2003, digital collage, acrylic & oil on stretched canvas, 25" x 20"
(not painted in Bimini)

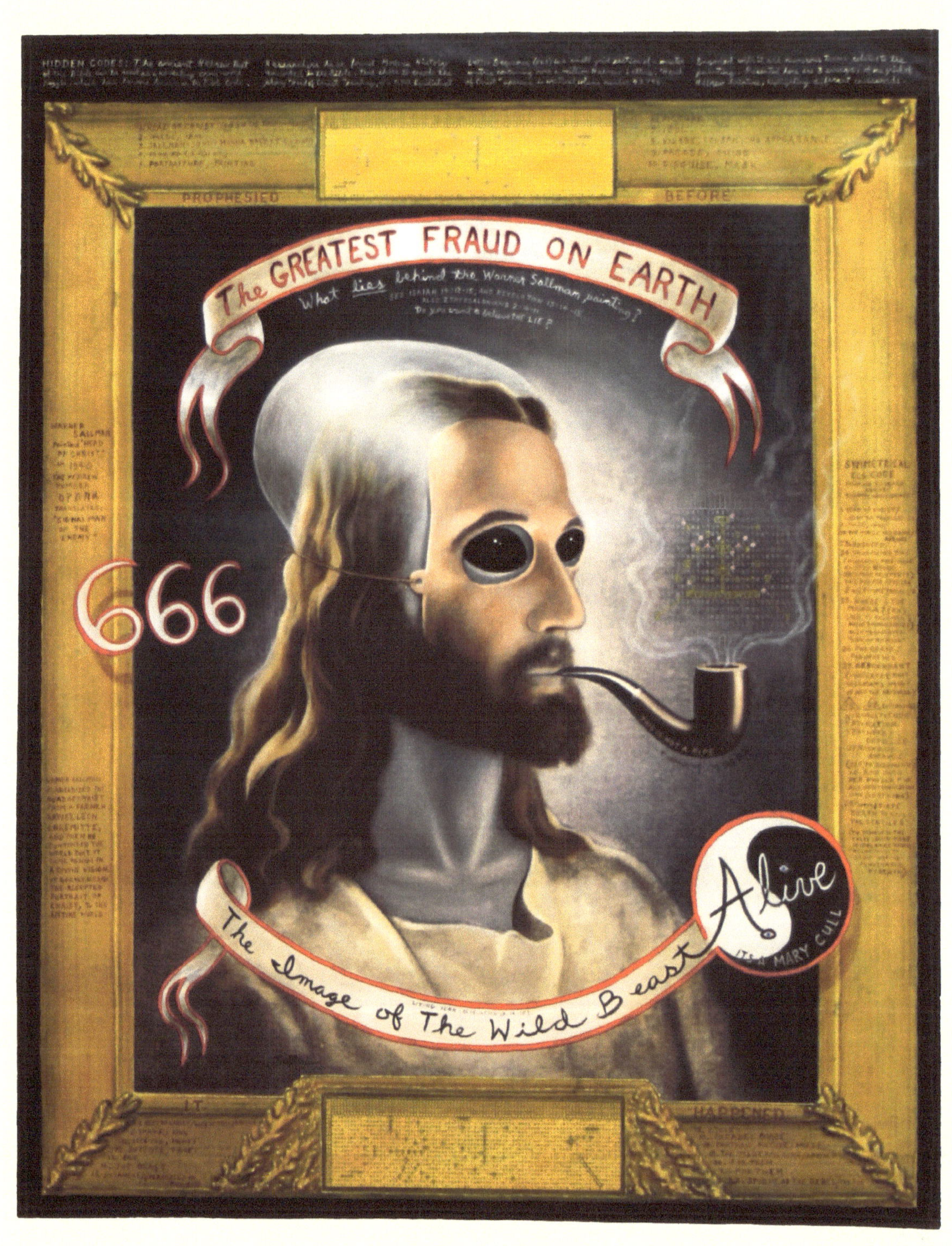

The Greatest Fraud On Earth, 2003-2004, acrylic on canvas banner, 50" x 42"

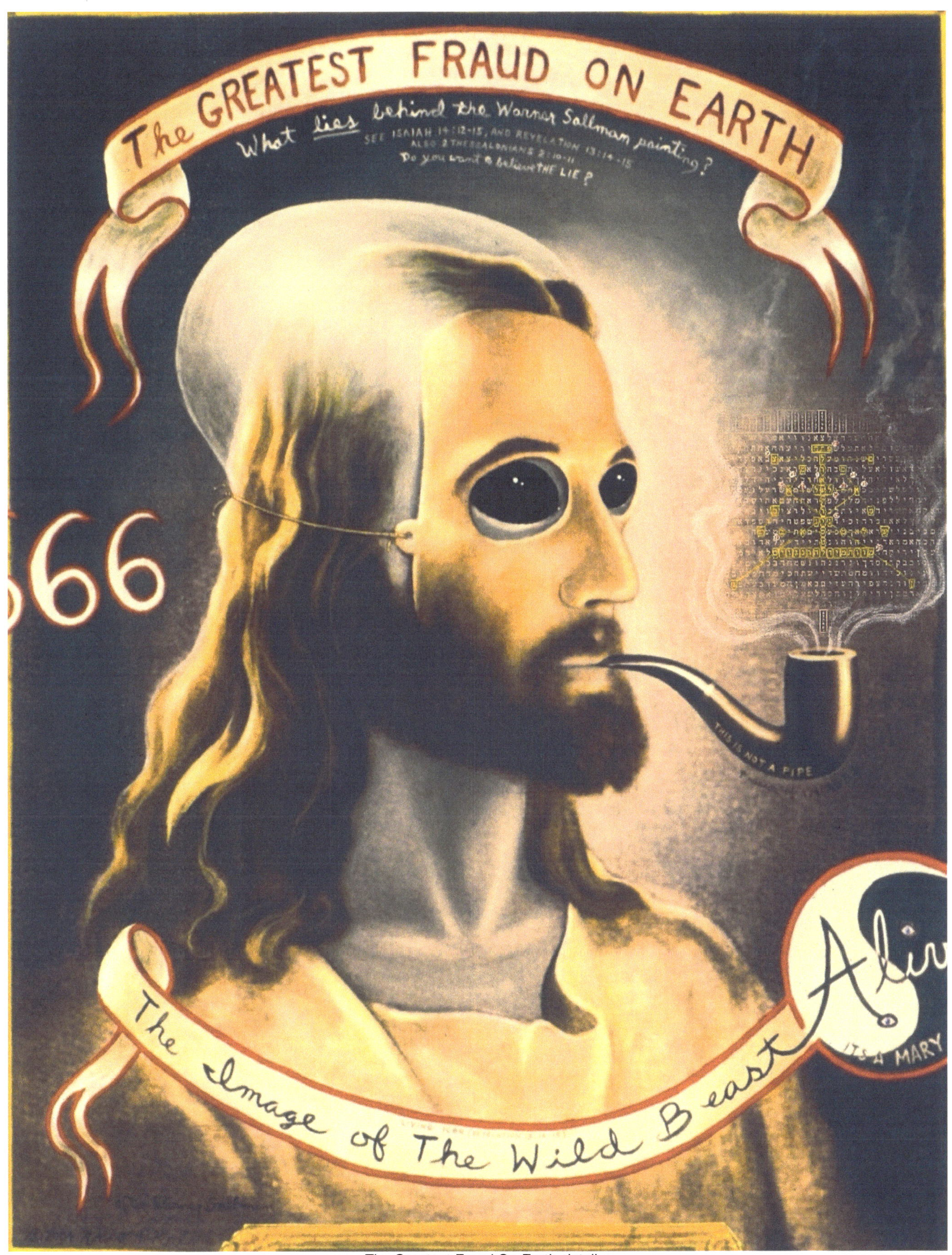

The Greatest Fraud On Earth, detail

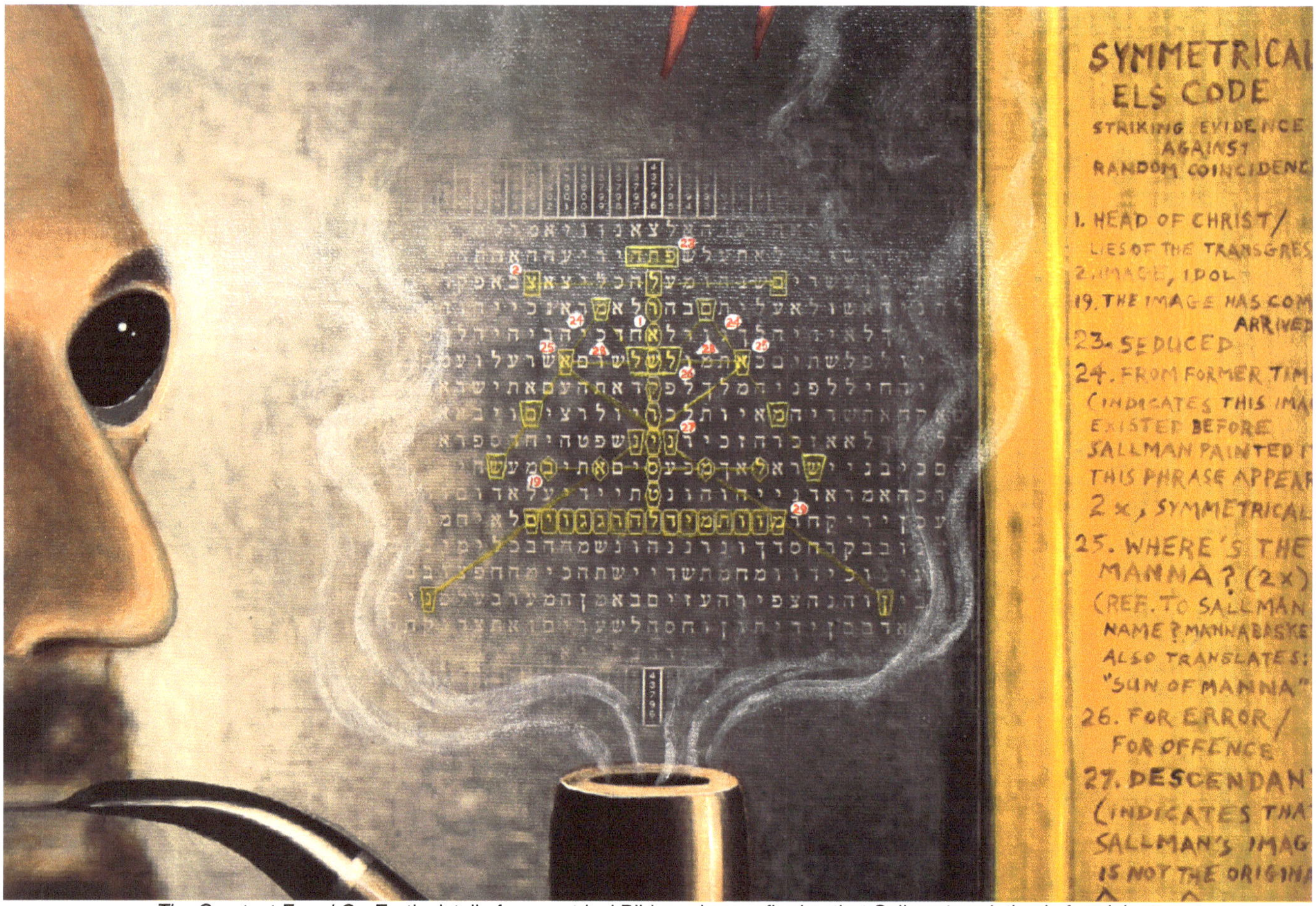

The Greatest Fraud On Earth, detail of symmetrical Bible codes confirming that Sallman's painting is fraudulent

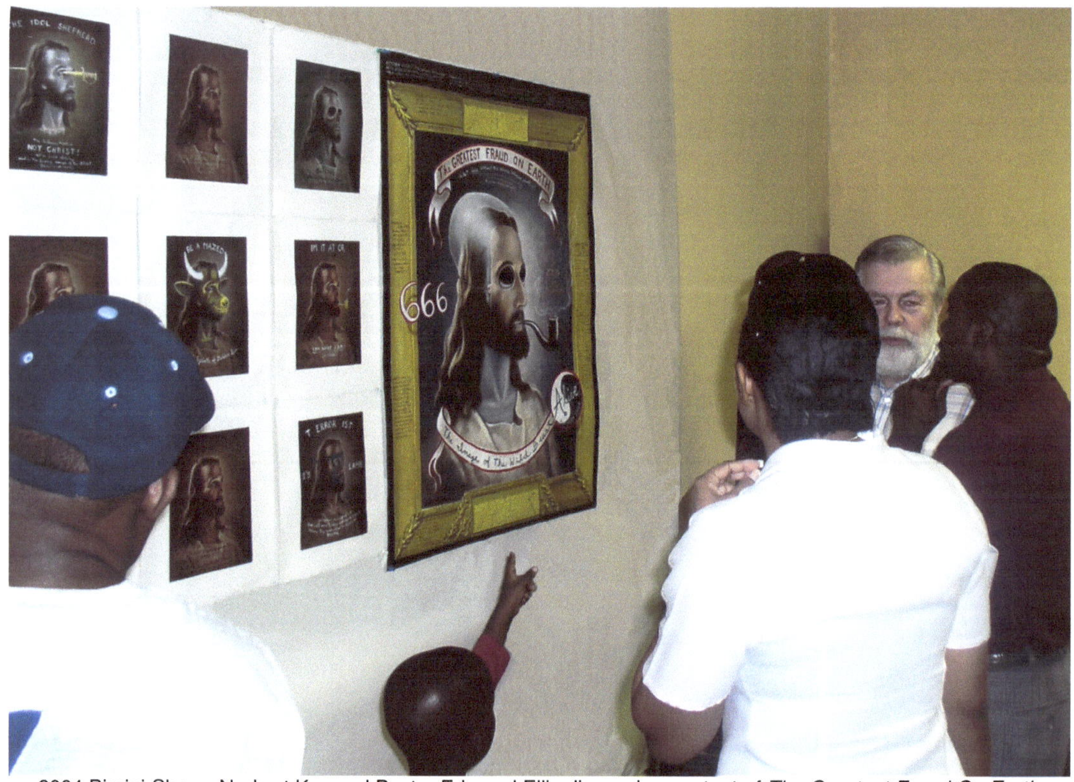

2004 Bimini Show, Norbert Kox and Pastor Edmond Ellis discussing context of *The Greatest Fraud On Earth*

(photo by James Pinder)

BIMINI ART EXHIBIT (2005)

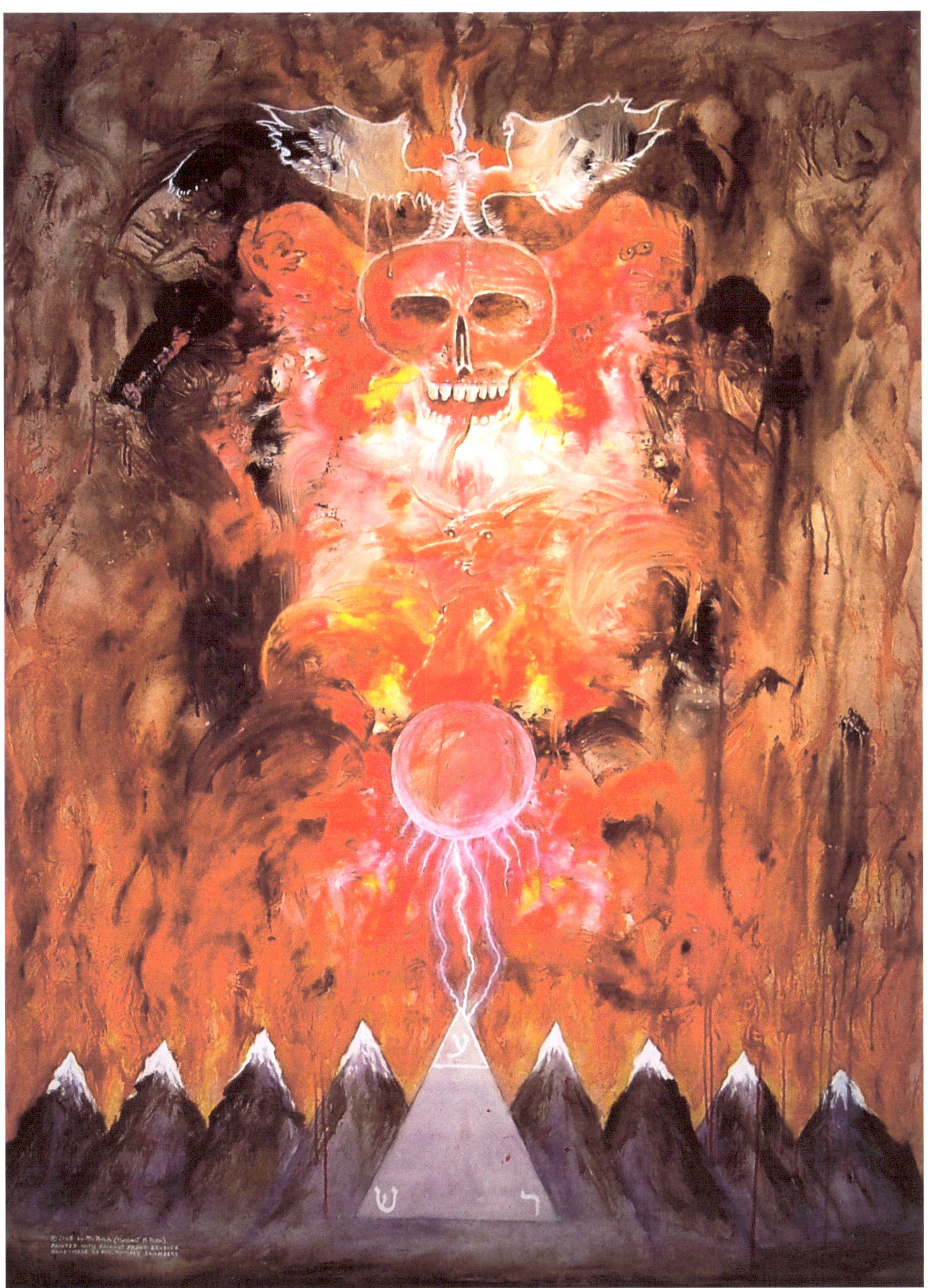

Portal of Doom, 2004-2005, acrylic on canvas, 64" x 47"
Painted in Bimini with coconut frond brushes made by Mr. Tommy Saunders.

Additional paintings, *Portal of Heaven*, and *Opening the Portal*, from the 2005 show can be seen on page 51.

BIMINI ART EXHIBIT (2007)

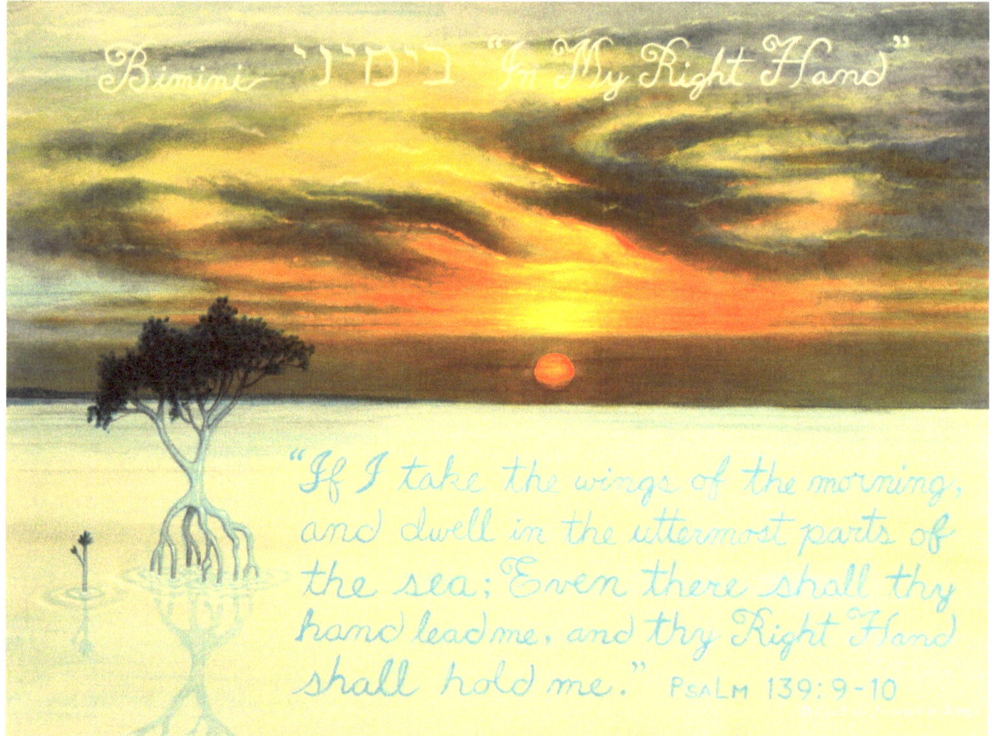

In My Right Hand, 2006-2007, acrylic on canvas, 18" x 24"

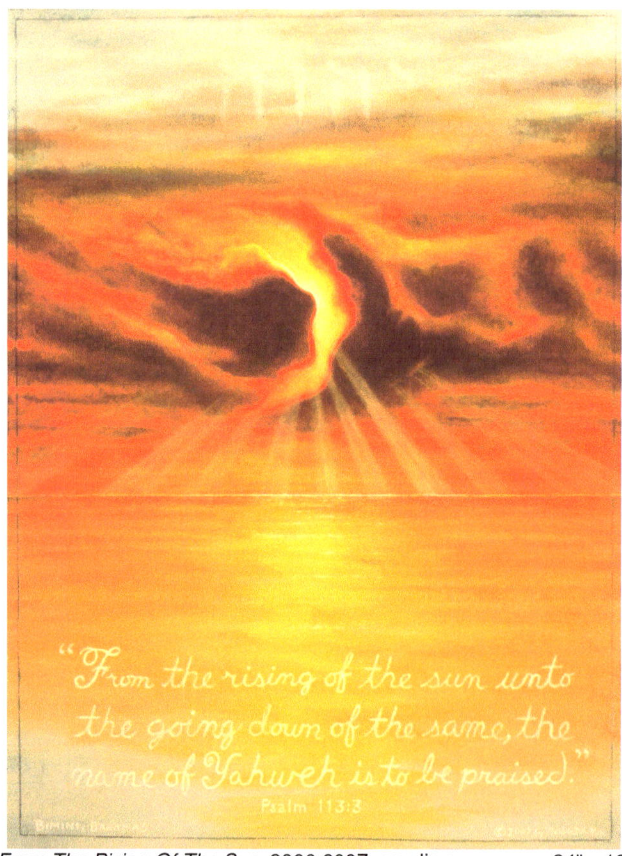

From The Rising Of The Sun, 2006-2007, acrylic on canvas, 24" x 18"

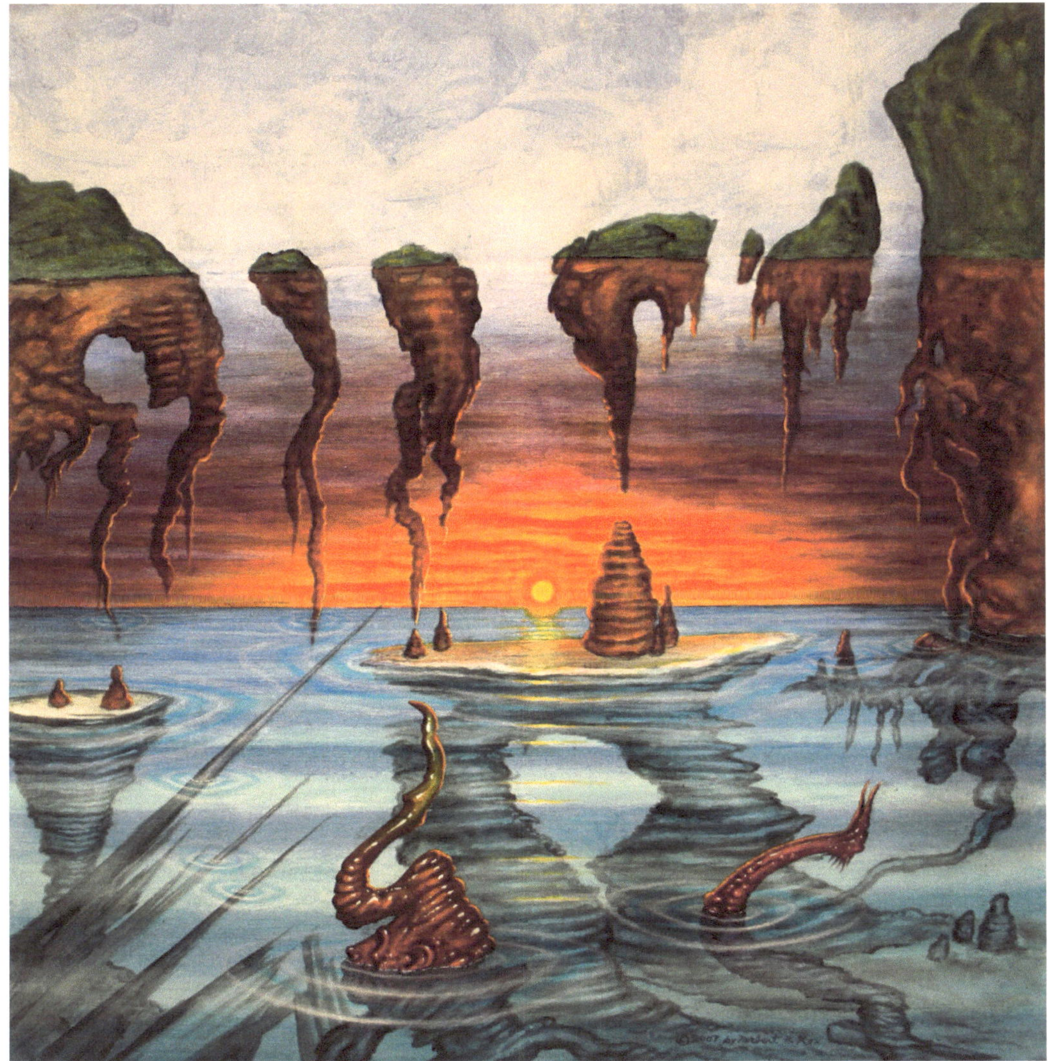

Primordial Pandora, 2006-2007, acrylic on canvas, 25" x 24" (unstretched)

Primordial Pandora (Floating Mountains) was originally untitled at the Bimini 2007 art exhibition. "In a previous painting demonstration, I had just painted whatever came to mind with no idea of the meaning." Those present at the exhibit offered several suggestions. One visitor said that it brought to mind Pandora's Box. Although it probably holds some deep hidden truth, on the surface this seems to have been a prophetic reference to the sci-fi movie *Avatar*, which was to come along just two years later.

> December 21, 2009 - The movie is set on the fictional Pandora, one of the many moons of a fictional Saturn-sized gas giant, Polyphemus... Tropical rainforests cover most of Pandora's continents... The draw that Pandora has for humans is a naturally occurring ore dubbed "unobtanium,"... Unobtanium is the best superconductor known, and apparently works at room temperature. Just as real-world superconductors can float in the presence of a magnetic field, mountains on Pandora apparently loaded with unobtanium can float in the powerful magnetic pockets that dot the moon's surface. (*http://www.surrealaward.com/avatar/science13.shtml*)
>
> The producer of "Avatar" is fond of saying that writer and director James Cameron does not write science fiction, he writes science fact... To be sure, Mr. Cameron likes to bring his fair share of Hollywood to the cosmos, painting his scenes with the brush of fantasy. But beneath some of his most outlandish visions is often a kernel of scientific possibility. (*ibid.*)
>
> "*Avatar's*" alien world of Pandora, it turns out, is simply a massive superconductor... entire mountains loaded with unobtanium float in the world's massive magnetic field. ...scientists say. On Cameron's Pandora, those tidal stresses have fractured the landscape, and, in the case of the Hallelujah Mountains, sent it up into the sky. (*ibid.*)

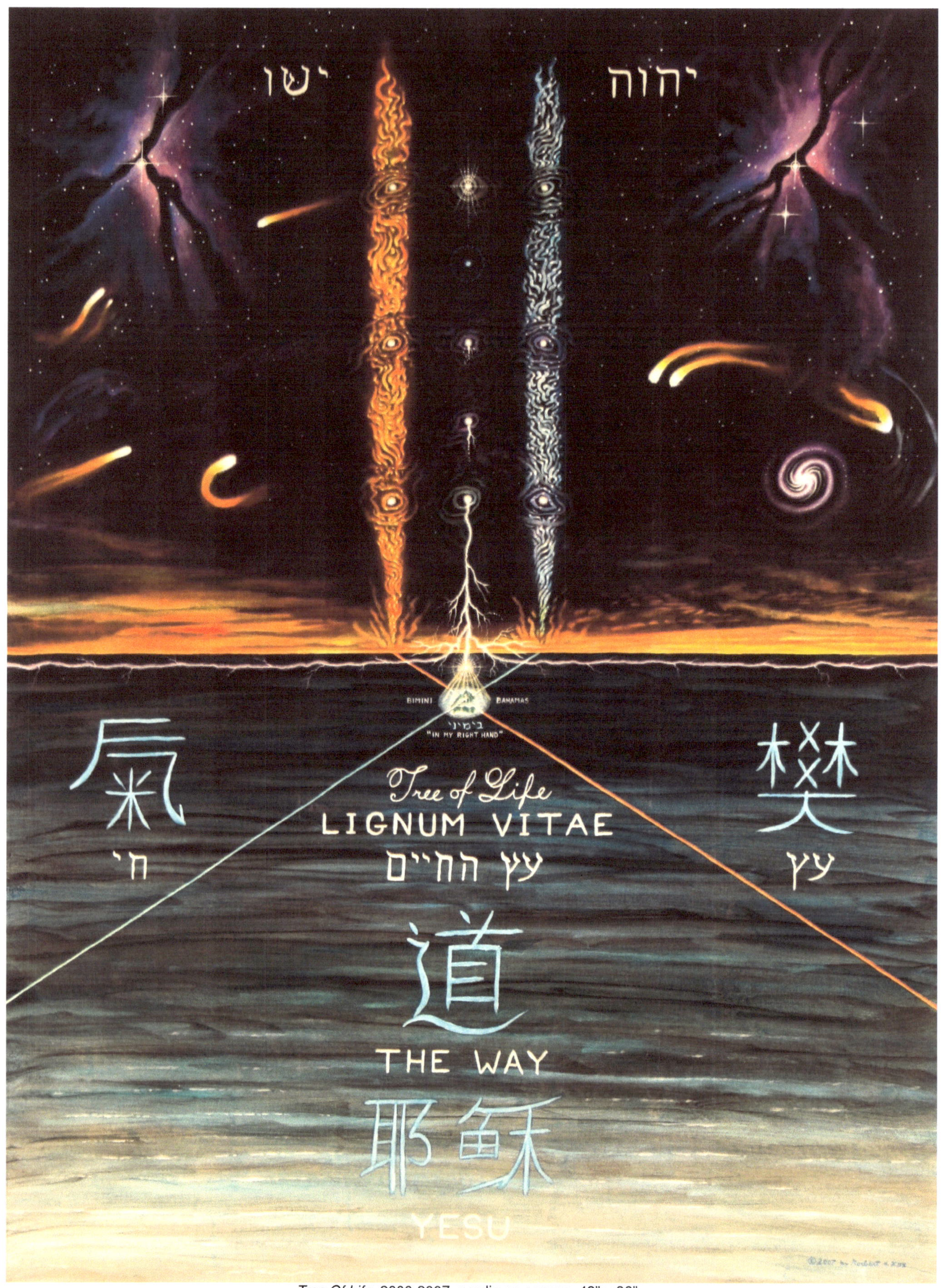

Tree Of Life, 2006-2007, acrylic on canvas, 48" x 36"

Exhibited also in England: *Sacred Pastures*, 2008, Horse Hospital, London, and *Eloquent Obsessions*, 2008, Orleans House, Richmond, England

TREE OF LIFE

The piece titled *Tree Of Life* [opposite page] is one of my recent glory paintings from the Island of Bimini in the Bahamas. The Source energy of the Universe is seen manifesting in fire and water, two natural symbols of power and cleansing. This painting ties together aspects of ancient Jewish Mysticism, Chinese Tao and Christianity. The Hebrew spellings of the names of Yahweh and Yesu border the pillars of water and fire in the Jewish Kabbalistic Tree of Life. The Source energy flows down the center of manifestation shining its light on Bimini, which in the Hebrew spelling means "In my right hand". Significantly, the national tree of the Bahama Islands and Bimini is the *Lignum Vitae*, "Tree of Life". The Hebrew and Chinese characters for "tree" appear on the right, and those for "life" are on the left side of the painting. The Chinese symbol for Tao is at the center, with its English translation, "The Way" (Tao is the way or the path, but actually encompasses the entire eternal Source). Beneath that are the characters for the name Yesu. The Chinese translation of the Bible says that Yesu is the Tao [see Canton edition of the New Testament, published in China, 1911, American Bible Society]. (London online magazine, *Fate*, "Norbert H. Kox and the End of The World," http://www.dontpaniconline.com/magazine/fate/norbert-h-kox-and-the-end-of-the-world)

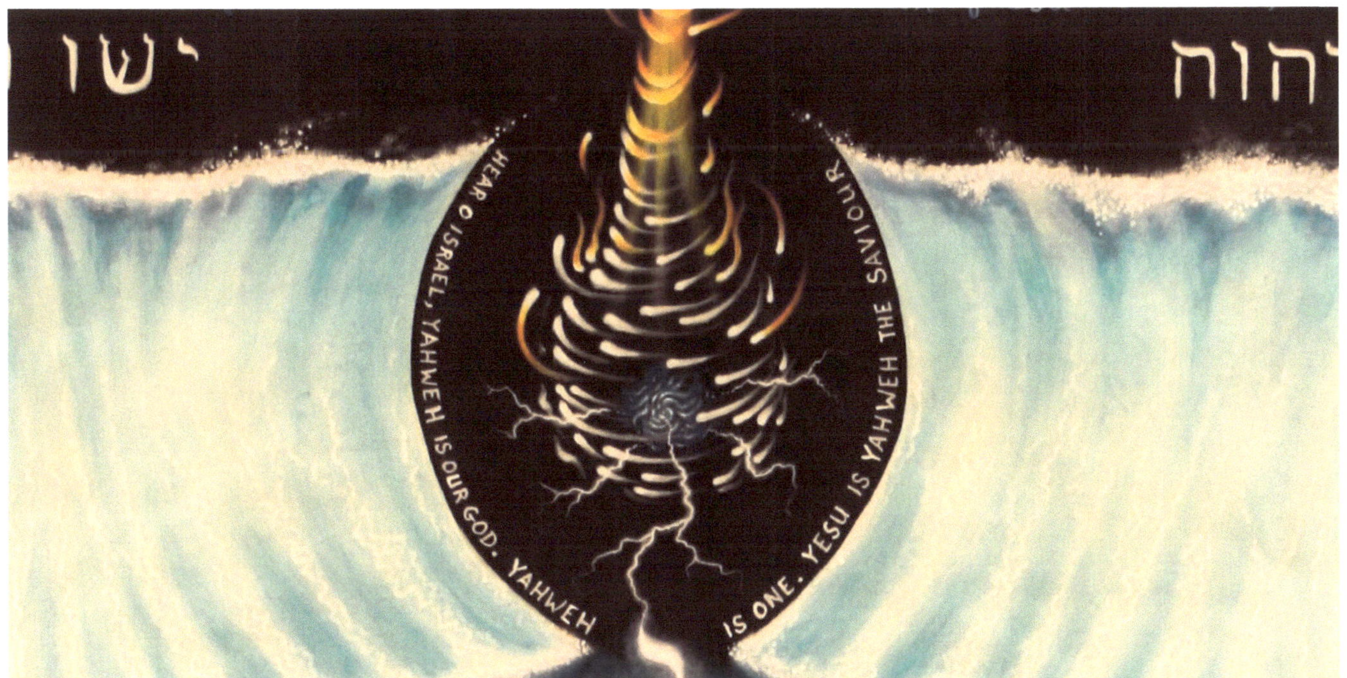

Crossing The Strait (detail, ball of energy representing the Source, Yahweh, in the pillar of fire)

CROSSING THE STRAIT

Straight Is the gate (*portal*) and narrow the way that leads to life and few there be that find it (Matthew 7:14). Many seek to enter and shall not be able (Luke 13:24). Scripture gives the analogy of the crossing of the Red Sea as a symbol of baptism. The Israelites crossed the parted sea under Yahweh's pillar of fire becoming a symbolic reference of the baptism of fire and water. "He that believes and is baptized shall be saved…" (Mark 16:16). "He that believeth not is condemned already, because he hath not believed in the name of the only be gotten Son of God (John 3:18). There is "one baptism" but we need to see that it is in two parts, the water and the spirit. If you have been baptized in water and not in the Holy Ghost you have only one half of the baptism, and if you have been baptized in the spirit but not in the water you also have only half of the baptism. Think about it.

The inspiration for this painting came after an underwater inspection of the area in the ocean near Spook Hill, where the X of God's mark appears in the waves. In 2006 I was compelled to perform a snorkel dive in that area to investigate the ocean floor for any anomalies that might be a clue to what is happening. I waded out to where the water was about five feet deep and began to snorkel around. Immediately I was met with a very strange sight. The sand bottom was riddled with potholes and mounds. The holes were each about two to three feet in diameter and about one and one-half feet deep. The mounds each appeared to be made up of the same amount of sand that came from each hole.

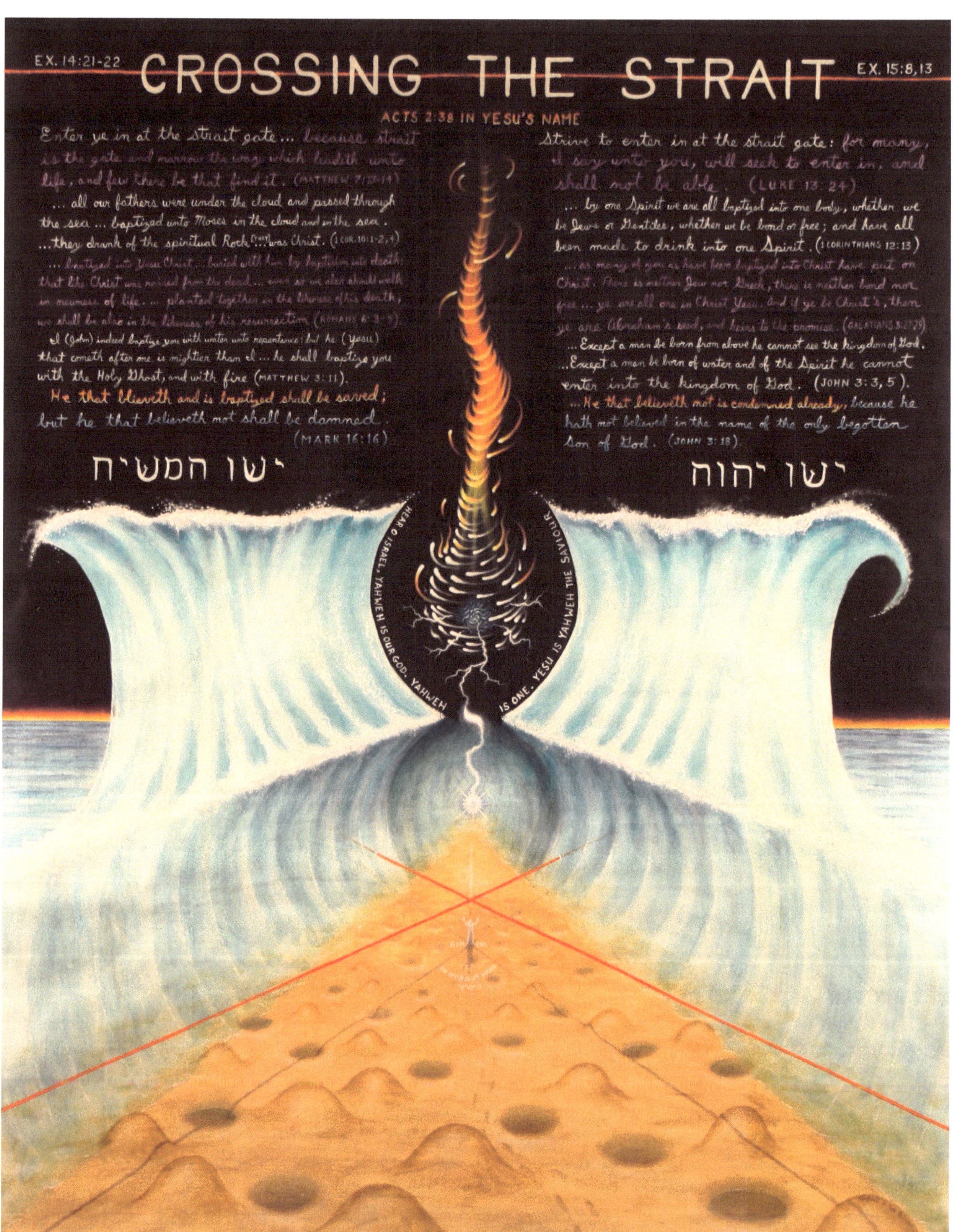

Crossing The Strait, 2006-2007, acrylic on canvas, 60" x 48"

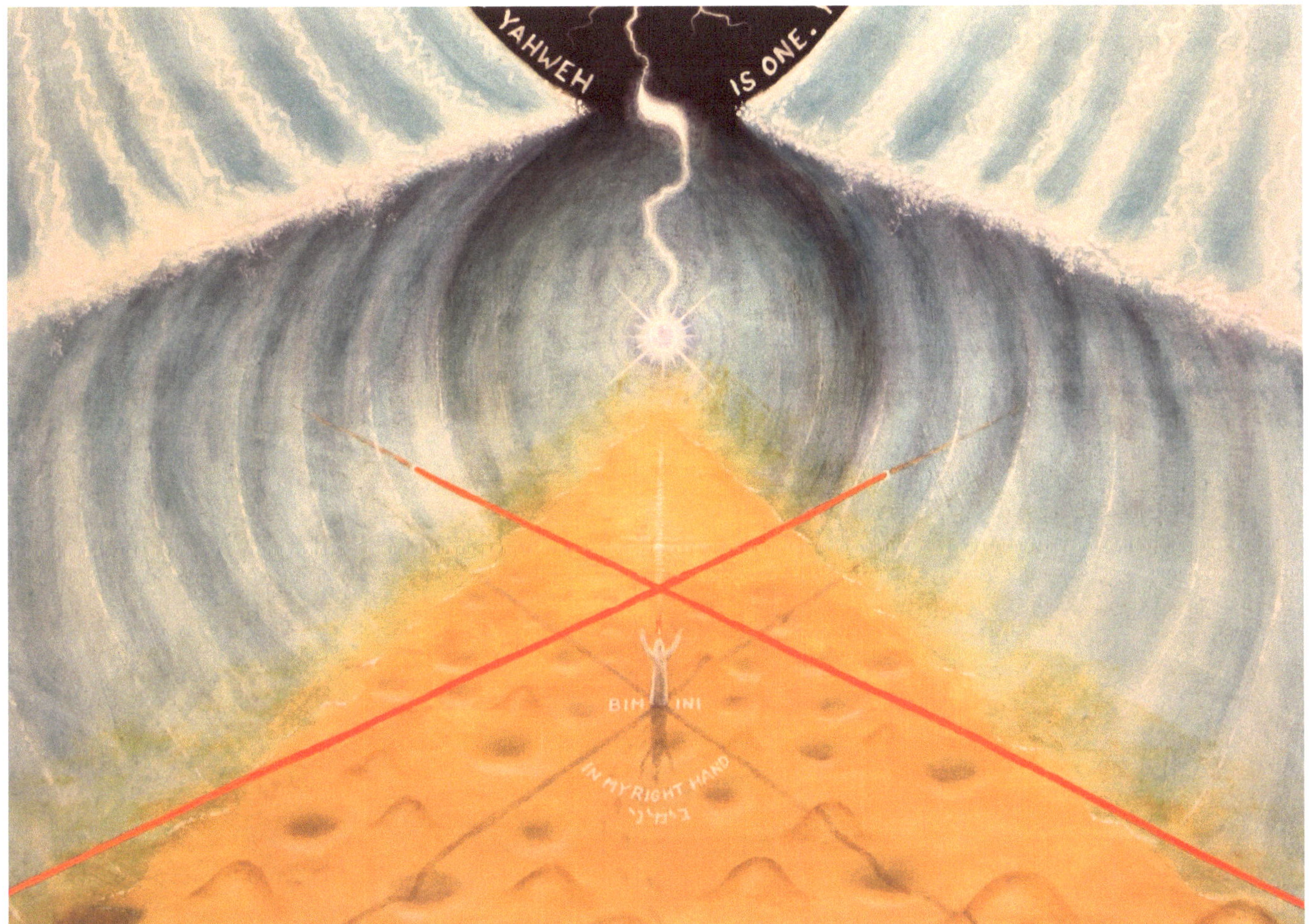

Crossing The Strait (detail)

The area of the potholes and mounds was about 100 feet wide. To the north of that area the sea floor was normal, and to the south it was also normal. It seems that whatever is causing the crisscrossed waves is also causing the strange configuration of the sand on the sea floor. At least the two must be somehow related. Is there something in this area disturbing the electromagnetic grid and setting up frequencies that would affect both the water and the sand? Could it be possible that, as some have speculated, there may be portions of Atlantis buried here with powerful crystals still emitting energy from somewhere beneath the sands?

BIMINI SHOW IN LONDON (2008)

Eight of the Bimini paintings were exhibited in London, England, at the Horse Hospital Art Gallery in the summer of 2008, in a three person exhibit titled "Sacred Pastures." Artists were Eric Wright, Cathy Ward and Norbert H. Kox. The Bimini works that were shown included, *Tree of Life*, *Crossing the Strait*, *Chariots of the Gods: Wheels of Fire*, *Bimini: Mountaintop of Atlantis*, *Delight of the Scribe*, *From the Rising of the Sun*, *Day Five*, and *We Are One*.

Some of the Bimini works have been placed with Henry Boxer Gallery, also of England, and a number of them are in Luxembourg, Europe with Armand Hein at Galerie Toxic.

ART EXHIBIT IN BIMINI (2008)

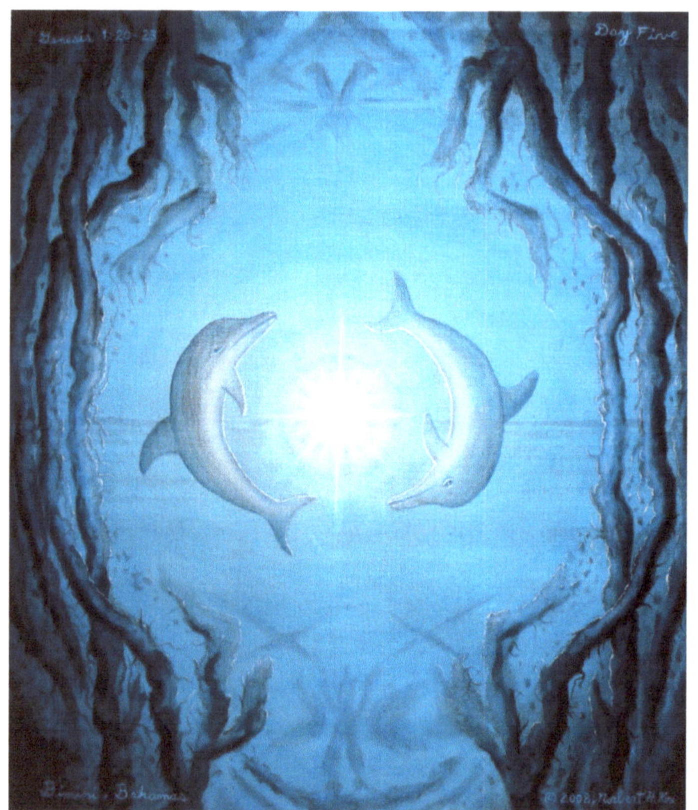

Day Five, 2007-2008, acrylic on canvas, 20" x 18"

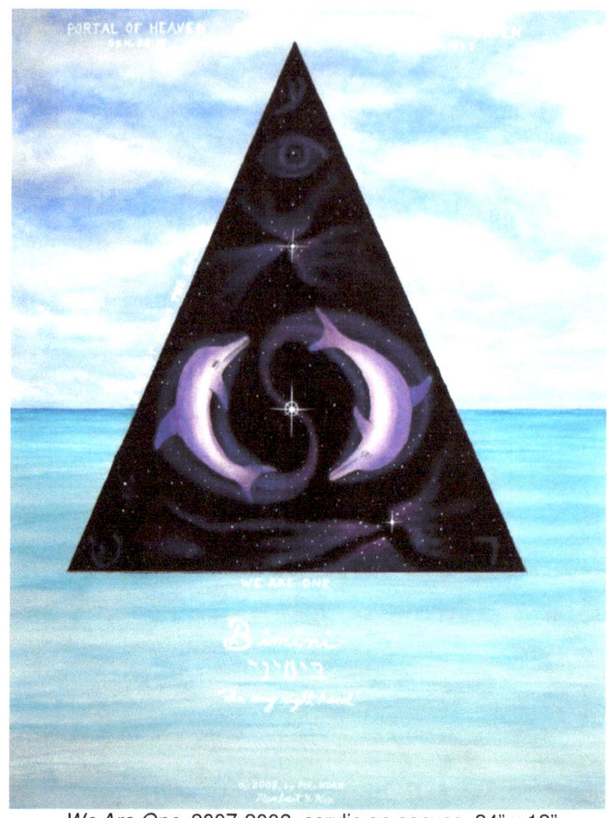

We Are One, 2007-2008, acrylic on canvas, 24" x 18"

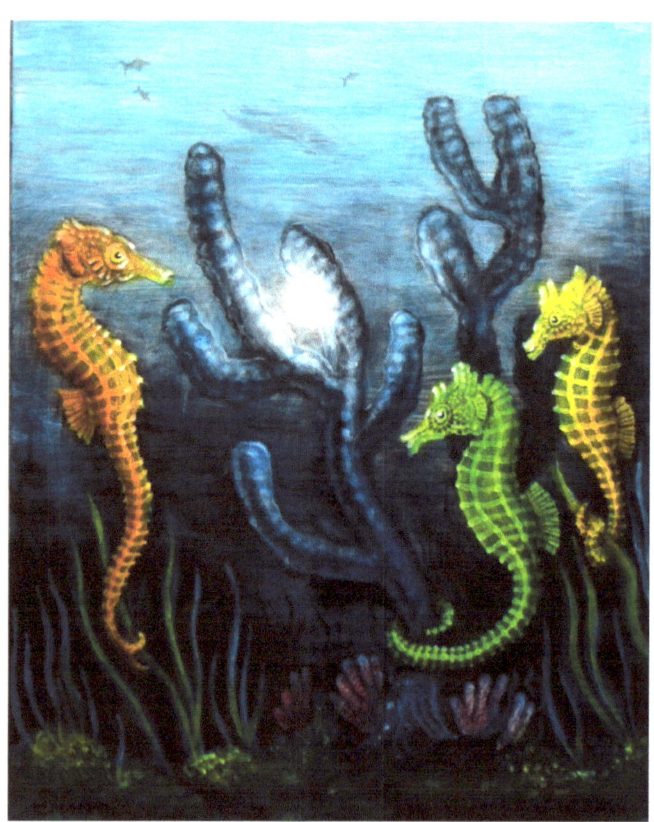

Guardian of the Deep, 2007-2008, acrylic on canvas, 10" x 8"

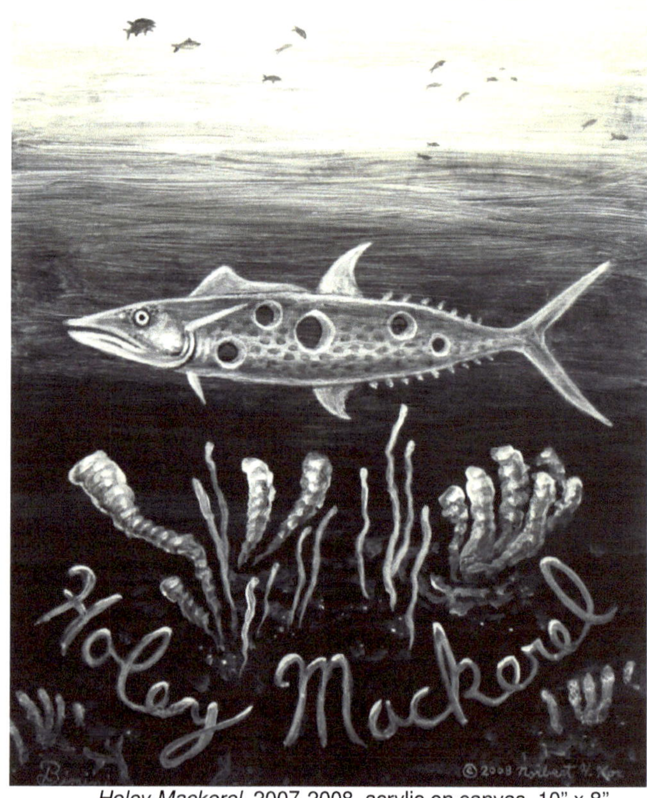

Holey Mackerel, 2007-2008, acrylic on canvas, 10" x 8"

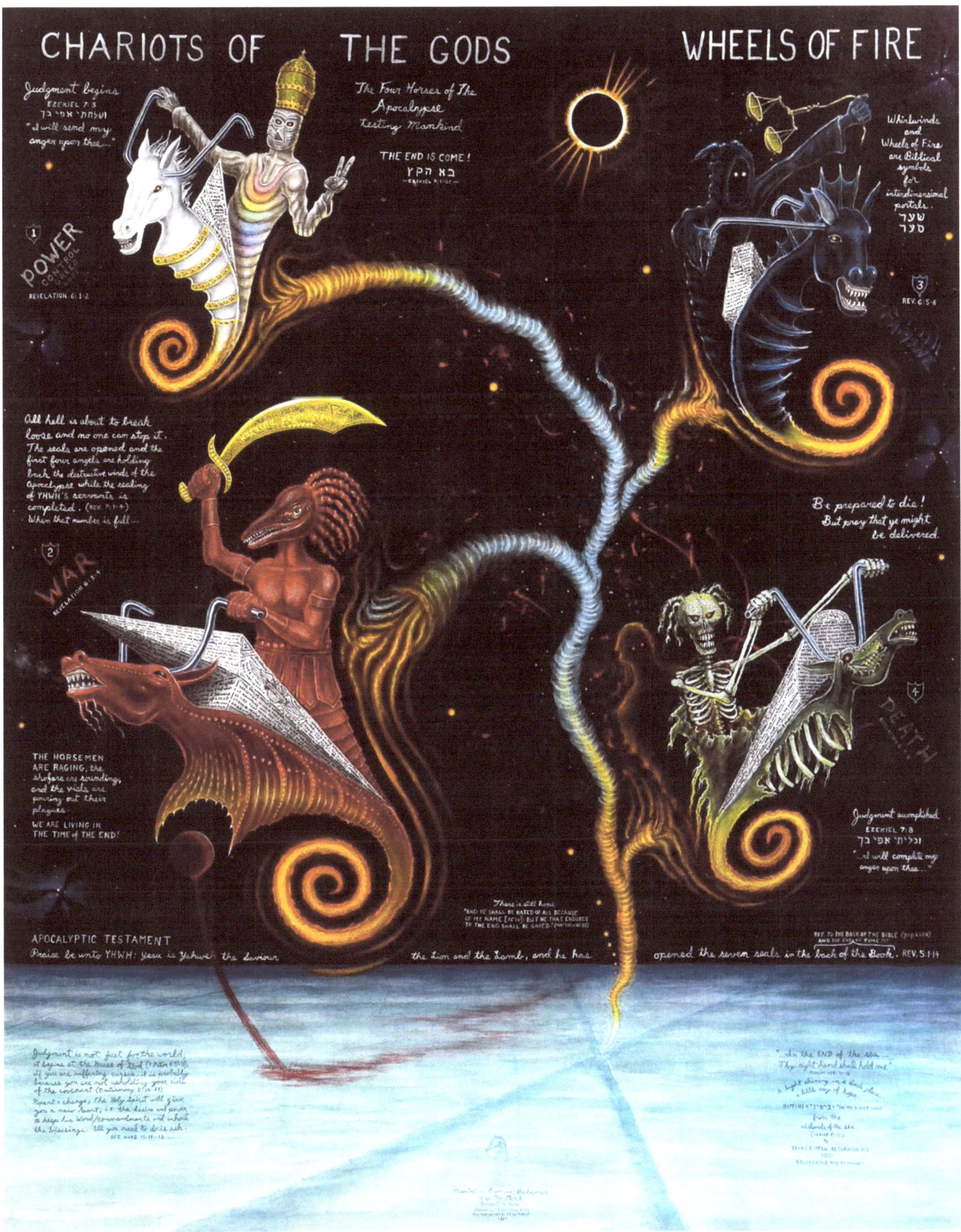

Chariots of the Gods: Wheels of Fire, 2007-2008, acrylic on canvas, 60" x 48"

This painting was also exhibited in London, England in the 2008 *Sacred Pastures* exhibition, and again in *Ete 08*, at Galerie TOXIC, Luxembourg, Europe. The inspiration for the piece followed the four-tank collaborative sculpture, *The Four Horsemen Of The Apocalypse* (2007) by David Damkoehler and Norbert H. Kox

BIMINI ART EXHIBIT (2010)

"Issues of Life and Death"

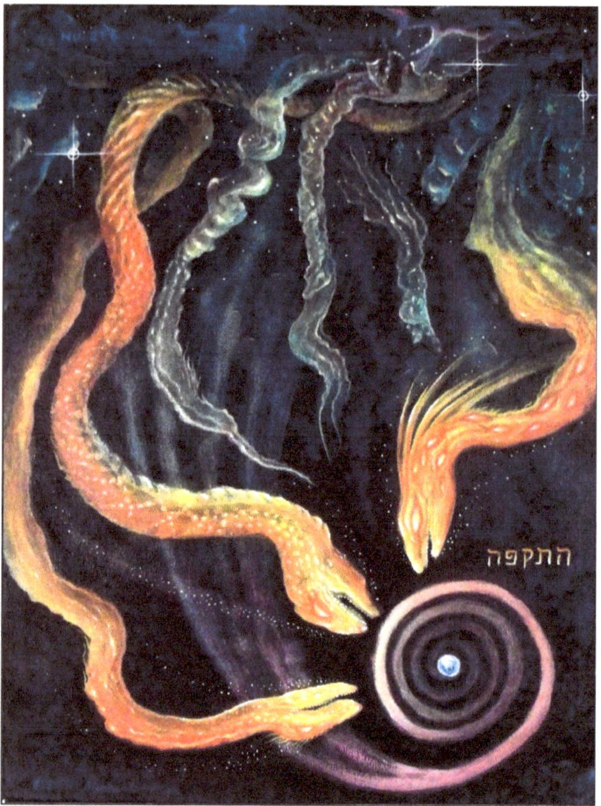

Attack, 2009-2010, acrylic on canvas, 24" x 18"

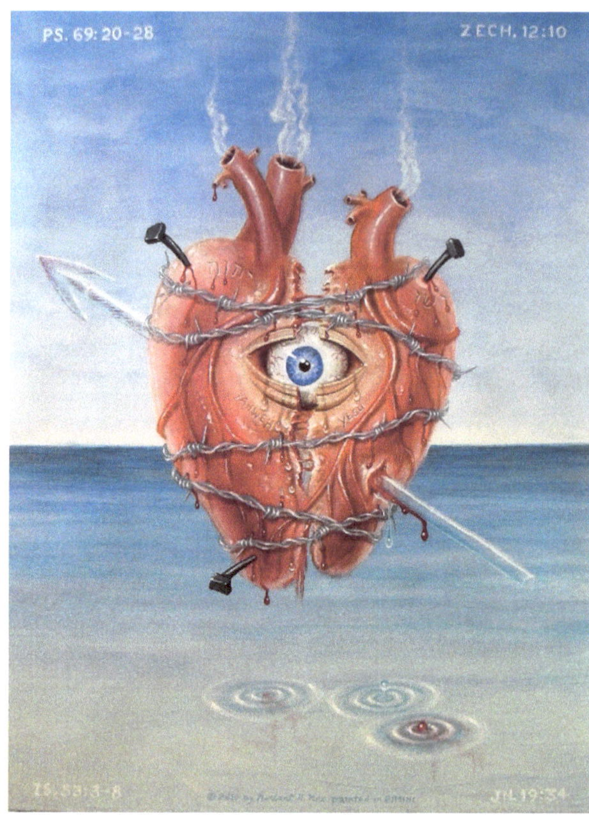

Blood and Water, 2009-2010, acrylic on canvas, 24" x 18"

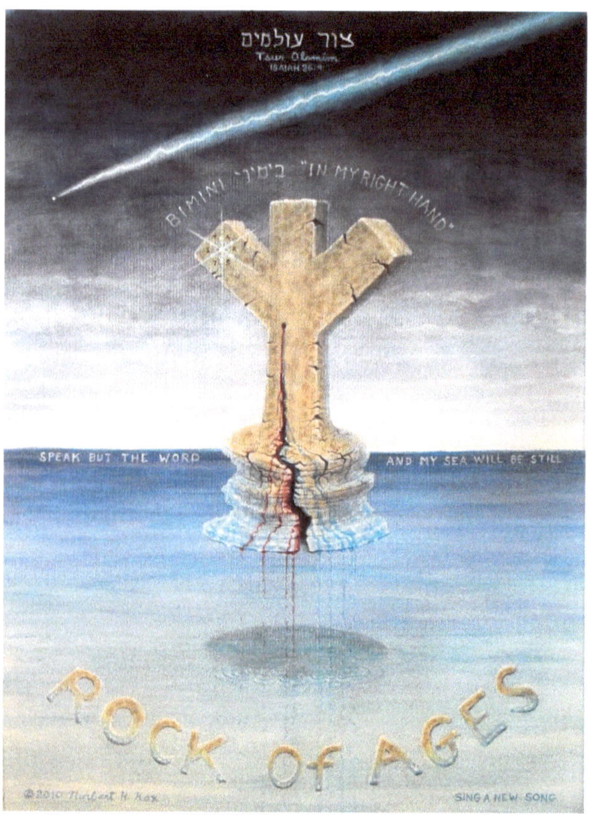

Rock of Ages, 2009-2010, acrylic on canvas, 24" x 18"

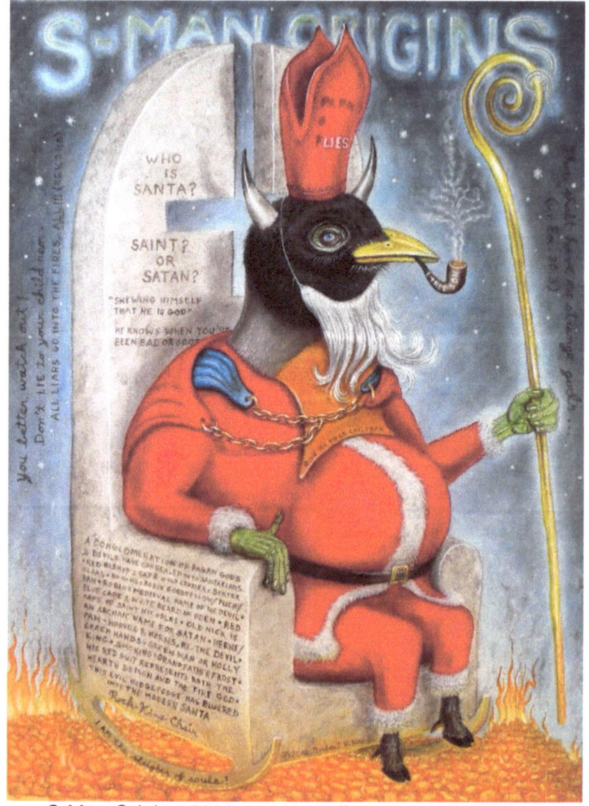

S-Man Origins, 2009-2010, acrylic on canvas, 24" x 18"

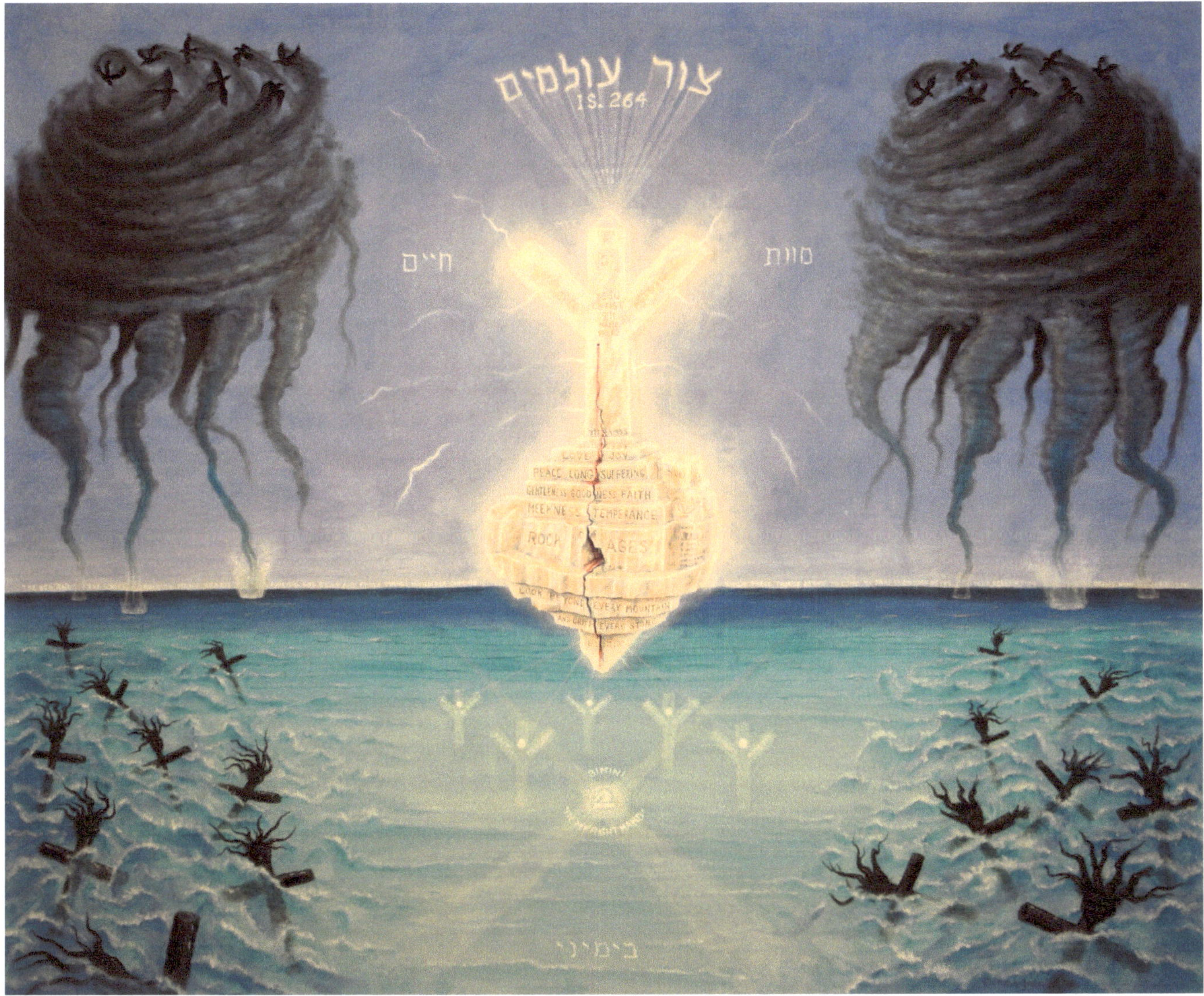

Rock of Ages: Issues of Life and Death, 2009-2010, acrylic on canvas, 48" x 60"

MOUNTAIN OF LIFE

Once more, in the *Rock of Ages: Issues of Life and Death*, is the concept of the island in the sky, the floating mountain of energy (*viz.* "...the stone was cut out of the mountain without hands" – *Daniel 2:45*). It symbolizes the kingdom of God coming down from above, bringing light and truth. Here the mountain/rock hovers over Bimini. Looking up from below we can see the stone base is bearing the names Yahweh-Yesu, in the Hebrew characters.

Written in Hebrew text, Bimini means "In my right hand." Although this painting centers on the Island of Bimini, symbolically it is more than just Bimini, it represents the world: "He's got the whole world in his hands."

Yahweh does have Bimini in his right hand, and has chosen to bring his hand to Bimini in a special way through his name.

In the painting we see the capstone, chief cornerstone (*i.e.* stone of the top corner – *Psalm 118:22*) as a crystal of light on top of the stone cross. Camouflaged within the light beams radiating from the crystal capstone is the reference, Is. 11:11, which indicates Yahweh returning his "hand" in the *Yod*, the initial of Yahweh and Yesu. His *Yod* is seen in the painting as a radiating light within the capstone. Yesu Christ is the light of the world as well as the capstone that was rejected by the builders.

The Hebrew words projected in light over the cross are equivalent to the English phrase "Rock of Ages," also translated "everlasting strength" (Isaiah 26:4).

The glowing rock of the ages is symbolic of the second coming of Christ, with death on his left hand and life on his right, separating the sheep from the goats, i.e. good and evil. The path of calm water dividing the turbulence is reminiscent of the parting of the Red Sea, and also the gentle waters of the Word of God and the Holy Spirit.

The X crossing Bimini is the mark of God. The X was the ancient form of the letter *tau*. It was the mark of salvation in the foreheads of those who cried out against the abominations/idols (Ezekiel 9:1-11).

Bimini represents the hope of the world with five angels manifesting the nine gifts of the spirit (ref. 1Corinthians 12:8-10). The nine aspects of the fruit of the spirit (Galatians 5:22-23) are carved into the rock stairs leading to the cross. The arms of the cross support the instructions of Acts 2:38 and Acts 4:12. The powerful energy bolting from the cross is life-generating for the children of light, but destruction to the children of darkness.

The root crosses in the turbulent waters are branded with the names of all the "works of the flesh" (Galatians 5:19-21). They may represent evil forces, but also the people who reject and disobey the teachings of Christ thus barring themselves from the kingdom of God. "For the wages of sin is death; but the gift of God is eternal life through Yesu Christ our Yahweh" (Romans 6:23).

The ravens are stirring the dark mist of death creating the enormous whirlwind-waterspouts that quickly approach the workers of evil like giant vacuum cleaners with menacing octopus tentacles, emphasizing the hopelessness of those who reject the Almighty.

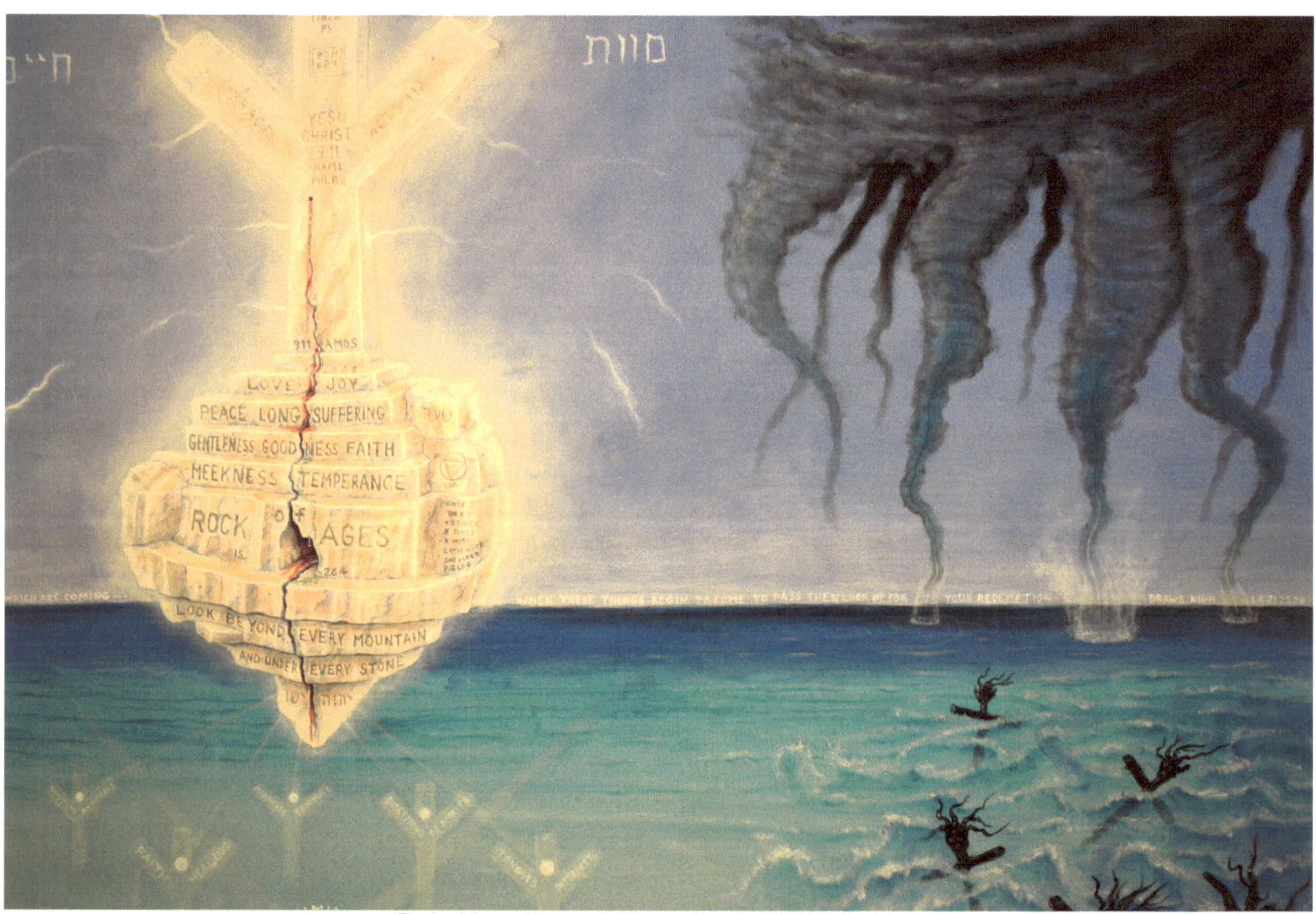

Rock of Ages: Issues of Life and Death, 2009-2010 (detail)

"Rock of Ages, cleft for me, let me hide myself in thee; Let the water and the blood, from thy wounded side which flowed, Be of sin the double cure, save from wrath and make me pure" (1763, Agustus Montague Toplady)

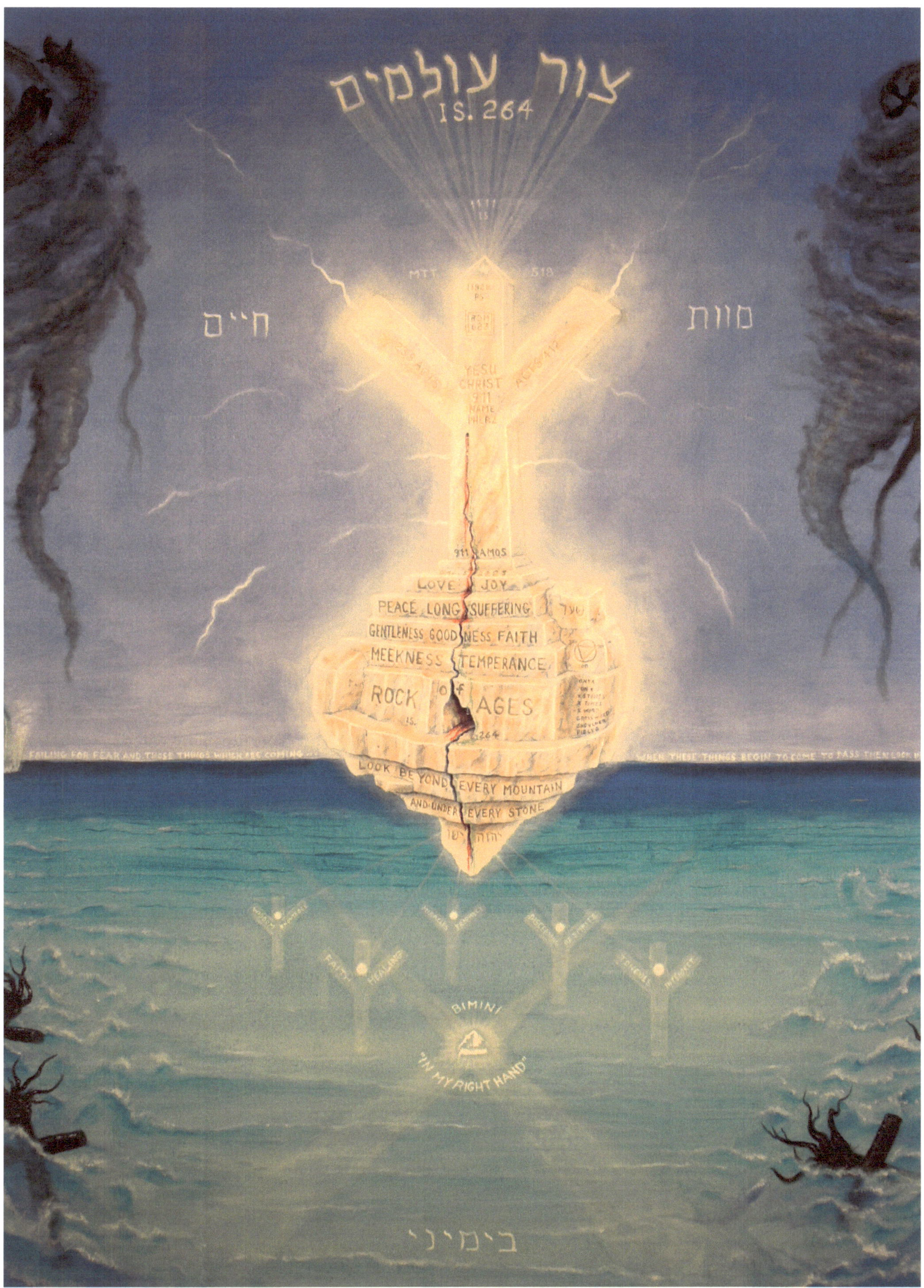
צור עולמים
IS. 264
חיים
מוות
YESU
CHRIST
911
911 AMOS
LOVE JOY
PEACE LONG SUFFERING
GENTLENESS GOODNESS FAITH
MEEKNESS TEMPERANCE
ROCK of AGES
IS.
264
FAILING FOR FEAR AND THOSE THINGS WHICH ARE COMING
LOOK BEYOND EVERY MOUNTAIN
AND UNDER EVERY STONE
BIMINI
"IN MY RIGHT HAND"
בימיני

JAMES PINDER

The 2010 show was the third annual Kox and Pinder exhibition.

Although trained in the fine arts, the works of Bahamian artist James Pinder have been described as both intuitive and visionary. His artworks are collected in Europe, the United States, Canada, Costa Rica, Jamaica and the Bahamas.

Bahamian Collections include, Former Prime Minister of the Bahamas Honorable Perry G. Christie, Former Deputy Prime Minister Honorable Cynthia Pratt, Member of Parliament For Bimini and West End Honorable Obadiah Wilchombe, Member of Parliament Honorable Larry Carthright, Bahamas Minister Of Education Honorable Desmond Banister, Former Member of Parliament for Bimini Mr. George Weech, Former American Ambassador to the Bahamas His Excellency Mr. John Rood, Former Ambassador to the Bahamas His Excellency Mr. Sidney Williams, Arch Bishop of the Catholic Diocese Bishop Patrick Pinder, Sir Michael and Lady Barbara Checkley.

His paintings are derived from dreams and Bible texts, ranging in themes from the Hebrew names of God to sculptured paintings of the "Armor of God". The complex imagery contains hidden messages that only emerge upon close examination. The stylized faces overlap each other to mysteriously form images within images.

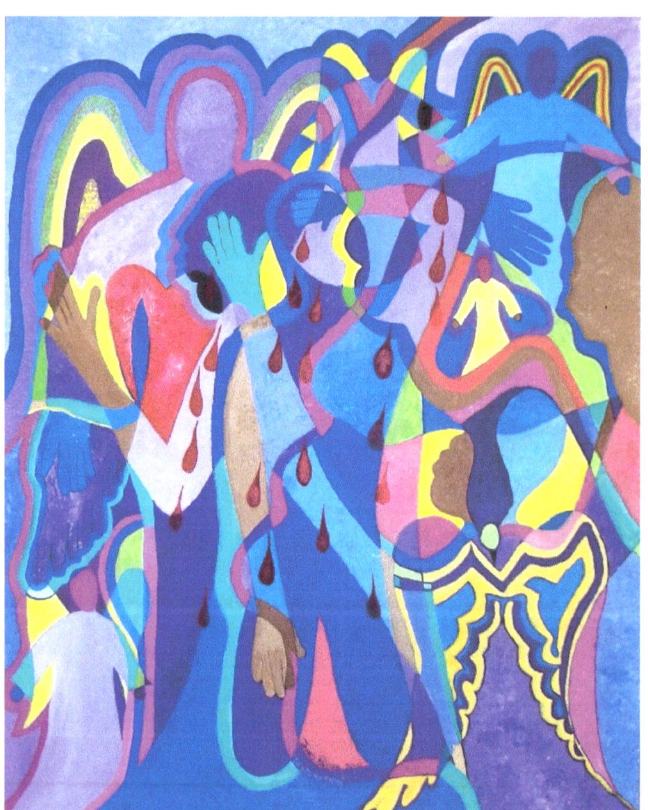

Restoration, 2010, acrylic on canvas

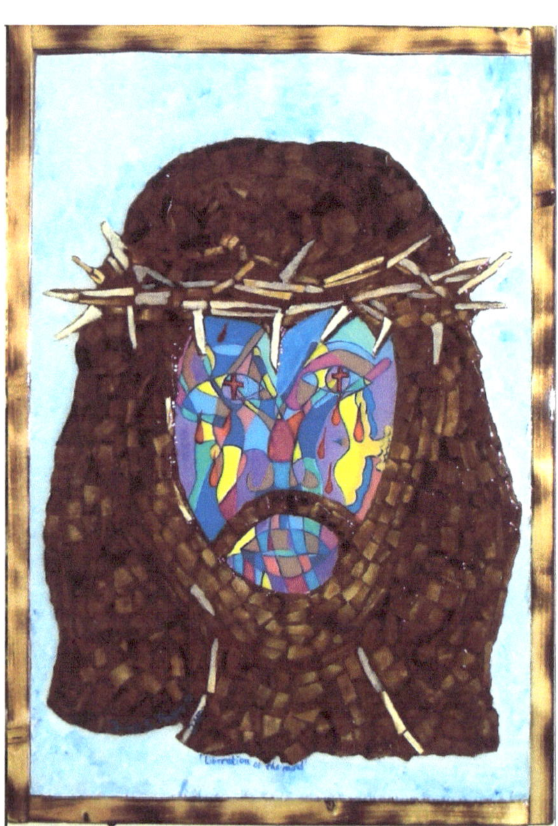

Liberation of the Mind, 2010, acrylic & wood tiles on board

Pinder's recent technique integrates both sculpture and painting. Various symbols are cut out and overlaid with small pieces of wafer-thin native wood ("horse flesh" and mahogany). Intricate designs are created with the light and dark slivers of wood that are placed like miniature tiles and grouted with a mixture of saw dust and glue. Sometimes paintings created on tile, canvas or wood are inserted into the constructions. When the work is thoroughly dried the wooden mosaic is sanded and coated with a clear epoxy finish.

Utilizing the Island's natural resources—drift wood, native wood, and sea shells of various shapes and sizes—sculptured tables and water fountains are created by James Pinder in a similar fashion to the sculptured paintings. The unique fountains incorporate melted glass bottles into their design along with drift wood and assorted sea shells.

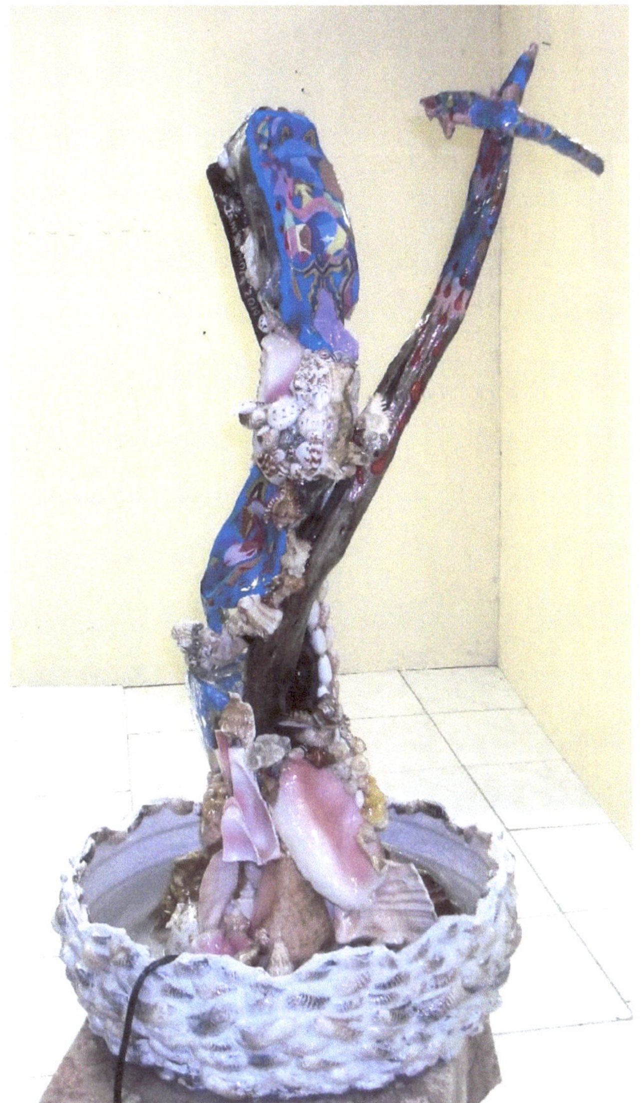

Fountain, 2010

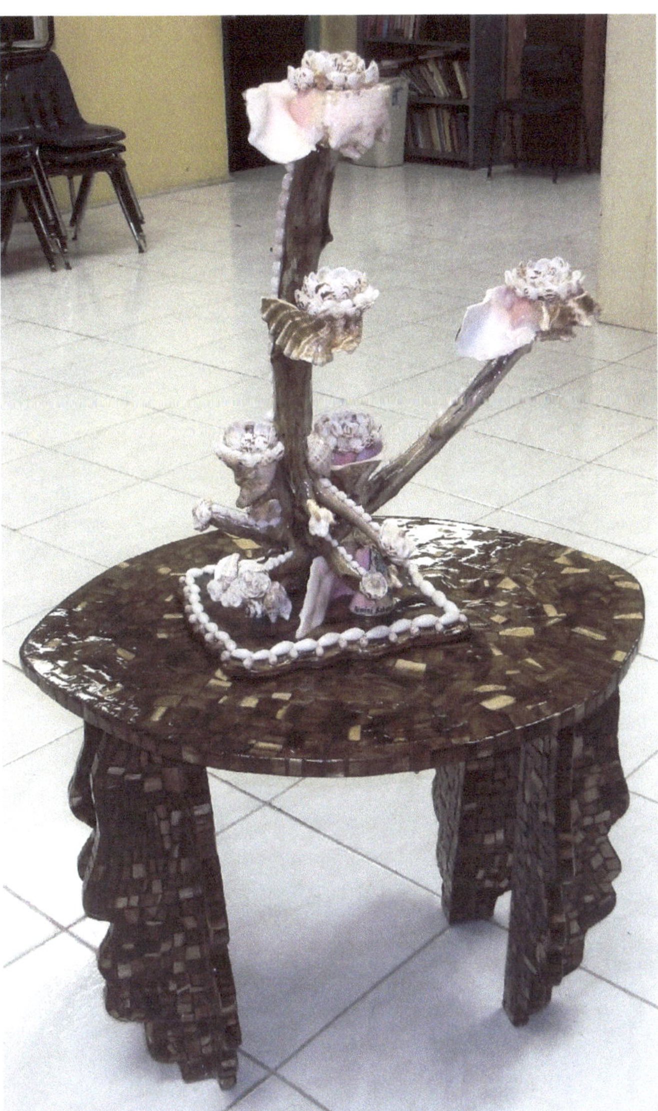

Sculptured Table, 2010, and Table-top Sculpture, 2010

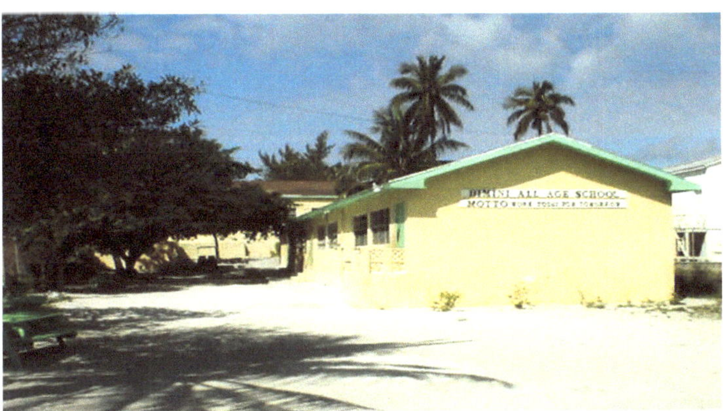

Bimini All Age School and Art Center

DOLPHIN HOUSE & MISCELLANEOUS PHOTOS

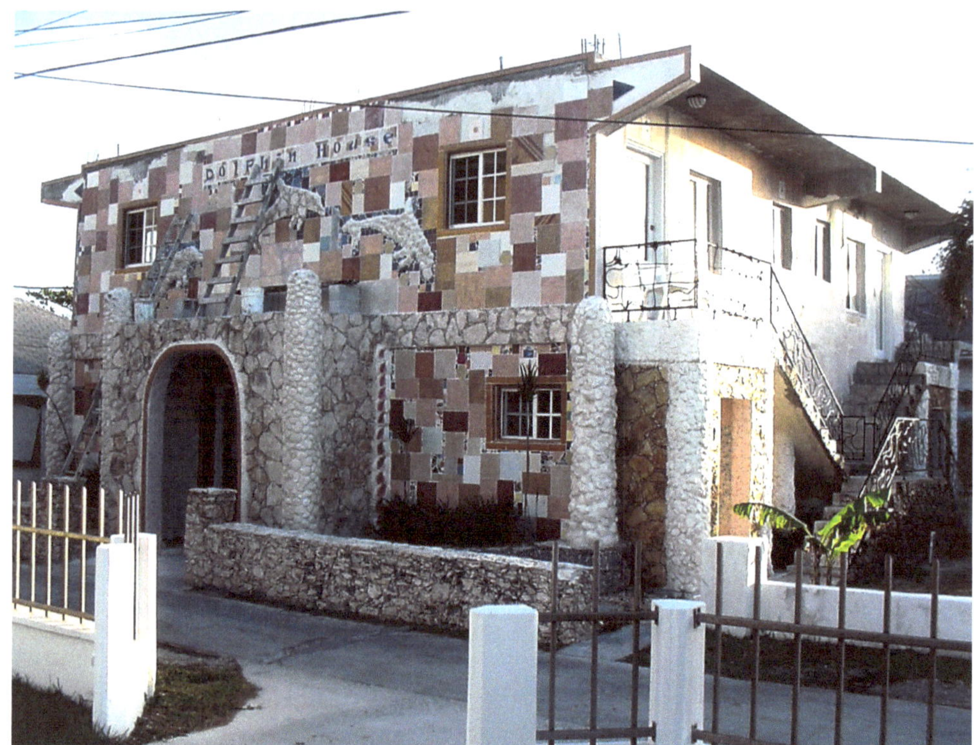

The Dolphin House is a continuing work of art by Island historian and artist Ashley B. Saunders

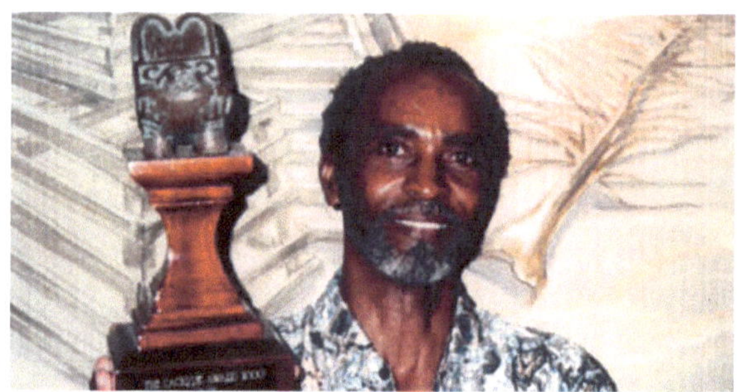

Dolphin House creator Ashley B. Saunders, recipient of the prestigious Cacique Award 2000 for achievements as writer, poet, and author of the volumes of *The History of Bimini* (for purchase/information contact *saundersa62@yahoo.com*)

Nine of my twelve stays in Bimini, as of February 2010, have been in the Dolphin House where most of my Island artworks have been painted. There is a high level of positive energy present in the house that is very conducive to artistic creativity. Mr. Ashley Saunders has certainly impressed his energy upon the house through his creative expressions, but the house also has its own inherent energy.

I have become sensitive to the subtle energies that surround us at all times. This is especially noticeable at the Dolphin House. I started to feel it very strongly during my 2004-2005 visit. The following year it was even more intense and I believe it is due in a large part to the stonework and shellwork that Mr. Saunders has artistically cemented into the walls. We know that stones emit frequencies from the energy they hold. Certain crystals even produce a strong electrical charge when placed under pressure. The build up of stones, coral and shells on the walls within the house retain a detectable level of energy.

After a great deal of testing within the Dolphin House, it is noted that the energy levels fluctuate significantly. The house seems to interact with us. Our own energy stimulates the stone house causing its level of energy to increase substantially. The energy can be felt as you enter the building and is usually felt quite strongly when you move a bare arm within a few inches of a wall, as it stands the hair on end.

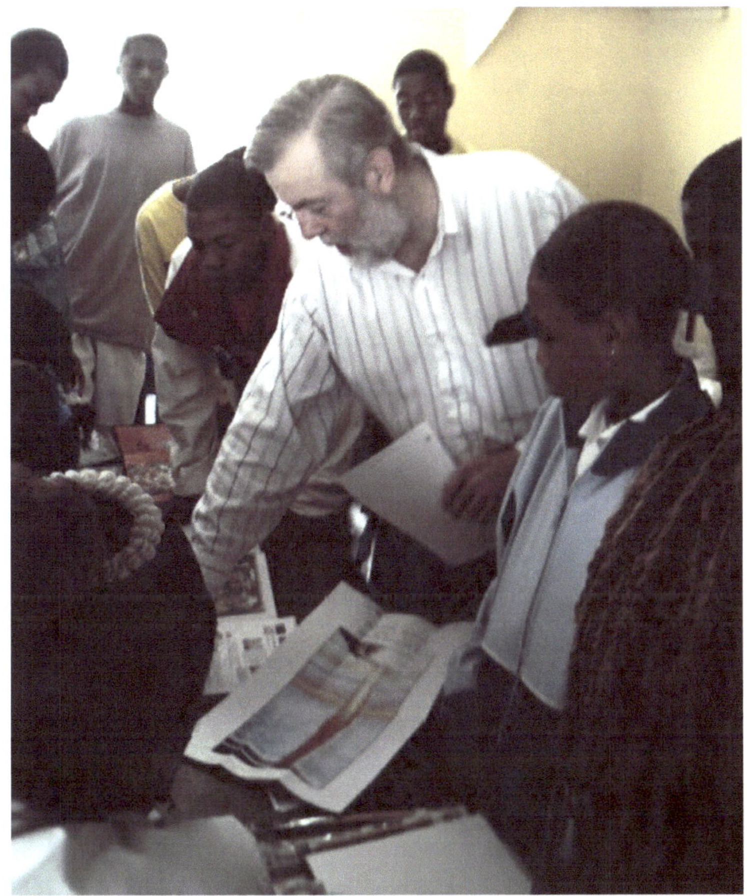

Nor working with students at Bimini All Age School

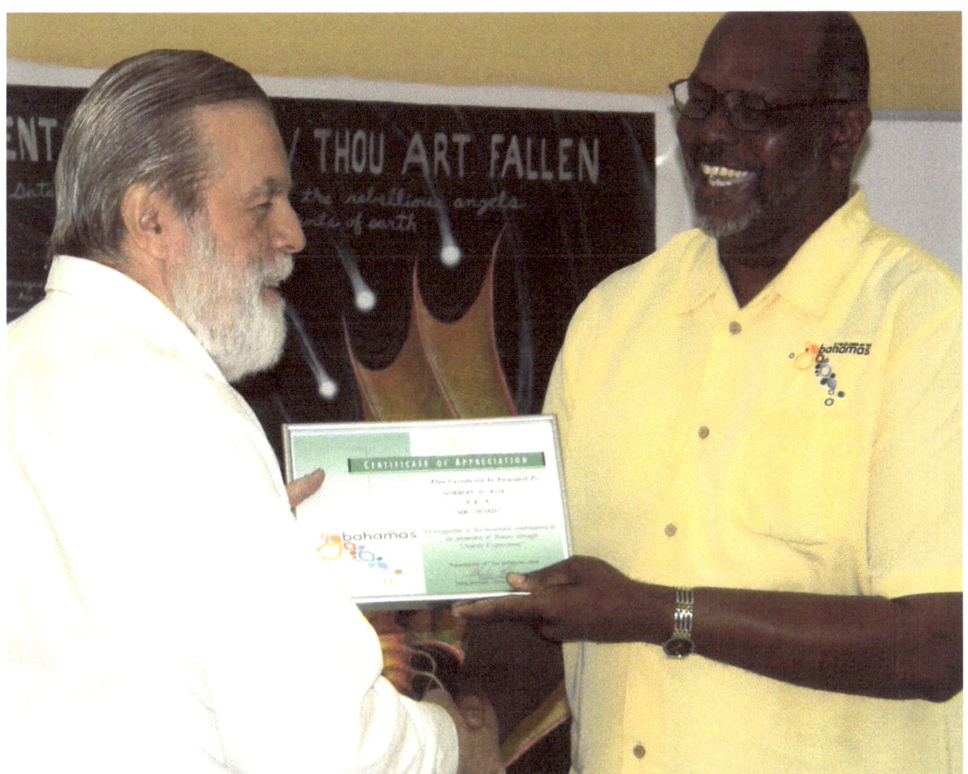

Norbert Kox receiving award of recognition from Charles Robins (Ministry of Tourism representative, Bimini) During the opening reception, February 16, 2009: *This Certificate Is Awarded To Norbert H. Kox, A.K.A. "Mr. Noah" In recognition of his invaluable contribution to the promotion of Bimini through "Artistic Expressions"* (photo by James Pinder). "My thanks and appreciation to all the people of Bimini." NHK

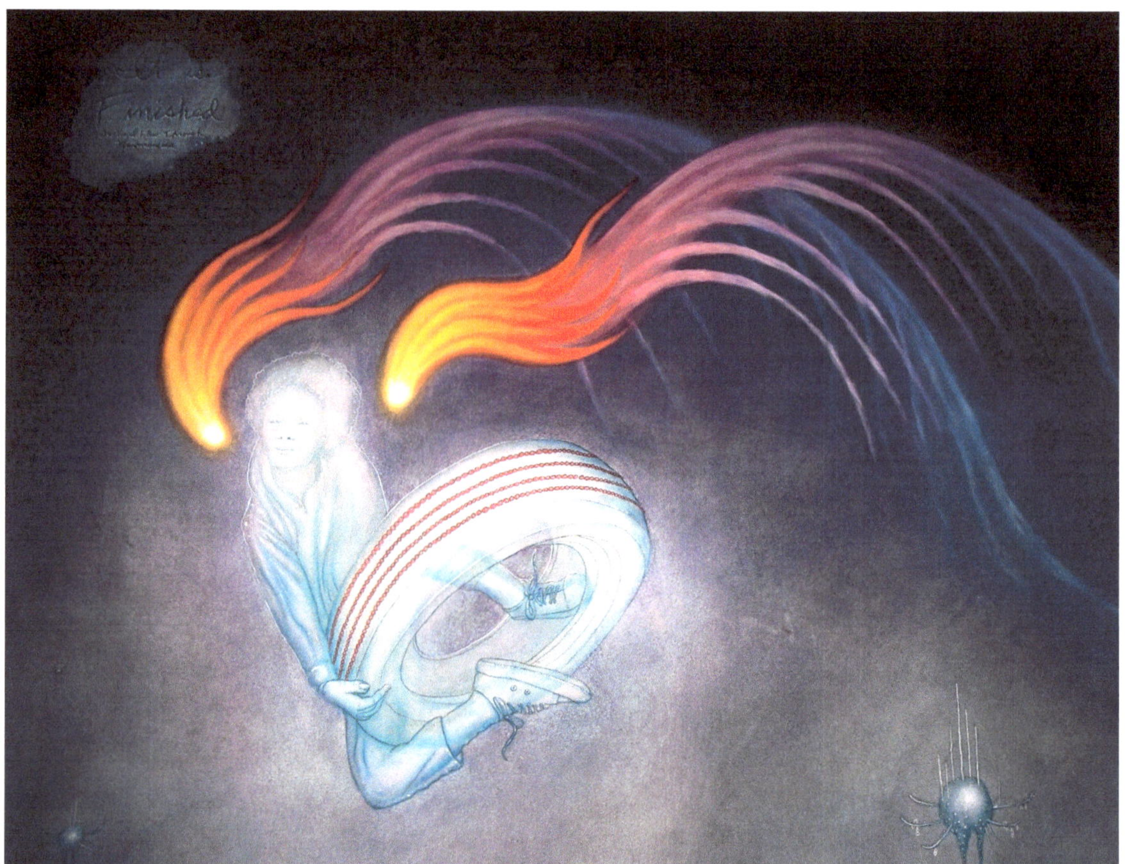

"It Is Finished" (detail panel of *Apocalypse to Eternity*) was painted in 1998, just prior to my first extended stay in Bimini. Many have commented on the change and feel of the work compared to anything prior. This change which even affected my color palette, was undoubtedly due to a subconscious anticipation of things to come, *viz.* Island painting.

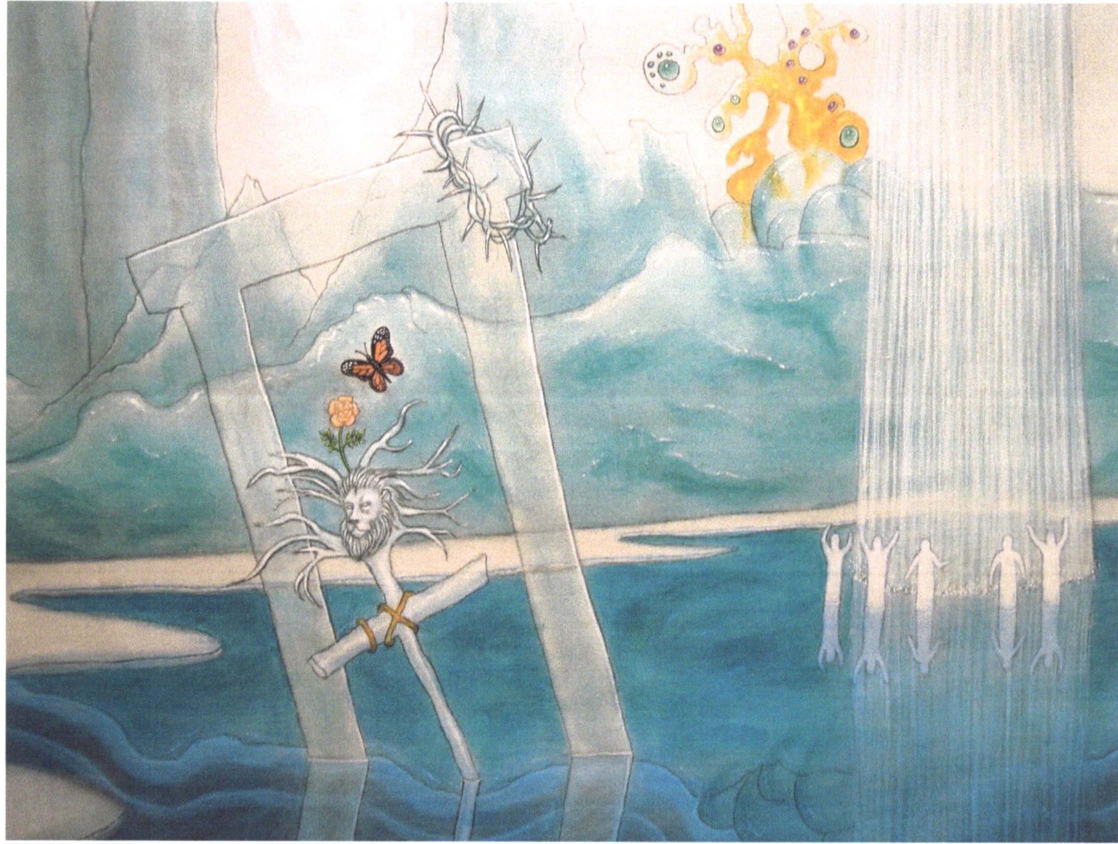

"No More Dying" (detail panel of *Apocalypse to Eternity*) The Isabella Rose, named after my Granddaughter, is a symbol of resurrection, along with the Monarch Butterfly. The redeemed of Yesu Christ are being refreshed in a waterfall of light.

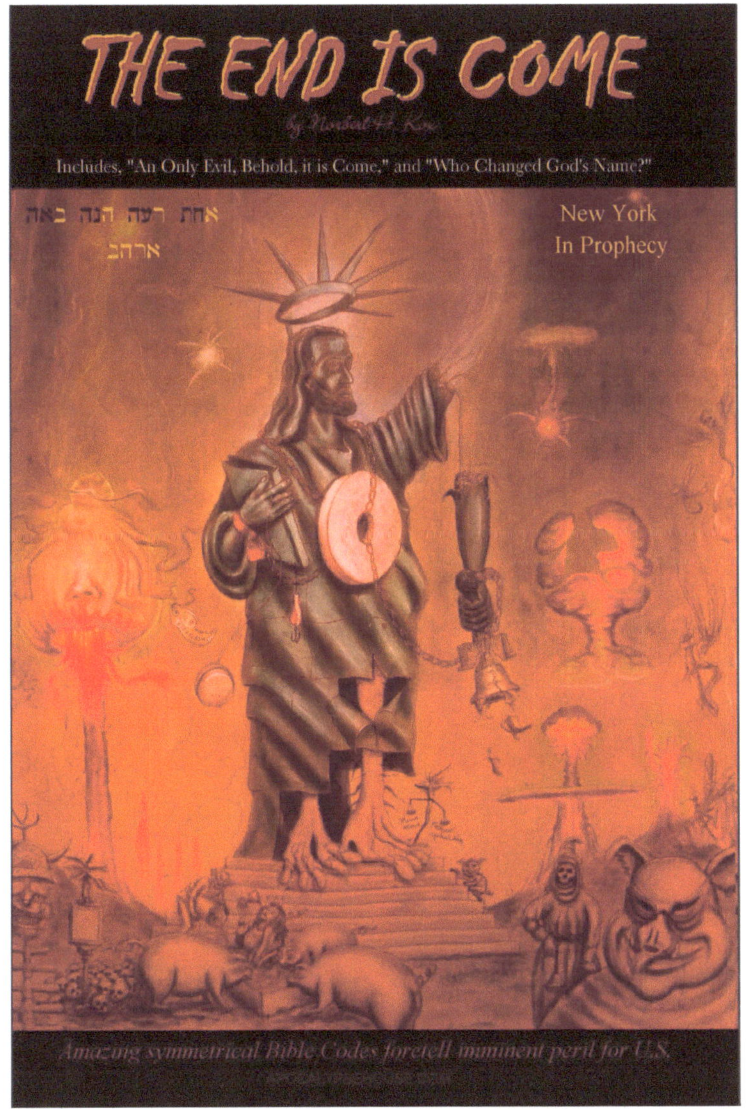

The End Is Come

New York is obliterated in Apocalyptic Prophecy
presented in the new, non-fiction book

What happens when the scientist's predictions of impending natural disasters fall on deaf ears?

The United States' most populated city is on course for ultimate destruction by not one, but two natural disasters and no one has heeded the warnings. In this book by visionary artist and author, Norbert H. Kox, a grim picture is painted regarding this inevitable scenario. Based on scientific studies, biblical prophecy, and newly discovered bible code research, Kox's book "The End Is Come" (221 pp, pb, 2007, Apocalypse House, $19.95) reveals what few are willing to face.

A horrendous destruction is about to consume the entire New York City area. Repercussions on the United States and the rest of the world will be horrifying. It is all detailed in "The End Is Come: An Only Evil, Behold, It Is Come. Who Changed God's Name?" The imminence of this great doom is prophesied in the Bible and confirmed by current warnings of seismologists and meteorologists. The Bible Code Has recorded virtually every major incident and important historical event since the beginning of time, all written and recorded before they happened. The September 11, terrorist attack on

New York is accurately recorded in great detail. Another devastating tragedy is recorded for New York also. If it is accurate, like the other entries, it may prove to be the worst human suffering since the great flood. It could conceivably be a destruction from which the land will never recover. The scientific evidence is in total agreement with Bible prophecy and symmetrical Bible code findings.

“The End Is Come,” is a compendium of two insightful books; the newest, “An Only Evil, Behold, it is Come,” and the newly updated version of his riveting expository thesis, “Who Changed God’s Name?" In “An Only Evil, Behold, it is Come,” Kox explores Biblical Prophecy regarding the 911 attack and scientific evidence of New York’s imminent destruction from Earthquake and Hurricane. His dutiful research provides the reader with “hair-straightening” facts and graphics that will open the eyes of even the most ardent pessimist.

In, “Who Changed God’s Name,” Kox reveals history’s attempt to erase the true names of God and why it is imperative that the names be manifest into daily use by Jews and Christians worldwide. Thirty years of research culminates in this authoritative treatise on how the names were hidden, changed, and eventually all but lost by time and treachery. This is a must read for all believers seeking the true face of God.

++

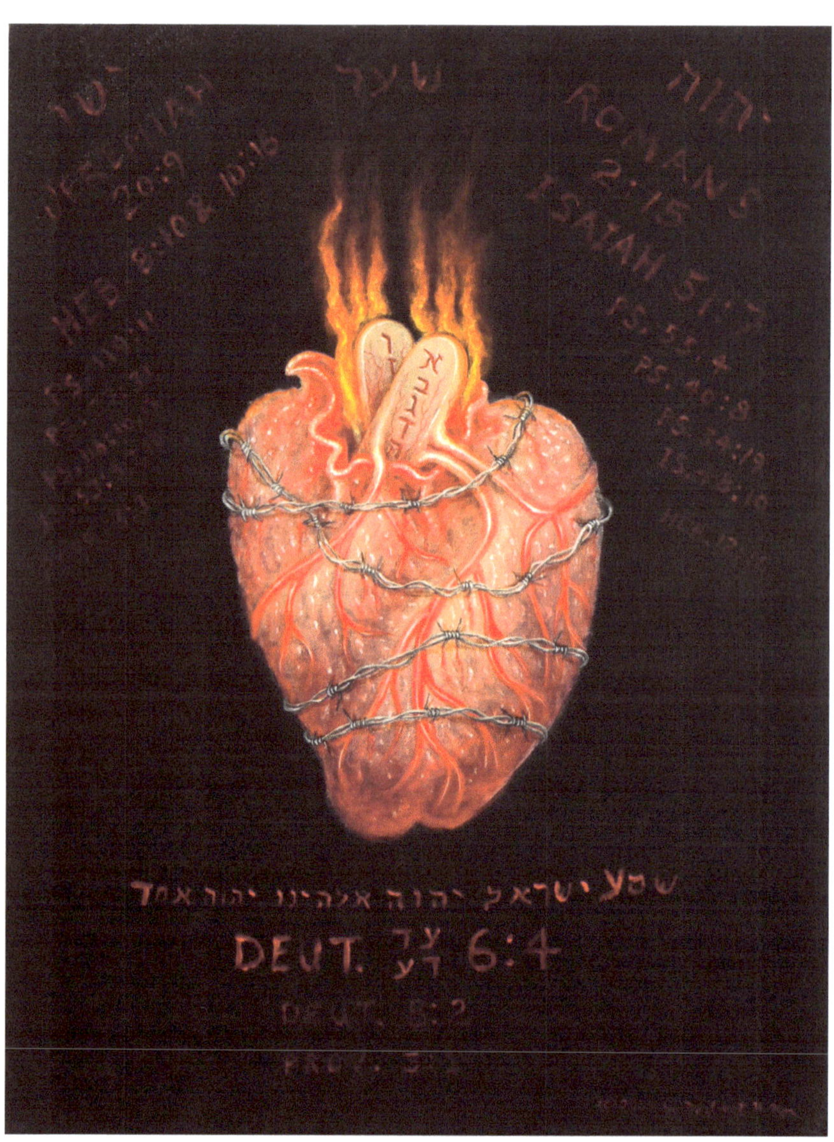

Six Four, 2009, acrylic on canvas, 24" x 18"

LUX IS LIGHT

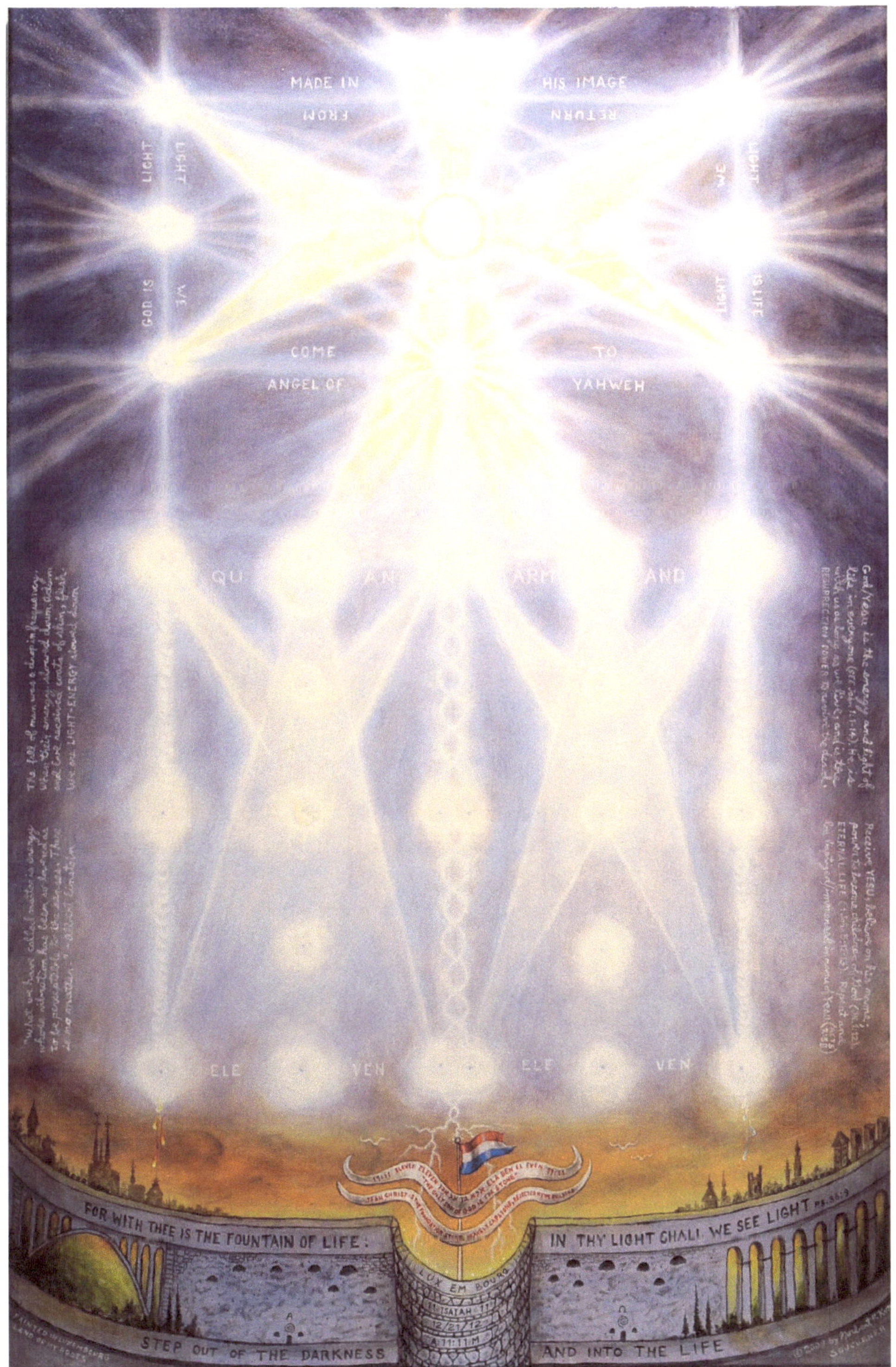

In His Image, 2009, acrylic on canvas, 48" x 30"

This piece was created in Luxembourg, Luxembourg, during the Last Chance Apocalypse exhibition. It was painted specially for Quan and Armand Hein, following in the pattern of the Bimini energy paintings, particularly the *Divine System of Spontaneous Regeneration* (pp. 56-58).

The concept: We are children of the Light. From light we come—to light we return. The lights hover above the Luxembourg cityscape. Each vertical pattern contains eleven power points, thus, the two combined are eleven-eleven (11:11 reference, p.16, "The Bimini Call," and p.19, "Islands of the Sea").

www.ingramcontent.com/pod-product-compliance
Lightning Source LLC
LaVergne TN
LVHW070128110826
845147LV00002B/211
9780578061047